First published in 2012 by Voyageur Press, an imprint of MBI Publishing Company, 400 First Avenue North, Suite 300, Minneapolis, MN 55401 USA

Voyageur Press titles are also available at discounts in bulk quantity for industrial or sales-promotional use. For details write to Special Sales Manager at MBI Publishing Company, 400 First Avenue North, Suite 300, Minneapolis, MN 55401 USA.

To find out more about our books, visit us online at www.voyageurpress.com.

Editor: Melinda Keefe

Design Manager: James Kegley

Designed by: Carol Holtz

Layout by: Helena Shimizu

ISBN-13: 978-0-7603-4245-9

Printed in U.S.A.

10 9 8 7 6 5 4 3 2 1

Library of Congress Cataloging-in-Publication Data

Barnyard confidential : an A to Z reader of life lessons, tall tales, and country wisdom / edited by Melinda Keefe.
    p. cm.
  ISBN 978-0-7603-4245-9 (hard cover)
  1. Family farms--Encyclopedias. 2. Home economics, Rural--Encyclopedias. 3. Farm life--Humor. I. Keefe, Melinda, 1982-
  HD1476.A3B37 2012
  630.3--dc23

                              2012004783

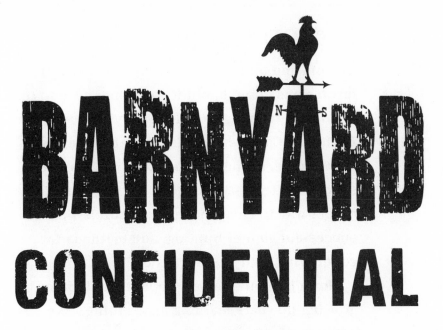

BARNYARD CONFIDENTIAL

An A to Z Reader of Life Lessons, Tall Tales, and Country Wisdom

FEATURING STORIES FROM
E. B. WHITE, MICHAEL PERRY,
ROGER WELSCH, GWEN PETERSEN,
AND **MANY MORE**

MELINDA KEEFE, EDITOR

Voyageur Press

INTRODUCTION

The ins and outs of rural living can be scary and mysterious enough, but if you're not wise to the lingo, you're in big trouble. Lucky for you, *Barnyard Confidential* discloses the secrets to country life, giving you the tools you need to survive by demystifying such riddles as the proper way to enjoy sitting on a porch, tips for successful gopher hunting, and methods for conquering your pressure cooker.

Iowa born and raised, I spent much of my growing-up years learning about things like *cross-pollinating* and *detasseling*, trying to understand the difference between a *crick* and a *creek*, and hiding blank looks when people started talking about sheep dipping and pasteurization.

I would say my farm education really began when I signed up as part of a detasseling crew one summer. With dreams of huge paychecks dancing in my head, I showed up before sunrise that first day, ready to honor my rural heritage. I should explain the concept of *detasseling* for those of you who may never have heard the word. Farmers plant three rows of one kind of corn next to one row of another kind of corn. When the corn reaches a certain height (usually just tall enough that you can't see over it), unsuspecting teenagers work their way down the three rows, fighting corn rash, claustrophobia, viciously sharp leaves, mud up to their ankles, and oppressive heat and humidity to pull the tassels off of each stalk, which allows the different varieties to cross-pollinate and create a hybrid seed. Trust me, after a summer spent detasseling, I wish I didn't know what that word meant, either.

As far as regional dialects go, however, rural terms can, surprisingly, allow for even more shades of meaning. For example, in the neighborhood where I grew up, we had a crick down the street. Now, a *crick* is not a *creek*, no matter what your dictionary may say. A crick, in the minds of Iowa children everywhere, is basically a trickle of water that runs through a giant cement tunnel under the street and along your back yard. It is a place to get a little wet but not soaked, a trickle that expands into a rushing stream in the spring and just about dries up by the end of the summer. A creek, however, is much larger and meanders through country pastures, creating picturesque views and providing livestock with water. Knowing these and other subtle differences just might save you from sounding dumb when your friends ask you to go cow-tipping or snipe-hunting out on the back forty.

Though by no means an exhaustive dictionary of farming terms, *Barnyard Confidential* brings to light some of the challenges unique to country living. In A-to-Z encyclopedia format with both humorous definitions and curiously informative stories, the authors featured here share their practical advice and their love-hate relationship with rural life, giving you a chance to see for yourself the ups and downs of the farm culture and to decode the mysteries of farm lore.

—Melinda Keefe

ACRE

A unit of land measure, originally the amount an ox could plow in one day. The number of acres in a given field varies, depending on whether the owner is collecting hail insurance (when they become smaller, and therefore more numerous) or paying for custom work (when they get larger and fewer).

(Terry Chamberlain, *The ABC's of Farming*, 1999)

ALFALFA

A hay crop developed by plant breeder Alf Jones; it was post-humously named in his honor by his wife Nellie, who stuttered. When in bloom alfalfa is a purple-blossomed plant; when converted into hay it is quite fragrant and is usually fed to cattle.

(Terry Chamberlain, *The ABC's of Farming*, 1999)

APPROACH

Method of access. The definition of a *good* approach depends on whether you are talking about (a) picking up a member of the opposite sex, (b) borrowing money, or (c) crossing a ditch to get to a field or farmyard. A "good approach," then, would consist of (a) flowers and a bottle of wine (b) a tear-jerker of a story, or (c) a culvert covered with several layers of packed clay and sand. Field approaches are an omnipresent feature of the rural prairie scene; they serve as indicators for giving directions ("Turn in at the second approach past the big slough"), as emergency pulloffs ("I better stop at the next approach and check that tire"), and, conversely, as traffic hazards ("He went into the ditch and hit an approach").

(Terry Chamberlain, *The ABC's of Farming*, 1999

AUGER

A machine which looks like a long-barreled (25–50 ft.) cannon with attached engine. It is used for moving grain or fertilizer from trucks to granaries to trucks etc. When I was a boy on the farm this was usually accomplished with shovels, which is why so many people my age had bad backs, damaged lungs, and a fanatical hatred of shovels. If you need to move grain around, take it from me: use an auger.

(Terry Chamberlain, *The ABC's of Farming*, 1999)

AXE

Perhaps the tool least regarded in America is the axe. Everyone has an axe lying around somewhere, but few axes have the same care lavished on them that is afforded other tools; almost none has the cutting edge that it deserves. You'll seldom find a man who will think twice before lending his axe. To find it he'll have to look in a dark corner of the cellar, or it may be clunked into a chopping block where it was left out in the weather. Yet a century ago the axe was the most important implement in America. There were manufacturers who made nothing but axes. There was a choice of some fifty designs, and every man had his favorite. He knew his axe handle length better than he knew his own shirt sleeve measurements.

You could once tell a man's character to some degree by his axe. Uniquely a man's own, like his signature, his axe handle design was often kept in the form of a blank pattern from which to fashion future handmade helves, as axe handles were formerly called. A man might season some special chunk of hickory by the fireplace all winter long, to prepare it for carving an axe helve in the spring.

The early axehead wasn't just one piece of metal; it had a "bit" of special steel hammered into the cutting edge . . . . Any experienced woodsman knew that axe bits chipped easily when they were very cold, so he heated the axehead and blade before using it in winter weather. A book could be written just on American axe lore for, with this single implement, the pioneer went into the forest and cleared the land; with it he split firewood, built a cabin, made furniture, and on occasion even used it for protection against marauding animals and Indians. But not many would read such a book, for few of us truly appreciate axes nowadays.

I always thought that to be a proper countryman, you had to start with a good axe, so when I first moved from the city, I stopped in at Abercrombie and Fitch's shop in New York to buy one. They hadn't had any calls for axes lately, it seemed, and outside of a folding axe and a mountain climber's implement, the only other one they could find turned up in an old catalog. After some searching they found this item in one of the storerooms. "Don't bother to wrap it," I said. "My train leaves in ten minutes and I have just enough time if I run for it." Luckily I knew the house detective, but even then he seemed startled at seeing me dashing out into New York's Madison Avenue with an axe. The conductor on the train, however, didn't know me. Probably there isn't a law forbidding passengers carrying axes; at any rate, he merely shook his head either in wonder or disbelief.

When I arrived home, I found that my nice new axe had a split in the handle. It certainly had to be returned, and this time I decided to wrap it. The same conductor stopped in his tracks when he recognized the telltale shape. He greeted me warily. "Hello again. You've wrapped it this time."

In New York, the store manager apologized and I was soon on my way to the country again with another axe in its axe-shaped wrapping. The conductor had become accustomed to me now. "How is your axe?" he asked. "Fine, thank you," I said.

But would you believe it? The store had given me a short-handled axe, not at all suited to my arm length. You can guess the rest. I became known as the commuter who carries an axe, and I didn't make many friends in the club car, even after I had obtained a proper implement and stopped toting axes.

("The All-American Axe" from *The Second Barrel* by Eric Sloane, 1969)

BALE

A mechanically formed, compressed bundle of hay or straw, bound by twine (a heavy cord). There are two basic kinds: square and round. Square bales are often picked up from the field by hand and tossed onto a truck or flatbed trailer. You won't load round bales that way, not even if your hired hand is Arnold Schwarzenegger, as they weigh several hundred pounds apiece. They are handled with a tractor-mounted, hydraulically operated front-end loader, which, by the way, is a wonderful device that has done more for the human back than anything else, except perhaps the grain auger.

(Terry Chamberlain, *The ABC's of Farming*, 1999)

BARBED WIRE

The old-time cowboys, used to the open range, hated barbed wire fences, and their attitude is shared by many a city-bred stroller who crosses over or through them, especially when they are electrified.

(Terry Chamberlain, *The ABC's of Farming*, 1999)

BEE FARM

a.k.a. **apiary**.
Keeping bees
has many
advantages over
cattle, pigs, sheep, and other kinds
of livestock:

1. No fences, big buildings, or haying
   equipment needed.
2. They are cheap to feed in the
   summer as they always eat out,
   often on other farmers' crops.
3. You don't have to call a veterinarian
   if one gets sick. If it dies, well,
   you have thousands more.
4. If one steps on your foot it doesn't
   hurt as much as when a
   cow does.
5 Your kids are not likely to name
   them, make pets of them, and get
   upset when they're gone.

Of course, as with any endeavor,
there are certain drawbacks. The
most obvious one is not as big a
problem as you might think: in
today's commodity markets farmers
are used to getting stung.

(Terry Chamberlain, *The ABC's of
Farming*, 1999)

BISON

More commonly called "buffalo."
Closely related to the barnyard cow,
though the cow is reluctant to admit
it, the buffalo being a rough, shaggy
creature with terrible manners. Once
they roamed wild on the prairies, but
now most are confined to game
ranches. In fact, the bison is
sometimes bred to the domestic cow,
usually, I suspect, without
her consent.

(Terry Chamberlain, *The ABC's of
Farming*, 1999)

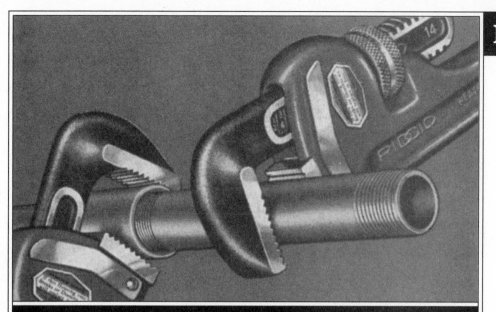

BORROWING

While that sort of practice resonates with Christian charity and is rarely anything but altruistic, I have grown a good deal less sanguine about the constant practice of rural lending and borrowing. I have had friends borrow everything from my tractor to my shotgun, from my power washer to my pickup truck, and in each and every case the item in question was returned in worse condition than it left, sometimes ruined. Often it wasn't returned at all. My Dad made a determined point of never loaning or borrowing anything and pounded into my head that if I should ever borrow anything, it had to be returned in better condition than when I got it. That is definitely not the attitude around here, where the feeling prevails that if you could spare this item long enough to loan it out, you probably really don't need it much anyway. One good friend asked to borrow a relatively expensive car-top luggage carrier for his daughter to use on a trip to Florida, where she was going to live for a while, until she moved permanently . . . to Africa! I wondered aloud how he planned on getting the carrier back to me if this was a one-way journey? He looked at me in puzzlement and then indignation. Obviously, he considered it downright un-neighborly of me to clutter my mind—and his— with such a consideration. He wanted to borrow the carrier; returning it hadn't come into the mix yet, if it ever would.

To this day my favorite example was the time a friend who had become an in-law asked to borrow a couple expensive, heavy-duty house jacks from me to raise the corner of his sagging house. For those of you who might not know about such things, these heavy screw jacks are put under a building and turned to raise the building, or in this case, a corner of it. The element you are lifting is pushed just a trifle beyond where you want it and then a permanent foundation like concrete blocks, stones, or wood pilings are put under the building and the jack is eased back down until the house rests on its new base. A couple more turns and the jack can be removed to be used the next time you need to do some heavy lifting. But my friend and kin didn't bother with those last few steps. He just used my jacks to lift his house . . . and walled shut the bottom of his house, thus making the jacks the new permanent foundation of his home. Did he apologize? Did he replace the jacks? Did he even bother to tell me where my jacks had found a new home? Why would he want to do something like that? I loaned him the jacks, didn't I? So obviously, I didn't need them.

It seems unfriendly of me, I realize, and I am sure I've gained something of a reputation for being selfish, unreasonable, and snooty, but after years of replacing broken items that had been borrowed, having to go out around town to retrieve loaned items (borrowed things are blithely loaned to someone else, and even then to a third party, who doesn't even know from where it came originally and therefore couldn't return it to the owner even if he wanted to, and simply loses things no matter how expensive or irreplaceable they may be), I've had to make a policy of loaning nothing to anybody. On one occasion a really good friend needed a tool and wanted to borrow mine. I knew that once that thing went out the door of my shop, it was gone forever and I would have to buy a replacement. So instead of losing the expensive tool I was fond of, I just went ahead and bought a less expensive example of the same item and gave it to my friend as a gift, saving the trouble of getting all hepped up about him not returning the one I would have loaned him. I didn't get the impression that the irony of what I had done made a dent.

("Neither a Lender" from *Forty Acres and a Fool* by Roger Welsch, 2006)

BOYS

Say what you will about the general usefulness of boys, it is my impression that a farm without a boy would very soon come to grief. What the boy does is the life of the farm. He is the factotum, always in demand, always expected to do the thousand indispensable things that nobody else will do. Upon him fall all the odds and ends, the most difficult things.

After everybody else is through, he has to finish up. His work is like a woman's—perpetual waiting on others. Everybody knows how much easier it is to eat a good dinner than it is to wash the dishes afterwards. Consider what a boy on a farm is required to do; things that must be done, or life would actually stop.

It is understood, in the first place, that he is to do all the errands, to go to the store, to the post office, and to carry all sorts of messages. If he had as many legs as a centipede, they would tire before night. His two short limbs seem to him entirely inadequate to the task. He would like to have as many legs as a wheel has spokes, and rotate about in the same way.

This he sometimes tries to do; and people who have seen him "turning cart-wheels" along the side of the road have supposed that he was amusing himself, and idling his time; he was only trying to invent a new mode of locomotion, so that he could economize his legs and do his errands with greater dispatch.

He practices standing on his head, in order to accustom himself to any position. Leapfrog is one of his methods of getting over the ground

quickly. He would willingly go an errand any distance if he could leap-frog it with a few other boys.

He has a natural genius for combining pleasure with business. This is the reason why, when he is sent to the spring for a pitcher of water, and the family are waiting at the dinner-table, he is absent so long; for he stops to poke the frog that sits on the stone, or, if there is a penstock, to put his hand over the spout and squirt the water a little while.

He is the one who spreads the grass when the men have cut it; he mows it away in the barn; he rides the horse to cultivate the corn, up and down the hot, weary rows; he picks up the potatoes when they are dug; he drives the cows night and morning; he brings wood and water and splits kindling; he gets up the horse and puts out the horse; whether he is in the house or out of it, there is always something for him to do.

Just before school in winter he shovels paths; in summer he turns the grindstone. He knows where there are lots of winter-greens and sweet flag-root, but instead of going for them, he is to stay in-doors and pare apples and stone raisins and pound something in a mortar. And yet, with his mind full of schemes of what he would like to do, and his hands full of occupations, he is an idle boy who has nothing to busy himself with but school and chores!

He would gladly do all the work if somebody else would do the chores, he thinks, and yet I doubt if any boy ever amounted to anything in the world, or was of much use as a man, who did not enjoy the advantages of a liberal education in the way of chores.

("No Farming without a Boy" from *Being a Boy* by Charles Dudley Warner, 1877)

BRANDING

On branding day (the day when your ranch mark is burned into the hides of all those fresh-faced baby calves), you do double duty. Not only do you act as hired hand, but you're also chief cook, hostess, and runner-after of anything anybody has forgotten. Sometimes a day of indescribable hilarity, sometimes laced with small tragedies, branding day is always a whole lot of work. As a thinking Country Wife, estimate how many neighbors and extra hands are coming to "help"; add fifteen, then lay in mountains of provisions, because country custom says you must feed all those hands promptly at 12:00 noon. All food must be home-cooked. Fortunately, some of the neighbor Country Women feel it is their duty to help out in the kitchen.

While you nestle cases of beer and soda pop among the rocks at the edge of the creek, the men and women riders are furiously busy. Calves are cut away from their mammas, branding fires are started, ropers swing loops. Calves are roped and dragged, bellowing, towards waiting cowboys and cowgirls who grab the north and south ends of the poor little things and stretch in both directions. Other cowboys leap to apply the hot iron, castrate the little bulls, notch the ears, and gouge out nubbins of horn.

You and the other women not smart enough to stay in the house (or if you're not a roper) are in charge of the vaccinating, the tally sheet, the disinfectant, the scour pills, the blood stopper powder, and keeping track of the de-horning spoons.

The watchwords for the Country Woman wielding any of the branding day implements are "Look out!" Exude confidence as you approach a calf captured firmly by north and south cowboys. Have the vaccine gun primed and ready. Pinch a bit of skin away from the calf's ribcage just under the foreleg. Thrust the needle in, making sure you don't poke through one side and out the other of the pinch, thereby squirting the vaccine in the air. Move quickly and try to keep out of the way of the man with the hot iron who is searing the brand into the calf's hide at the same time you are doing your needlework. The second you've finished injecting, pull needle out and turn nonchalantly away.* While being nonchalant, do not dawdle. Those two cowboys holding the calf will turn loose all at once. Being struck by flying hooves can take the enthusiasm out of the day.

About your person, hang a small notebook and pencil. Remember to tie these items on. Merely stuffing a notebook and pencil in your pocket won't do. At the wrong moment it will fall out and into a fresh juicy pile. Fish it out and use it anyway. As each critter is vaccinated, it's up to you to tally heifer or bull in your little book.

When you tally the bulls and heifers, you always get mixed up, but NEVER admit it. Always answer promptly and confidently even if you have to make it up.

Once or twice a lull occurs in the feverish activity. The men sag against the corral posts or flop on the ground, beer cans in hand. At this point, race for the house, make sure the big coffee urn is full and functioning, check the roasts, stuff a bushel of potatoes in the oven to bake, mentally count the chairs around the dining-room table and decide some people will have to eat from laps in the living room.

Then race back to the corral where the thoughtful husband has saved you one last swallow of warm beer.

At the noon break, pick up the bucket of Mountain Oysters** and dash for the house ahead of the men. While they "wash up," load the food on the table. No matter how starved, the men will politely hang around outside in the yard till you ring the come-and-get-it bell. Once seated, absolutely no sound is heard for the first ten minutes besides the clinking of the eating utensils. When the first panic subsides, limited conversation begins to trickle around the table. By dessert, the morning's funny episodes and catastrophes have been repeatedly analyzed and all bachelors have been teased about their girlfriends.

Naturally, you and the other women keep the coffee pot pouring and serving dishes full. Between trips, you get to eat, standing up, in the kitchen.

("Branding" from *The Ranch Woman's Manual* by Gwen Petersen, 1976)

Caution: Although nonchalance is the key attitude, alert attention must be the Country Woman's prime focus.

** *Mountain Oysters, sometimes referred to as Prairie Oysters: Those items separated from the bull calves. To be laboriously cleaned, egg-battered, crumbed, and deep-fried at a later date. (Freeze 'em till then.) Old timers claim they're delicious as well as having certain rejuvenating powers. It is not a good idea to dispute this claim.*

BUMPKIN

Name used by city folk for farm people. It implies they are unsightly, ignorant, unintelligent, and awkward. Which is ridiculous, of course; farm people are not awkward.

(Terry Chamberlain, *The ABC's of Farming*, 1999)

CALVING TIME

Generally prairie farmers and ranchers, or their spouses and offspring, must attend the births of calves in order to assist in the deliveries and/or make sure the newborns survive. They usually arrange for the calves to arrive in February or March, but within that timeframe the cows have considerable leeway to choose the specific day, hour, and minute. They generally pick the colder, wetter days (driving rain or snow if possible), late evenings (after dark), early mornings (before daylight), and bonspiel weekends.

(Terry Chamberlain, *The ABC's of Farming*, 1999)

CHICKENS

The new warmth of spring meant the chickens could be let out to run free. When I opened the door for them, they poked their heads outside cautiously for the first time in four months or more, then with a wild flapping of wings they ran out into the yard.

"Just like you boys on the first warm day," Mother said.

The chickens chased and leaped and cackled for a few hours, then settled down and began scratching for seeds, eating the new grass and looking for insects. Almost immediately they began laying more eggs. These eggs were different, the yolks much darker yellow. Mother's cakes were a richer color and everyone said the eggs tasted better.

For me there was a problem in the chickens being let out. As far back as I could remember I had been the official egg-gatherer. In winter I had only to go into the chicken house and reach into the nests for the eggs, sometimes doing it twice a day in the coldest weather so the eggs wouldn't freeze and burst. But starting with spring the eggs might be just about anywhere. Something about being free brought out a secretive side of the chickens. At least half of them seemed determined to hide their nests from me. So with spring, egg-gathering became a battle of wits.

"All you have to be is smarter than the chickens," Lee said, laughing at me. "That shouldn't be too hard, even for you."

It was, though. Either I wasn't very smart or the hens were a lot smarter than most people figured. Any sporting hen is supposed to cackle when she lays an egg. We had hens that would lay an egg and run halfway across a forty-acre field before they'd cackle, some that laid eggs and never did cackle, and some that cackled and ran but never did lay an egg. With hens looking pretty much one like another it was hard to get very scientific about egg-gathering.

Some years we had two breeds of hens and that helped. The smaller white leghorn had a more excited cackle and liked to hide nests in high places such as the haymows. The heavier Plymouth Rocks stayed on the ground and had a deeper-voiced cackle.

Mother helped by observing; "One cackled down in the orchard today," she'd say.

"What kind of cackle?"

"Sounded like a Plymouth Rock."

That meant the hidden nest would likely be on the ground. But the hiding places on a farm were endless. Hens used the soft sawdust under the protruding ends of the post pile, sheltered fence corners, feed boxes of unused horse stalls,

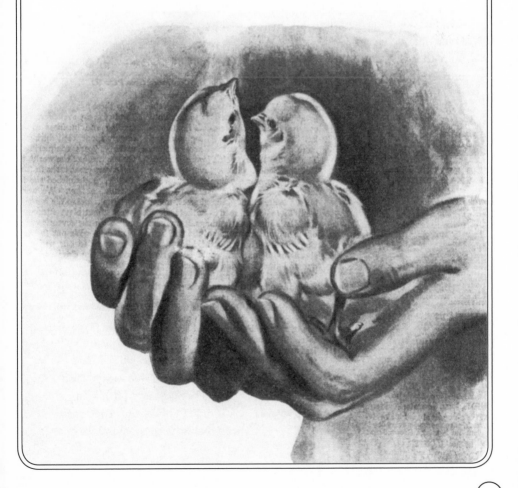

hidden corners of the haymows, and a hundred nooks and crannies in every outbuilding, weed patch, and sheltered spot.

They especially liked dark and secret corners. Where one week I reached in to find a fresh egg, the next week I might find the nest taken over by bumblebees. Once, poking into a dark tunnel in the haymow, I felt something cool and smooth. But the shape was wrong. I took hold and hauled back. Out came a hissing, five-foot black snake, lumpy with swallowed eggs. I jumped back. My full bucket of eggs and I went crashing down the hay chute. I don't know what happened to the snake (were the eggs inside him already broken?). Mother said it was the best job of scrambling since the time the buck sheep butted me when I was climbing over a board fence.

There was a time she may have forgotten. That was when I was coasting downhill toward the open barnyard gate, a bucket of eggs in the wagon with me. Just as I got to the gate, the wind blew it shut.

I remember once at breakfast when it seemed everybody was reporting cackling that I was supposed to investigate. I began to feel the whole purpose of the hens was to give me a bad time.

Father laughed at my grumbling. "Ever stop to think those poor hens are just following their natural instincts? Probably all they want to do is get a batch of eggs together and hatch out some chicks. So the smarter you get, the smarter they have to get."

"Actually," Mother said, "it's kind of a compliment to you. It shows they respect your ability."

Well, that may have helped my bruised ego a little, but it didn't make the nests any easier to find.

For every reported and suspicious cackle I had to set up a strategy. Fortunately, each hen tended to lay her eggs at about the same time every day. I would hide and watch for one beginning to move in the direction of the reported cackle. They were very good at it. A hen would keep pecking and scratching, as if all she had in mind was more food, and all the time be slowly moving off from the other chickens. I shadowed the hen, keeping out of sight, trying not to make any noise. Of course, a hen never went straight to her nest. There was some kind of "natural instinct" that took care of that, too. She'd move off in one direction, double back, go around buildings, head into the deep weeds. At some point when she was half hidden, she stopped being casual and I knew she was getting close. Crouching low to the ground, the hen would creep forward so slowly that I might lose her if I took my eyes off her for a second. Then, if I was lucky, she'd move to her nest and I had won.

I didn't always win. There were hens that seemed to know I was following them. They just played a game with me. They would follow the standard routine, moving off casually, then beginning to creep, but after about fifteen minutes of leading me on they would just walk out of the weeds and rejoin the other hens. Were they just practicing or did they know exactly what they were doing? I wanted to ask Mother if she knew of any way to tell if a chicken was laughing, but I couldn't think of a way to ask without giving away more information than I got back.

Sometimes hens were all too easy to outsmart. They overacted. I remember one who reminded me of how Lee and I tried to look very innocent when we were staging a raid on Mother's shredded coconut in the pantry. Sort of humming a little song, this hen would poke along toward the horse-barn door, acting as if she didn't have a thought in the world, or maybe was just out for a morning stroll. But she kept moving right toward the barn. Finally, with a little look, as though to see who was watching, she would hop through the door. About twenty minutes later she'd come walking out, still humming her little song. Slowly she would stroll halfway across the barnyard, and only then would she suddenly run and cackle. But I knew from experience that her egg would be where it always was—in the third horse stall from the door.

Other times, weeks went by before I located a nest. Then I'd find it, full of eggs. Such eggs were not to be trusted. I put them, a few at a time, into a bucket of water. If they didn't float, I took them to the house and put them in the basket reserved for what Mother called "the questionable eggs." Eggs from that basket had to be broken, one by one, into a cup for observation before they were used. For years I thought the phrase "don't put all your eggs in one basket" had something to do with separating good eggs and questionable eggs.

> If I took the eggs away from the hen maybe she'd stay on the empty nest anyway. Some hens were just natural-born setters.

If the eggs floated, I either buried them or threw them against the side of the silo to see how they smelled. It was a way of checking the reliability of the water test. Usually they smelled pretty bad.

Sometimes a hen would be setting when I finally found the nest. Then I had to make a decision. How long had she been setting? Did we want more baby chicks? Was it too late in the season?

I had to sit down and think about it. If I took the eggs away from the hen maybe she'd stay on the empty nest anyway. Some hens were just natural-born setters.

One thing to do was see if the eggs were shiny. If they weren't, they'd been set only a few days and were worth putting to the water test. For the set-on eggs, the test was helpful but not conclusive. An egg that floated might be too old and going bad, or it might have a baby chicken forming inside. So when set-on eggs didn't sink, I had to run back and put them under the hen to stay warm while I made up my mind.

It was a weighty decision. How was the hen going to feel? Was there a beginning live chick inside each egg? I had to be careful about getting too sentimental. If I made a wrong decision too late in the season, there would be a whole bunch of little chicks running around in the frosty grass to feel sorry for. A late batch of chicks was always a mark of my failure, not easy to hide either, with chicks hopping and cheeping all over the place.

I can recall exactly how egg-gathering became a thing of philosophy for me. It was a warm spring day when I was in the second grade. All the boys were lined up at lunchtime, leaning back against the warm south wall of the schoolhouse. I carefully cracked a hard-boiled egg against the edge of the half-gallon syrup pail I used as a lunch bucket.

"Which came first, the chicken or the egg?" one of the big boys asked.

I hadn't been initiated to the riddle. I just stared at him.

"Which came first?" he repeated, laughing.

I thought about it. "The chicken hatches out of the egg."

"But the chicken had to be there already to lay the egg," he said.

I could see that all right, but where had that chicken come from if not from an egg? I sat there eating my hard-boiled egg, dipping it into the mixture of salt and pepper Mother had wrapped in waxed paper for me. The argument went on around me. The majority opinion was for the chicken being there first. Somehow chickens were more real.

I thought about it all afternoon. When I went out with my bucket that evening, I picked up a smooth white egg and turned it over and over in my hand. There was life in there. Inside that cool and motionless white egg, which made a silly hen cackle, was the start of a new chicken. And that new chicken would grow up, lay an egg and cackle, and the new egg would . . .

It was too much for me. I could see an unending line of eggs and hens stretching out of sight in both directions (I don't remember when I caught on to the importance of roosters). Still holding that white egg firmly in my hand, I went to consult Mother.

"Which came first, the chicken or the egg?"

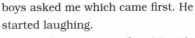

She didn't laugh. She thought about it for a moment and said,

"Neither."

She went over to my blackboard, next to the kitchen range, and drew a circle. "The chicken and the egg are both part of the same circle of life."

"Oh," I said.

I went back out and finished gathering the eggs. A circle was certainly better than a line. A circle stayed right where you could see it.

The next day at school I had a hard-boiled egg again and one of the boys asked me which came first. He started laughing.

"Neither one came first," I said. I picked up a stick, brushed the wood chips aside and drew a circle on the soft ground. "The chicken and the egg are both part of the same circle," I said with great authority.

"Oh," the boy said.

Everyone sat there looking at the circle. No one ever brought up the question again. There's something about a circle that puts a stop to things. Maybe that's all that philosophers really do—just bend the straight lines into circles, the lines coming back to meet each other so there aren't any loose beginnings or endings any more.

Now that I come to think of it, I guess my mother was a pretty good philosopher.

("Which Came First?" from *The Land Remembers* by Ben Logan, 1975)

CHORES

On most farms this means small jobs that must be done on a regular basis: milking the cows, for instance, or weeding the garden. There are many such tasks on the average farm or ranch, and they are often done by the children. It is a well-known fact that these chores teach responsibility and the work ethic, and that they are the main reason why farm kids are always honest, hard-working, self-reliant, and respectable while city kids are mostly self-indulgent, irresponsible, disorderly, lazy bums.

Another thing about chores: each generation they get easier. I know this is true because certainly I had more of them than my kids did, and my father assured me mine were nothing compared with what he had to do. I can only conclude that in my great-grandfather's time the kids did all the work while the adults did nothing but think up more chores and issue orders for them to be done. A fellow who should know tells me that in his day parents often prescribed heavy chores as an effective hangover cure for wild farm boys on the morning after.

(Terry Chamberlain, *The ABC's of Farming*, 1999)

COLT

A baby horse, especially a male one. (A she-colt is properly called a filly, which Webster's dictionary also defines as "a wanton young woman." Thus you can expect the Department of Political Correctness to soon ban the use of the term except where it can be proven that a young horse is wanton.)

A colt can grow up into a stallion (a co-producer of colts and fillies) or a gelding (a surgically altered stallion who often pretends he is still a great lover but can't come through in the crunch; therefore he shares the same low status as the **steer** and the **capon**.

A filly grows up to be a mare. "Mare" is the Latin word for "sea" or "ocean"; you'll understand the connection when you see a horse urinate (they must have gigantic bladders).

(Terry Chamberlain, *The ABC's of Farming*, 1999)

COMBINE

A harvesting machine that came into general use over the past 60 years or so. Since then one combine operator can accomplish in a few hours what three binder operators, five stookers, a thresher operator, two spike pitchers, two field pitchers, and six teamsters needed two or more days to complete. If the Agricultural Labourers' Union would have had any sense they would have murdered the inventor of the combine and destroyed his prototype before he could get it on the market.

(Terry Chamberlain, *The ABC's of Farming*, 1999)

COUNTRY MINDED

To be country-minded and chained and riveted to city living when the spring comes to the fields is woe indeed!

They say that an expatriate is one who is absent by choice, while an exile is one who is absent by compulsion. City slaves of rural origin belong to both classes. There is, of course, a third class to consider—those who never lived in the country and yet who yearn for it constantly when they can find the time for yearning.

To some city-bred folks "country minded" means being ornery and unwilling to think in a definite mold or pattern. It means being "permickety" and stubborn, resistant to modernity, inconsistent and untamed. To illustrate this scrambled idea of theirs, they point to cooperative squabbles and the insistent and never satisfied cry for farm relief and equality. They dub this as being "country minded" when it is only a manifestation of a very common human trait influenced by environment, native habits and politics.

What is it that makes country-minded men come from city offices with a smile when rain breaks a dry spell and causes them to scan the skies, like sailors, during hay time? What is there about being country minded that gives such a fraternity of feeling to folks who openly rejoice in their rural origin?

Memory is the only answer. You can take any topic under the sun, almost, and test it out under the influence of country minded memory. The power of that early environment to color the ways you approach a subject is amazing. Take religion or piety, self control or decency—whatever you choose to call this moral fiber of one's nature—and you find it has deep tap roots in the memory of country minds.

Perhaps this is why so many have observed that the city is full of successful folks who originated in the country. No doubt this is why farmers have been willing to remain underpaid and have not insisted upon union hours. This is why we cannot prove cost of production in so many specified "man-hours" at every turn of the dial in the country. So much of life and work on farm lands is a tribute to the soil itself, to the pulse of nature, dedicated to the task done to a finish, rather than to the tune of a paymaster. This is why memories of the hired help blend so closely with our own family life, instead of being some remote tool of profit-making such as too many city employees become.

One fault of country mindedness remains as a relic of copy-book days. It uses sentiment when hard sense would fill the bill to better advantage. The tendency to glorify all that is bucolic with tender allegory and plaster it with mawkish praise is as unseemly and untrue as to claim that the country is the only refuge of the pure and the meek.

The age-long struggle against bugs, blight, frost, flood and hail makes for a rather stoic sort of inward philosophy.

Arising from that same trait in the country mind is the saving grace of good humor. There is more broad, man-sized appreciation of the ridiculous and the laughable in our country communities than almost anywhere else. It is possibly this homeopathic method of treating our mental ills with a dose of risibility which enables me to accept the crowded street car, the fly-specked lunch counter, the traffic jams at night and the blunders of the janitor with more or less equanimity.

So probably the country mind is one that has been both ventilated and insulated, and hence escapes some of the contagion and the false attitudes of the passing moment. At least we who think we have it yearn to mingle with those who possess it, and we long to live once more under the sky and the stars, clasping the plow-handles, feeding the livestock and braving the elements, with the mortgage and the tax bill as the only reminders of Adam's original sin and his banishment to a bucolic livelihood.

("On Being Country Minded" from *The Land: Volume 5* by E. R. McIntyre, 1945)

COUNTRY MUSIC

A type of song, originally associated with rural regions, with lyrics mostly about ridin', truckin', hurtin', cheatin', losin', boozin', bleedin', leavin', lyin', cryin', and dyin'. If you are the bizarre and perverse kind of person who can listen to that kind of downer and actually feel good about it, then you are, like me, a country music fan. But if you are the type who gets depressed easily, stay away from it; it'll push you over the edge.

(Terry Chamberlain, The ABC's of Farming, 1999)

COURTING

"My father took great delight in questioning my boy friends and I always wanted him to be on his best behavior. One of his little questions was inquiring what their intentions were. And one time I had a young man who invited me out to the movies and I was upstairs getting ready, and I heard Father at the front door letting him in and I thought, 'Oh, I'd better get down there in a hurry.' I was coming down the stairs when I heard Father launching into his speech:

" 'Now, young man, just what are your intentions towards my daughter? Are they honorable or dishonorable?'

"Most times when he said this, the young men were always very shy and got all flustered and said:

"Well . . . nothing really, just want to take her out.'

"But this young man was really up to the occasion. He looked at my father and said:

" 'You mean I've got a choice?'

"Father never did repeat that little one again."

("Young Man, What Are Your Intentions?" from *Remembering the Farm* by Allan Anderson, 1977)

COW

An animal that looks something like a buffalo but better groomed. She-cows are factory machines: hay and grain are delivered to the Input end; milk, ice cream, butter, and yogurt are obtained from the Output end in four convenient spigots, with organic fertilizer as a by-product.

He-cows are called bulls, and they have the best job on the farm, which is to assist in the production of baby cows, though for some strange reason a few leave to take employment in the entertainment industry chasing cowboys and matadors around arenas. At birth, however, a bull's future status, indeed his future, period, is rather precarious.

The farming industry in Canada for years depended on a few tried-and-true breeds: in dairy cattle, for instance, the big black-and-white Holstein and the smaller, prettier red Jersey (known for producing milk rich in butterfat); in beef cattle, the Black Angus and the white-faced Hereford. In recent decades, however, the trend to the fancy and the foreign has come to cow country, particularly in beef breeds. The Charolais—larger and beefier than the traditional breeds—was one of the first to gain favor.

(Terry Chamberlain, *The ABC's of Farming*, 1999)

COW PIE

Not, as urbanites may suppose when hearing the term, a beef pastry, but an equally delightful and honorable symbol of Western rural life, it has enlivened the evening stroll of many a city-bred visitor.

(Terry Chamberlain, *The ABC's of Farming*, 1999)

CULTIVATOR

The thing you cultivate with. It is basically a long, rectangular frame on wheels with dozens of small shovels hanging down from it. When the machine is pulled across a field the shovels dig up the dirt, of course, and thus wear out rather quickly and must be replaced (another tedious job I hated when I farmed). As a result most farms possess a pile of used cultivator shovels. (A tip: three or four used shovels welded together make a dandy boat anchor.)

(Terry Chamberlain, *The ABC's of Farming*, 1999)

CYCLONE

Dorothy lived in the midst of the great Kansas prairies, with Uncle Henry, who was a farmer, and Aunt Em, who was the farmer's wife. Their house was small, for the lumber to build it had to be carried by wagon many miles. There were four walls, a floor and a roof, which made one room; and this room contained a rusty looking cookstove, a cupboard for the dishes, a table, three or four chairs, and the beds. Uncle Henry and Aunt Em had a big bed in one corner, and Dorothy a little bed in another corner. There was no garret at all, and no cellar—except a small hole dug in the ground, called a cyclone cellar, where the family could go in case one of those great whirlwinds arose, mighty enough to crush any building in its path. It was reached by a trap door in the middle of the floor, from which a ladder led down into the small, dark hole.

When Dorothy stood in the doorway and looked around, she could see nothing but the great gray prairie on every side. Not a tree nor a house broke the broad sweep of flat country that reached to the edge of the sky in all directions. The sun had baked the plowed land into a gray mass, with little cracks running through it. Even the grass was not green, for the sun had burned the tops of the long blades until they were the same gray color to be seen everywhere. Once the house had been painted, but the sun blistered the paint and the rains washed it away, and now the house was as dull and gray as everything else.

When Aunt Em came there to live she was a young, pretty wife. The sun and wind had changed her, too. They had taken the sparkle from her eyes and left them a sober gray; they had taken the red from her cheeks and lips, and they were gray also. She was thin and gaunt, and never smiled now. When Dorothy, who was an orphan, first came to her, Aunt Em had been so startled by the child's laughter that she would scream and press her hand upon her heart whenever Dorothy's merry voice reached her ears; and she still looked at the little girl with wonder that she could find anything to laugh at.

Uncle Henry never laughed. He worked hard from morning till night and did not know what joy was. He was gray also, from his long beard to his rough boots, and he looked stern and solemn, and rarely spoke.

It was Toto that made Dorothy laugh, and saved her from growing as gray as her other surroundings. Toto was not gray; he was a little black dog, with long silky hair and small black eyes that twinkled merrily on either side of his funny, wee nose. Toto played all day long, and Dorothy played with him, and loved him dearly.

Today, however, they were not playing. Uncle Henry sat upon the doorstep and looked anxiously at the sky, which was even grayer than usual. Dorothy stood in the door with Toto in her arms, and looked at the sky too. Aunt Em was washing the dishes.

From the far north they heard a low wail of the wind, and Uncle Henry and Dorothy could see where the long grass bowed in waves before the coming storm. There now came a sharp whistling in the air from the south, and as they turned their eyes that way they saw ripples in the grass coming from that direction also.

Suddenly Uncle Henry stood up.

"There's a cyclone coming, Em," he called to his wife. "I'll go look after the stock." Then he ran toward the sheds where the cows and horses were kept.

Aunt Em dropped her work and came to the door. One glance told her of the danger close at hand.

"Quick, Dorothy!" she screamed. "Run for the cellar!"

Toto jumped out of Dorothy's arms and hid under the bed, and the girl started to get him. Aunt Em, badly frightened, threw open the trap door in the floor and climbed down the ladder into the small, dark hole. Dorothy caught Toto at last and started to follow her aunt. When she was halfway across the room there came a great shriek from the wind, and the house shook so hard that she lost her footing and sat down suddenly upon the floor.

Then a strange thing happened.

The house whirled around two or three times and rose slowly through the air. Dorothy felt as if she were going up in a balloon.

The north and south winds met where the house stood, and made it the exact center of the cyclone. In the middle of a cyclone the air is generally still, but the great pressure of the wind on every side of the house raised it up higher and higher, until it was at the very top of the cyclone; and there it remained and was carried miles and miles away as easily as you could carry a feather.

It was very dark, and the wind howled horribly around her, but Dorothy found she was riding quite easily. After the first few whirls around, and one other time when the house tipped badly, she felt as if she were being rocked gently, like a baby in a cradle.

Toto did not like it. He ran about the room, now here, now there, barking loudly; but Dorothy sat quite still on the floor and waited to see what would happen.

Once Toto got too near the open trap door, and fell in; and at first the little girl thought she had lost him. But soon she saw one of his ears sticking up through the hole, for the strong pressure of the air was keeping him up so that he could not fall. She crept to the hole, caught Toto by the ear, and dragged him into the room again, afterward closing the trap door so that no more accidents could happen.

Hour after hour passed away, and slowly Dorothy got over her fright; but she felt quite lonely, and the wind shrieked so loudly all about her that she nearly became deaf. At first she had wondered if she would be dashed to pieces when the house fell again; but as the hours passed and nothing terrible happened, she stopped worrying and resolved to wait calmly and see what the future would bring. At last she crawled over the swaying floor to her bed, and lay down upon it; and Toto followed and lay down beside her.

In spite of the swaying of the house and the wailing of the wind, Dorothy soon closed her eyes and fell fast asleep.

("The Cyclone," from *The Wonderful Wizard of Oz* by L. Frank Baum, 1900)

DAIRY FARM

Place where dairy cattle are kept. They are much like beef cattle; both kinds come equipped with four legs, four stomachs, split hooves, twin horns, leather upholstery, and voracious appetites. If given a choice of career, however, most cattle would opt for the dairy industry, since it is easier to part with your milk than it is to part with your hocks, ribs, and rump roasts. That is why dairy cows look so contented: they love life, hay, well-warmed milking machines, and supply-managed markets.

(Terry Chamberlain, *The ABC's of Farming*, 1999)

DARES

It was risky to dare this one boy because he'd do anything.

Betcha don't dare hang by your heels from the top of the windmill.

He did that, no questions asked. He did it for so long his face turned blue and the other boys screamed at him to please stop.

Betcha don't dare stuff that whole hamburger in your mouth at one time.

He stuffed the whole thing in, onions, pickles, and all. So much hamburger stuffed up in his cheeks made his eyes water, but he reached for another and was going to stuff that in too before one of the other boys said, No, don't, you'll choke.

Betcha don't dare eat a live earthworm.

He took a big one and didn't just swallow it quick like bad medicine. He sucked it in slow like a long strand of live spaghetti until some of the boys were gagging on the words they dared him with.

Then one big boy—and he must have thought about this dare for a long time, because he made sure lots of other boys were around—he said, Betcha don't dare sit on your knees and get a drink of milk from that cow without using your hands. Just your mouth. Betcha don't dare. And you gotta swallow some of it.

It was an old tame cow that was locked in a stanchion and chewing her cud. She was so tame she probably wouldn't have kicked at a rattlesnake, let alone a boy on his knees with his mouth open.

The boy looked at the cow and didn't say anything. Something about this dare made him think for a while. Then he took a deep breath, got down on his knees, and did just what they said, down on his knees, using nothing but his mouth to get at the milk.

The cow turned her head in the stanchion and looked back. She probably had never felt anything like this before. But she didn't kick.

The boy stood up with his cheeks bulging with milk.

Swallow! yelled one boy.

He took a big swallow, then spit the rest of the warm cow milk at the boy who said that.

How did it taste, huh? How did it taste? teased another boy.

Same as always, he said. No different.

("Betcha Don't Dare" from *The One-Room Schoolhouse* by Jim Heynen, 1993)

DIRT

A much-maligned and unappreciated substance (think of the expressions "dirty tricks," "digging up dirt," "dirt poor," etc.). But always remember: of all the assets a farmer has— hundreds of thousands or more dollars in tractors, combine, implements, trucks, grain bins, shop, barn, tools, and other equipment; agricultural skills galore; access to professional expertise in marketing, pest control, and crop science—all these pale to insignificance and are totally worthless without the most vital ingredient of all: lowly, messy, grubby, ugly, socially unacceptable, universally despised, plain old **dirt**.

(Terry Chamberlain, *The ABC's of Farming*, 1999)

DIVERSIFICATION

In agriculture this term refers to farmers getting into the kinds of crops and livestock they have never raised before and therefore know sweet nothing about; doesn't that sound like a clever idea? Some of the more exotic plants now making an appearance on the prairie scene are canary seed (many older farmers think it's for the birds), coriander (which I always thought was a female rock singer), fenugreek (which apparently is a good source of galactomannan gum, a fact that certainly got me all excited), and cumin (cumin soon to your area).

Some of the specialty livestock showing up on Western farms and ranches are buffalo, elk (large, economy-size deer), llamas (like camels but smaller, fuzzier, and more arrogant looking), ostriches (big turkeys that can kick the bejesus out of a horse, or farmer), emus (which look like poorly groomed ostriches), and exotic

rabbits (I promised not to say learning to look after them is a hare-raising experience).

(Terry Chamberlain, *The ABC's of Farming*, 1999)

DOCTORING

Our farm was twelve miles from the nearest doctor, hospital or veterinarian, so we became early do-it-yourselfers. We generally didn't have the money to pay for those services anyway.

Early in life, at Mom's insistence, we developed a sort of "if you don't think about it, it will go away," or "pick up your bed and walk with it" attitude. And, aside from an extremely acute case of appendicitis which I developed when I was in sixth grade, the system worked fairly well.

As children, our first encounter with a real doctor probably came about the third grade. We were lined up one morning at school and told to roll up our left sleeve. At the end of the line was a lady in a white dress and cap who turned out to be a nurse humbly taking orders from a man dressed in white who was, naturally, the doctor, we figured. The doctor held a long sharp instrument which looked to us like something one might use on a horse. It was the very early beginnings of what will probably one day turn out to be a national health program. We got free shots for diphtheria, and later free small pox vaccinations.

Other than these two incidents in school we were without much professional medical attention. The same went for the animals. But this is not to say we were without remedies, aids and help.

One of our major remedies was carbolic salve which we purchased from a man who came around twice a year. He was known to us simply as The Raleigh Man. He sold salves and vanilla and other things in bottles, jars and interesting little round tin boxes which are collector's items today. There was also the Watkins Man who also sold things to us from time to time.

Besides the carbolic salve which was used on man and beast, probably from the same orange and black striped can, we had an evil smelling liniment which was rubbed on horses and people. I never had occasion to use that hateful stuff, but my brothers did when they had aching muscles. And, the horses needed it all the time.

Goose grease was exactly that— fat from a goose. The bird served as a meal and left its fat behind for winter use. It was said to be a remedy for colds and chest problems. A layer of goose grease on the skin topped off by a piece of scratchy flannel seemed to heal where modern medicine fails.

When we had the money, we also had Vicks Vapo Rub which came, as it does today, in a dark blue jar. Rubbed briskly on a throat or chest, the vapor cleared sinuses for miles around including the victim's.

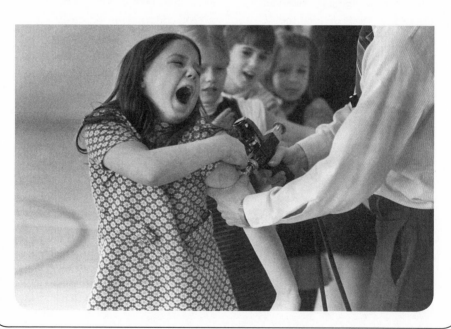

I would never dream of going into a winter now without a blue jar of Vicks handy, and I would put my lack of sick days record against anybody's.

Liverwurst sandwiches with raw onions also were eaten as a great preventive medicine. I expect today doctors would claim the reason onions helped is that they kept those with colds away from the ones without colds and that may be part of it.

If carbolic salve didn't work on wounds, turpentine would do. Holes in our bodies which demanded liquid medication were treated with turpentine. Sometimes the cure hurt worse than the wound, but we never lost a child or a parent due to these home remedies, so something worked.

There were ten of us in all and we bragged for years about never having had a broken bone despite the dangerous occupations we engaged in and the hazardous play areas we used.

One sure-fire remedy, a Saturday morning dose of castor oil, was discontinued, despite my parents' firm belief in its benefits, after I suffered appendicitis. The castor oil was administered to me when I turned up very ill about mid-day. By the next morning, I was sicker and by noon my appendix had ruptured. Dad and Mom were given a severe dressing down and a firm lecture about castor oil by the doctor who managed to pull me through.

Dad always said it was easier to give a horse a dose of something than it was to get that tablespoon full of castor oil into a thirty-pound kid anyhow. That's saying something, too, because horses are not all that willing to open their mouths to accept a foreign substance.

One method of administering pills to a horse is to put the king-size pill into a tube. One end goes into the administrator's mouth and the other end into the animal's mouth. Everything works dandy, unless, of course, the horse blows first.

The other method which involves the other end of the horse is far too grim to discuss here, but the same hazard exists in that method, too.

Sickly chickens got something in their drinking water. Sometimes it helped, and sometimes it just seemed to speed their demise. They have no staying power or positive thinking vents, of course. As baby chicks they will stand there looking cute as buttons and the next minute they are flat on their backs, feet in the air, totally dead without a sign of plague, disease or natural disturbance.

Hogs, a prime source of cash and meat for our own table, were pampered to the extent that they were vaccinated against cholera by a real veterinarian. Sheep seemed to seldom become ill. Sheep simply died, usually at lambing time, leaving us to hand-raise their offspring, if any.

The first five of us were born at home in the front bedroom, often with only the help of a lady who came for that purpose. She was a midwife, of course, but we didn't know that. We only knew we should stay outside and keep quiet until it was over. In fact for some time we didn't even know until what was over.

As the family grew the arrival of yet another little one was hardly cause for alarm, celebration or change in the daily routine. If the weather and season were right, Dad would often be in the field during the longest part of the drill. I recall one long afternoon, it was summer, when the three of us older ones placed ourselves on evenly spaced logs in the barn yard where we could keep close watch on the back door of the house. We sat there or stretched out on our stomachs saying little but just waiting. Not a sound came from the house where the woman who had been called in waited with Mom.

As the sun crept behind the barn and the end of the day approached, the woman came out and called to us. We were allowed to see our new brother, red, wrinkled and sound to sleep at Mom's side in the big bed in the front bedroom. The woman, meanwhile, carried out her orders which were to hang a white towel on the line if it was a baby girl or two towels if it was a baby boy. Two towels went up that day.

Later babies were delivered in the hospital twelve miles away, and we often didn't view the newest addition for a week or ten days later. By then we were old hands and actually could have waited two weeks if need be.

Usually a woman from the area came to cook while Mom was gone, but later we managed on our own with Dad directing the operation. By then I was capable of many household chores having been initiated early and well by need alone.

Once or twice we all fell ill with some childhood disease or other and thus forced to take to our beds for some days. But only a severe case of scarlet fever which overtook one of my brothers while the rest of us escaped for some reason was cause of alarm. But he recovered in no time.

When we came down with some contagious illness, as we did, of course, the county sent around a man who nailed a bright orange or yellow sign on the front door which meant we were under quarantine, sometimes for as long as two weeks. If we were lucky we all came down with the illness at the same time, if not we could be quarantined for weeks while we all went through it, one by one.

Quarantined meant nobody was to leave the farm or enter the house but us. Grandmas didn't count, however, so ours came and went as they pleased, daring the authorities to stop them if they cared to do so.

They did not. Both were formidable women.

There's much to be said for attitude, as some of the experts are now proclaiming. Smile and the world smiles back, a positive attitude goes miles toward recovery, but surgeons have their place, too, and the deal is to be smart enough to know which to use to achieve a cure.

We had, of course, plenty of outside exercise, lots of natural foods, not much candy, and perfect good reasons to stay on our feet. Not a bad way to go. I still use it today and find it still works.

("Castor Oil, Carbolic, and Courage" from *Rainy Days Are for Pulling Weeds* by Virginia MacKay, 1996)

DRESS CODE

Yes, there is a dress code for the prairie farmer. Many city folk still picture him as a long, lean fellow with a straw hat and overalls chewing on a straw and leaning on a pitchfork. That portrayal has become obsolete in recent decades, however. The straw hat, overalls, and pitchfork have gone the way of the dodo bird, replaced by the tractor cap, jeans, quilted vest, and front-end loader. And he's not necessarily that lean anymore either; what with all the power equipment found on most farms today, it's not just his pickup truck that's likely to be carrying a spare tire.

(Terry Chamberlain, *The ABC's of Farming*, 1999)

EDUCATION

My formal schooling began when I was six years old—at home.

Our farm was between two country schools, each two miles away. Normally, in such a situation, parents were allowed to choose which school their child would attend. But we had no car at that time and the roads we lived on were mud a good share of the year, making any passage difficult. Mom had been a country school teacher before her marriage and she asked permission from Mr. Henderson, the county superintendent, to teach me my first year at home.

I WONDER IF MISS HONEK WOULD LET ME GO FOR A PAIL OF WATER— WE DON'T NEED COAL FOR THE STOVE, AND I'VE ALREADY BEEN TO THE PRIVY THREE TIMES SINCE RECESS

IT SEEMED LIKE AN AWFUL LOT OF SPRINGTIME WAS WASTED INSIDE OUR LITTLE SCHOOL HOUSE — UNLESS WE COULD DEVISE WAYS OF GETTING OUTSIDE

He agreed and every morning, from nine o'clock to noon, five days a week, school was in session in our kitchen. It wasn't easy for me or Mom in such a familiar and family-used place. I looked forward to Saturday as much as any schoolboy anywhere. My school desk again was our table, my schoolroom again the kitchen and my teacher was again my Mom. I wasn't easy to teach and balked at the regimen of textbooks and slate and tablet.

The fall I became seven we had a car and Mom had had enough of teaching school in the house. It was decided that I would enter second grade at the north school where I knew one of the pupils.

As the end of summer approached and the fateful first day of school came ever closer, I could not bear to even look at a school house, any school house, as we passed them on the road. Even having new clothes, a new lunch pail and a new wooden pencil box with its wooden ruler, pencils and eraser didn't sweeten the situation for me.

The morning of my first day I had no appetite for the breakfast Mom prepared. Dressed in my new school clothes and with tears streaming down my cheeks I pleaded to be allowed to stay home. I promised to study hard and not balk at going to school in the kitchen. That arrangement seemed pretty good to me after all.

But fate moved relentlessly on and I soon found myself standing beside my mother being introduced to my new teacher—pretty, red-haired Miss Morgan. All the kids seemed to be old hands at this school business and gave me the impression I was an odd intruder into their tight association. Even the boy I knew previously seemed to desert me. I wanted to go home.

> Dressed in my new school clothes and with tears streaming down my cheeks I pleaded to be allowed to stay home.

During the next few weeks my resistance to becoming educated wore down and gradually the daily trip to school was made with less apprehension. I began to feel accepted by the other school kids— by all except Otto, who seemed to have something against me—and he carried quite a bit of influence in the school yard. When winter came he brought his new sled to school. Everyone was permitted to play with it except me.

But time has a way of healing hurts and changing things. As the end of the winter term approached, Mr. Henderson asked my parents to send me to Marion number seven, the school which was rightfully in our district anyway. He explained that the school population there had dropped to only three and that they needed four to keep the school open. So the beginning of the spring term found me, with my lunch bucket, wooden pencil box and second grade reader, moving into a new situation where I was to remain until I finished eighth grade six years later.

That spring term at Marion number seven was almost like being privately tutored when at home the year before, only that in addition to myself I had Wilbert, Rex and his sister Marjorie as school mates.

The following year the population increased and in a year or so we had nearly filled our one-room school. And going to school with its scholastic and social aspects pretty well filled my life a good portion of the year. My world was expanded beyond the boundaries of our farm and near neighbors to include the school district. Before long the extracurricular activities such as school programs at Halloween and Christmas and playing in the school yard (in which our imaginations had full reign, since we had a minimum of playground equipment—a softball and a bat) were something that helped to make me less reluctant to spend so much time at school. We played games such as "anty over" the school house, "pump, pump, pullaway", "red light", "run sheep, run" and other hand-me-down folk games. In the winter there was "fox

and goose", snowball fights with snow forts, and just plain frolicking in the snow. When the weather was bad we played inside at such games as "spin the bottle" and chalk games on the blackboard.

After Dean began school I was much happier. The two of us walked the two miles to and from school together. Our playground was extended to include the road between the farm and the school.

The walk to school was usually a "forced march" to get there before the nine o'clock bell rang. Sometimes when we were late, if one of our friends were on the bell rope, we were able to get into the school house before the bell stopped ringing and thus were not marked "tardy". It got so the neighbors knew when they heard an extended ringing of the school bell in the morning that the Artley boys were running the last few rods to the school house.

Going home after school was a much more leisurely time, however. Sometimes we were even tardy getting home and late getting at our chores. This could be worse than being late to school.

There was much to explore and examine along the rutted, often muddy, country roads. There were bridges to tip-toe over, "just in case a tramp was asleep under it". Roadside trees and shrubs were hosts to small wild creatures that we could sometimes spot if we were quiet. In season there were wildflowers, grape and plum blossoms along the fence rows that filled the air with their scent—adding to that of clover blossoms in the fields nearby. In September there were sweet wild plums with which we filled our lunch pails and fed upon along the way.

There was a period of time when Rodemeyer's dog intimidated me as I passed by their place. One time during my first year when I walked the road alone, Mrs. Rodemeyer had to rescue me from behind a roadside tree and accompany me safely past their driveway, assuring me that their dog, which seemed friendly enough then, was all bark. Nevertheless for some time after that I took another route home.

More frightening than any dog was an experience I had another time when I was going home alone by the alternate route which included a mile of graveled Iowa Highway number ten. A car pulled up and stopped and the lone man driver asked if I would like a ride. My parents had warned me to never accept rides from strangers, so I declined. He insisted and even started to get out of the car, whereupon I started running down the road toward Ed Mahncke's place hoping our good neighbor would see my plight. But about then the man who was so insistent upon giving me a ride apparently decided I wasn't worth his bother and took off in a cloud of dust.

That experience made me even more cautious of strangers. A few weeks following that episode another car pulled up beside me on the same stretch of highway. With my heart in my throat I refused the offer of a ride from the middle-aged couple, even though they said they were going right past my driveway. Sometime later the pastor of the Lutheran church about two miles from our place, vesper bell of which often could be heard on the evening air, told Dad about how he and his wife had tried to give me a ride. He thought my parents had me pretty well trained.

Most of the time our schoolyard gang was an amiable group, but occasionally there were fights. Too often I was one of the protagonists and Roy Spangenburg the other. I have no idea what we fought about—I'm not even sure we knew then.

> In September there were sweet wild plums with which we filled our lunch pails and fed upon along the way.

The last few years I attended country school, Dad served as director of our school. It was with a great sense of pride that I walked into our schoolroom, still reeking from the smell of cigar smoke from the meeting of the night before, knowing that Dad was now director of our school.

It was up to the director to hire the teacher, provide the coal and other supplies, and mow tall grass in the schoolyard each fall before school opened. During Dad's term of office a fence was put up around the school-yard and a well was drilled and a pump installed on the school grounds so that we no longer had to go across the road to Mahncke's for drinking water.

But being of the family of the director had its drawbacks as well as its glory. We became aware of this when Dad rehired a teacher that some in the district had expressed dissatisfaction with. This action of Dad's brought about a breach of relations between our family and several of our neighbors. For several months we were made to feel as outcasts in the neighborhood, and we couldn't even go to town without being aware of having fallen from the grace of our neighbors. When we met on the streets, they looked the other way. It was some time before this unpleasant situation healed, even though the scars remained.

On the whole my years at Marion school number seven were happy years, rich in things rural and human. The only adverse result of my years at country school was being made to feel inferior when I entered high school in town. Those of us from the country schools were breaking into a class that had been together since kindergarten in town.

We were the outsiders and rightly or wrongly, we felt we were being looked down upon.

But if I had to do it all over again, I would choose to spend those early, formative years in a one-room country school, just the way I did back then.

("School" from *Bob Artley's Memories of a Former Kid* by Bob Artley, 2002)

EGG

You will find these in the dairy section of your local grocery store along with milk, cream, yogurt, etc., which is strange because cows do not lay eggs. Hens do. In fact, an egg would have become a baby chicken, would have grown up to be a fine hen or rooster if you hadn't eaten it for breakfast this morning. But now it never will. I hope you're proud of yourself.

(Terry Chamberlain, *The ABC's of Farming*, 1999)

A fence strung with electrified wire to shock animals that touch it and thereby discourage them from trying to go through it. It has a secondary function of providing entertainment for farm families at the expense of visiting urban relatives. ("Sure you can pick yourself a tiger lily, Madge, there's one over there. Just bend down and lift that wire a bit . . .")

(Terry Chamberlain, The ABC's of Farming, 1999)

ELECTRICITY

The boys remembered the night electricity came to the farm. At least the oldest did, and the others pretended to. Or they'd heard the story so often they thought they remembered it. After a while, it didn't matter who really remembered it and who didn't. They all knew the story.

It was the night the big switch was thrown somewhere at some big dam. This was long after the electrician had spent weeks wiring all the buildings, putting switches on walls where only wallpaper had been, putting a long fluorescent light like the ones they'd seen in town right in the middle of their kitchen ceiling so that the old lantern had to hang on a new hook until the big switch was thrown.

The night of the big switch: that's when all these dead wires and gray light bulbs were supposed to come to life. Could it really work? Could electricity get all the way out here from that big switch at that big dam hundreds of miles away?

A letter had come telling how to get ready for the big night. Five o'clock p.m. on such-and-such a day the big switch would be thrown.

Have all switches turned off, the letter said, and turn them on one at a time. As if the big dam couldn't stand to have all of its electricity sucked out at once. Which made sense to the boys. Cows kicked if you tried to milk all four teats at once. And a horse would take more easily to four riders if they didn't all get on at once. Imagine a chicken laying ten eggs in one shot. It made sense.

So the night of the big switch they sat around the kitchen table waiting, switches turned off. Waiting for five o'clock. Then they saw it happen—a light on the horizon where there hadn't been a light before. Then a light in the neighbor's window, about a half-mile away. Then lights popping on everywhere. It looked as if the whole world was covered with fireflies. The new light was not the yellow light of lanterns but the white clear light of electricity. Light clear as water from the big dam, wherever it was.

One of the boys flicked the kitchen switch. And it happened right there. The big switch worked, even here. It was as if the ceiling opened with light. A fluttering fluorescent angel of light. A splash, a woof, a clatter of light. And in one second there was more light in that kitchen than had ever been there. Light brighter than high noon on the Fourth of July. They looked at each other in this new light—every freckle, every smudge, every stringy hair, every ring around the collar clearer than ever. Then they looked around the room—the cupboards, the wainscoting, the wallpaper, the ceiling where the old lantern dangled like a hanged man.

And out of the throat of one of the horrified light-stricken grown-ups came the words, My goodness! Look how dirty this place is!

So the first night of that great fluorescent light they spent washing the walls. Every one of them. Every inch.

That was the story the boys knew. That was the story they would always be able to tell, whether they remembered it or not.

("Electricity" from *The One-Room Schoolhouse* by Jim Heynen, 1993)

ENVIRONMENTALIST

Environmentalists are people who are specially trained to worry about the environment, and to make sure the rest of us worry about it too. They do not approve much of farmers and ranchers; their pesticides pollute the soil, they say, their cattle pollute the air (see **flatulence**), and their machines and vehicles have a ravenous appetite for fossil fuels. In return, of course, most farmers aren't too crazy about environmentalists either, especially those who lecture us about Canada's—and particularly the West's—high energy consumption, with no regard to our climate, our small population spread over vast distances, and the very high productivity and efficiency of our grain and livestock producers. The next time one of those smug experts tells us there should be a special energy tax on gasoline and diesel in order to "encourage" us to use "alternate modes of transportation," I think we should seize him, lock him in a prairie farmhouse, make him stay there until he develops a raging toothache, then let him out, hand him a bicycle, and say, "The nearest dentist is just 57 miles down the road. *Bon voyage* and toodle-oo!"

(Terry Chamberlain, *The ABC's of Farming*, 1999)

FARMER

One who farms, i.e., raises crops and/or livestock. Also known, in various times and places, as sodbusters, stubble jumpers, plowboys, peasants, pig sloppers, dirt grubbers, villains (which originally meant "farmers," check your Webster's) and numerous other unflattering and often unprintable terms. Funny thing about farmland: throughout history, those who owned it, never touched it, and knew sweet tweet about working it were elevated to high social status (dukes, barons, earls, and the like), while those who had the skills and know-how to make it produce the stuff of life were treated with contempt, impoverished, used, and abused. Today's ruling classes—corporate, financial, and governmental—are much wiser. They treat farm folk with respect: praise them, romanticize them, call them "the backbone of the nation" and such. They've discovered, you see, that it's much easier to shaft a guy who's grinning at you, unsuspecting, than one who is mad. Safer too.

(Terry Chamberlain, *The ABC's of Farming*, 1999)

FARM LABOR

Traditionally prairie farmers have depended on three main methods of obtaining farm labor: (1) Marry it. (2) Conceive it. (3) If all else fails, hire it.

All three methods have their drawbacks. Farm wives have, over the years, developed the unreasonable attitude that just because they do half or more of the work on the place they should also have a voice in the decision-making. Also, they do not come as cheap as many a young rube thought they would.

As for method #2, kids don't come particularly cheap either, and just when you get them trained to the point where they might be worth their keep, they fly the coop.

The third option, hiring someone, was once fairly easy, but not anymore. Getting someone with the skills to operate today's high-tech, expensive equipment is a real problem. If you do find an individual who won't drive your $150,000 tractor through the machine shed wall or put your prize boar through the combine you probably can't afford him or her. And of course, keeping up with labor regulations, figuring out payroll deductions, and doing all the related paperwork threatens to take up more time than the hired help is likely to save.

(Terry Chamberlain, *The ABC's of Farming*, 1999)

FARRIER

A person who shoes horses. No doubt a bit of downsizing occurred in this profession with the invention of the automobile and tractor, but farriers are still very important people in the racehorse, saddle horse, and show horse fields. Not a job for cautious people. This, after all, is the guy who holds a 2,000-pound Clydesdale's hoof between his (the farrier's) legs and pounds nails into it. He or she no doubt thinks driving Indy racers is a sissy job.

(Terry Chamberlain, *The ABC's of Farming*, 1999)

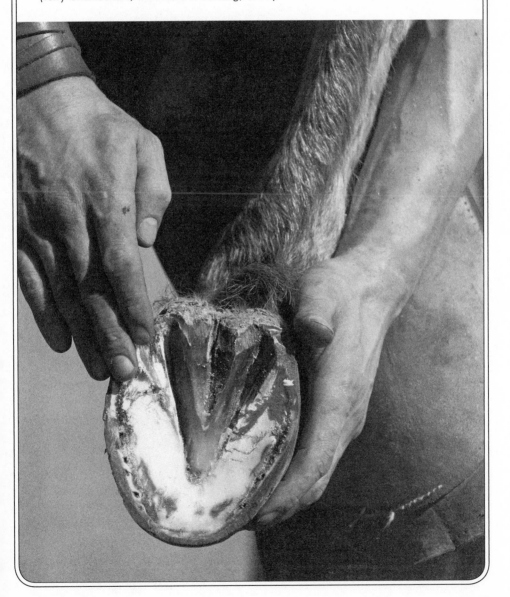

FENCE

A structure which is generally used on the farm to keep things (cows, horses, sheep, etc.) in, and in the city to keep things (dogs, burglars, perverts, in-laws, etc.) out.

(Terry Chamberlain, *The ABC's of Farming*, 1999)

FERTILIZER

Substances you put on or in the soil to make crops grow better. Once upon a time the manure of farm animals was good enough, and you had to haul the stuff out of the barn anyway. But that won't do anymore, oh no. It's too . . . *free*, for one thing. So a few decades ago researchers invented chemical fertilizers, which make plants grow much better, which increases the yield, which gives farmers more product to sell, which brings in more money. Therefore the more fertilizer used, the richer the farmer. That's the theory. Damn good one too, except for a few other considerations, such as the unpredictability of prairie weather, insect pests, diseases, etc. and the fact that every time grain goes up 10% in price fertilizer goes up 50%. Thus there is a Critical Line that marks the exact amount of fertilizer needed to increase yield to a point beyond which it would not pay to increase it further because of the cost of the fertilizer. Agricultural economists have been searching for the location of that critical line for 50 years now but haven't yet found it.

(Terry Chamberlain, *The ABC's of Farming*, 1999)

FISHING

A farmer who lives near a pond and keeps ducks, ties short fish-lines, with hooks and bait, to the duck's legs when he lets them out of the pen in the morning. While the ducks swim the fish bite. This scares the ducks, who hurry ashore and into their pens, dragging the fish after them. The farmer's wife releases the ducks and appropriates the fish, and when the farmer comes to dinner he enjoys the reward of his ingenuity.

(*Farm Journal*, 1886)

FLATULENCE

The passing of intestinal gas, normally expressed with a less fancy F-word. It contains methane, a "greenhouse gas," and therefore some environmentalists say that to protect our atmosphere we should raise fewer cattle, which are high-volume flatulaters. So are sheep, goats, deer, and moose, plant-eating animals being worse offenders than meat-eaters. Now it is the fashion these days for human beings to eat less meat and more grains and vegetables; that trend has to be bad news for the environment, to say nothing of small, crowded rooms.

(Terry Chamberlain, *The ABC's of Farming*, 1999)

FOOD

Food is the magnet around which so many of my farm memories cluster. Small wonder. Hearty food in vast quantities was needed three times a day. I remembered the obstetrician who had looked at Anne—newborn, long and slender—and said, "Babies are like empty stockings. Just fill her up." I hadn't appreciated the remark at the time, but I had been at the job of filling people up ever since.

You've heard of a "generous hand" in cooking? Well, Mother Douglas certainly had one. Her largess extended even to the pets, and items like leftover pork chops and dressing were broken up for the dogs' and cats' dishes. Under her hand, cream and butter and seasonings transformed even plain old carrots into a succulent treat. Thick sour cream and extra eggs fluffed her waffles. Long after her death, Papa would still beg me for pork hocks and noodles or small-curd cottage cheese "like Vivian used to make." I never thought I got it quite right but he apparently did.

One food I could never replicate for him was the justly famous specialty of Don's grandmother. It was known as Grandma Moats's Hot Sweet Chopped Green Tomato Piccalilli. The tomatoes had to be harvested just before the first killing frost. Then you had to collect red peppers, onions, condiments, spice bouquets, and, of course, mustard and vinegar. Even Mother Douglas did not know the complete list nor the exact proportions, because the recipe was a tightly guarded secret.

When the Douglases lived in Benson, Grandma Moats lived with them, as did her frail sister whom we called Aunt Belle. From my visits to Don's house as a college student, I remembered the two white-haired women in their dark, practical housedresses, knees spread to support the dishpans of potatoes they always seemed to be paring for dinner. I understood that Grandma Moats had sworn her sister to secrecy about the recipe.

Grandma Moats had not always been so tight-lipped, but as her delicious mix steadily gained fame at home and at church suppers, people constantly asked for it. Papa began to tease that he was going to steal the recipe, market the relish, and gain fabulous wealth. Grandma, a widow concerned about money, began to guard her secret jealously, especially from Papa (or, as time passed, from any possible spies).

Mother Douglas reminisced about the controversy one day as we sat in the sunny kitchen peeling tomatoes we had scalded for canning.

"The relish was sweet and sour, too," she began. "It was too tart for a sauce and too hot. I know there was plenty of red pepper in it. Wonderful with meat, especially pork. And a little bit went a long way. I've seen it bring tears to a grown man's eyes." She almost giggled. "We canned it in pints, and a pint lasted for days even with extra men at the table."

"But you said a whole relish dish of it disappeared?" I prompted.

"Yes. Once at threshing time the men gathered at that long harvest table we used at Benson. The men joked and laughed as they seated themselves—all except for Frank, a quiet fellow who was new to the bunch. My mother and Aunt Belle had helped all morning and I made them sit down with the men. Mother would not sit until she found a place for her precious bowl of piccalilli among the crowding trays of bread and dishes of butter, jam, and cabbage slaw. I brought platters of pork roast, mashed potatoes, baked beans, and tomatoes. In a second, the noise stopped and they all started in."

"You didn't sit down?"

"No, I had just got busy pouring coffee when I noticed a look of real distress on my mother's face. I soon discovered why. The new man had started on her dish of relish, which was near the edge of his plate, and he did not pass it on to the others. He must have assumed it was his side dish. He was eating it like a dish of applesauce, and it seemed to have no effect on him."

"I'll bet Grandma was wild! Didn't she say anything?"

"No, I was afraid she'd choke, but she kept still. He'd have been so embarrassed if he'd realized what he'd done."

Mother Douglas was laughing now, but her quick fingers worked as rapidly as ever. "Then I was afraid Frank would choke," she continued. "He was really gobbling that hot stuff—he must have been brought up to clean his plate!"

"Papa didn't notice?"

"Oh, trust him! But it was too late. Frank had laid down his spoon by an empty dish."

"Now, are you going to tell me that Frank had enough fire in his belly to do the work of two men that afternoon?"

"That's what Papa claimed—said he'd use the story in advertising. His motto would be 'Grandma Moats's Hot Sweet Chopped Green Tomato Piccalilli is energizing and safe in any amount.' "

Her story reminded me of when my friendliness had been tested by two hired men, a Mexican and an Indian, who were with us for two or three weeks. Inspired, I put my small bottle of Tabasco sauce on the table,

> Sometimes hired hands shared more than our food, though. They shared hopes, disappointments, and daily life.

thinking our food might seem bland. Apparently it did! I had used that same bottle from the time we were first married, measuring exactly ten drops in a celebrated salad dressing. They showered it on meat, potatoes, and vegetables, and sopped it up with bread. When I asked Don to get another bottle on the next grocery order, I told him, only half joking, "If I ever see them put that stuff on my pie, they will never come back, I mean it."

It was feeding the neighbors who came to help and the hired men, of course, that created most of the work in the kitchen. When neighbors were our helpers, there was news and friendly gossip. Sometimes they joked and told stories about the community that I enjoyed, as I waited on them and the children, snatching a bite when I could. Hired men were more a part of the farmers' world, and Don always found a basis of comradeship with his men. I tried to visit with them at meals, but mostly their talk was of the fields and machinery. Still, I remember them best through food. Sometimes I packed up iced tea in a thermos bucket and sandwiches and cake or cookies and rattled out to the field with the toy wagon. The children often trailed along, and a short picnic made a pleasant, albeit dusty, break in the day.

To this day I can't see a pork chop without thinking of Red. He was a big, powerful, good-natured bachelor from town who played in a German band all winter and lived on unemployment benefits most of the summer. Don talked him into becoming temporary crew foreman because of an unusual problem.

We had hired two young men from town after rain had delayed the cultivating. They ran the machinery well enough, but the work proceeded very slowly. Don suspected they were taking naps in the sunshine when their tractors were out of his sight, but he couldn't afford to stop his own work long enough to prove it. Their bad habit abruptly ceased when Red joined us. Coincidentally, we noticed a couple of freshly

blackened eyes. The arrangement got us over the hump and is the only time I can recall when Don's relationship with his helpers needed strong-arm tactics.

Red was fond of my pork chop casserole. Thus, when he agreed to work Easter Sunday so that we could keep a long-promised dinner date at the Lundgrens', I made this favorite dish for his dinner. I browned eight large pork chops, covered them with raw rice, generous slices of raw onion, and tomatoes, and left them in a slow oven to stew. I assumed that I'd have leftovers ready for Monday. Suffice it to say that Red loved to eat, and we did not begrudge him a single pork chop.

Sometimes hired hands shared more than our food, though. They shared hopes, disappointments, and daily life.

For several years, Andy Larsen lived with his family in one of our houses. His three small children and our kids played together. One day he indicated to Don that he was trying to save to buy a little land of his own. Hearing that, we gave them garden space and paid him extra for odd jobs. During a spree one weekend, he accidently let his wife discover his secret. Once she knew, nothing would do except to turn over the savings to her to squander. Thoroughly discouraged, Andy began frequent excessive drinking bouts and sought a job in town.

The following year a lively young fellow asked Don for work so that he could be married to the daughter of a well-respected German farmer just northwest of us. Don offered to supply paint, lumber, and wallpaper for them to decorate a two-room building that had been used as an office before we came. Hank proved to be an excellent farmer and well worth the higher wages he had requested. They stayed only a year before a better job called, but our friendship has lasted.

Old Joe was different. He came to the farm one day in his old Ford pickup, with the door on the passenger side tied shut with rope. His eyesight was failing, and he assured us he never drove over fifteen miles an hour, and then only on the shoulder! We didn't really need a man at the time, but he apparently had nowhere else to go. He eagerly offered to work for us at a low wage that Don promptly raised, as Joe became both useful and trusted. We had assumed he would not handle machinery nor take much initiative. Only later we discovered, through stories he told the children, that he had once been an assistant agent on an Indian reservation and carried considerable responsibility. He proved to be easy with the stock, prompt, and reliable at chores, and he watched out for the children's safety when they followed him about. Finally we felt enough confidence to go to the Twin Cities for a

long-postponed overnight with my parents, leaving Joe in charge of the farm. On our return we found that he had sold last year's hay (which he knew we didn't need) to farmers who had come by seeking some. There on the kitchen table lay the money with his careful notations.

Don could remember with fondness a hired man who had been like a member of his family and had taught him to read the newspaper before he started school. But this was my first time of sharing our daily life with a person who had no close family of his own. Joe's discharge from the agency, due to the frailties of age, must have been traumatic for him, but I never heard him talk about it. How lonely and useless he must have been feeling when he turned up at our farm seeking work. His two-year time with us met a real need for him, and he proved to be a contented, useful employee. Eventually he was welcomed into the home of a nephew in South Dakota for his final years.

Perhaps I noticed Joe's loneliness more because I could see Don's circle widening. While Papa and Mother Douglas kept a low profile, seldom even attending church, Don radiated the confidence born of his comfortable upbringing; he was liked and trusted. Often on Saturday evenings, we made popcorn and read aloud or played games with the children. Don, however, sometimes had errands or needed to visit Perry's

Barber Shop. That often ended with a shared bottle, but serious drinkers went to Correll, as Appleton always voted dry.

When I occasionally served hot gingerbread with applesauce or chocolate cake and the eternal coffee for one of Don's informal committee meetings, I could see his feeling of belonging through these contacts—and not only belonging. It became clear that people sought out his opinion, people from a wider community, less stratified than the one we had known in the city. (He continually encouraged the merchants of Appleton to admit a big chain store to increase their trade area, but they feared the competition and had to watch the neighboring town of Montevideo grow and thrive instead.)

My work of preserving, preparing, and serving food remained constant, however. I always had some hired help to feed during the crop season—except for our last summer when Don offered the job of hired hand to Anne and Bill. Bill got up early and ran a tractor till noon, Anne worked from noon till late supper. Each was faithfully paid one half of full wages every Saturday night. Anne later went to college, cherishing the knowledge that her daddy had said she "could disc in a dead furrow better than he could."

Life should have been simpler for the distaff side when big machinery replaced some of the hired men and threshing rings. Food was served in much smaller quantities than in the old days—but often at strange hours. Many times when bad weather threatened, but the crop was dry and right for harvest, Don ran our big combine all night. He stopped in for hot lunches or carried sandwiches and coffee with him to keep him safely awake. I had to agree with Mother Douglas, who insisted that headlights on tractors should never have been invented. They robbed farmers of their rightful rest—to say nothing of farmers' wives.

When winter weather was severe, Don arranged with Willy, who was the International dealer and also drove the township plow, to watch for our yard light. If he found it on after a storm, he stopped and plowed us out, knowing I would have roast beef sandwiches ready and lots of hot coffee. Of course Don paid him, but it was the food, I think, that lured him to come so promptly—and it saved us hours of hard work. If the snowfall was especially heavy, Don joined his friend as he went back to plowing out the county roads. They roared through the night. While Willie guided the big blade, Don kept his eyes fastened on the sloping wingblade as it swept the roadside and yelled a warning if an obstruction loomed in the swirling whiteness.

I would snuggle back into bed, thinking of Mother Douglas again and her saying to me as a newcomer that farm people worked hard and deserved the best food and lots of it. I ruefully added to myself—yes, and apparently at all hours!

("Food and Those Who Ate It" from *Eggs in the Coffee, Sheep in the Corn* by Marjorie Myers Douglas, 1994)

4-H

A youth organization (the letters stand for Heart, Head, Hands, and Help) that illustrates one of the many basic paradoxes of prairie farming: The same men and women who constantly bitch that uncontrollable forces have combined to make farming a futile and nerve-wracking occupation, which only a fool or a masochist would take on, then turn around, form clubs, and volunteer their time to teach their own children and others the skills that will prepare and encourage them to get into the same painful cycle all over again.

My own two sons work in the city and lived there for years but always longed to move their families to rural communities. They both finally did just that and are now condemned to the inconveniences of country life and of commuting daily. I put much of the blame for that squarely on the shoulders of the 4-H leaders in the community where they grew up, who taught them such things as horse handling, leather work, and outdoor living. Those leaders were wonderful, patient, competent folk who gave unsparingly of their time and talents, but that doesn't excuse them.

(Terry Chamberlain, *The ABC's of Farming*, 1999)

FUNICLE

This is "the stalk of a seed": I looked it up. What a relief it is to know this. All my life whenever other people were discussing their funicles I wondered, "What the hell are they talking about?" I always worried that someday someone would offer to give me some funicles, and I wouldn't know what to say. Now I know. Whew!

(Terry Chamberlain, *The ABC's of Farming*, 1999)

GATE

Gates in the rural West serve two functions. One is to allow access through fences. The other is to serve as an indicator of social status: If you were to follow a pickup truck traversing a farm or ranch you would note that the dominant individual drives while the subservient one opens and closes the gates. It is also possible to judge the relationship of a farm couple as follows: If the wife does the gates it is a Traditional Marriage. If the husband does them it is a Politically Correct Marriage. If they take turns it is a Democratic Marriage (or, more likely, they're newlyweds or not yet wed).

(Terry Chamberlain, *The ABC's of Farming*, 1999)

GENETICS

Study of inherited characteristics and its application. Genetics has been important to agriculture ever since a Stone Age farmer noticed that two white chickens are more likely to have white offspring than two black chickens are. Well, then, why not use the fattest pigs, strongest donkeys, etc. for breeding stock? As a result of this *selective* breeding, modern beef cattle look about as much like their ancient ancestors as sumo wrestlers look like jockeys, and some of the poorest yields of wheat today would have looked like a bumper crop back in King Solomon's time.

A new wrinkle has been added in recent years with the development of *genetic engineering*, which includes the introduction of genetic material from one species into the reproductive cells of another, e.g. rabbits' into tomatoes'. Disgusting, unnatural, and a threat to civilization, you say? Could be. However, that hasn't stopped many other clever ideas once they catch on. The possibility of creating a germ or bug that will wipe out all the higher forms of life seems a small price to pay for juicier tomatoes, apparently. Certainly at a glance the future would suggest that if your kid wants to be an engineer you should steer him or her toward the genetic kind rather than the railroad kind.

(Terry Chamberlain, *The ABC's of Farming*, 1999)

GOAT

A small hoofed animal, useful as a supplier of milk for special needs, such as lactose-intolerant diets. Not particularly popular on prairie farms and ranches for three reasons: First, though the milk is quite valuable, daily milking of an animal that stands only two feet high is a sure-fire guarantee of chronic back trouble. Secondly, they have a rather startling body odor problem. Thirdly, they are designed by nature to do a lot of climbing, and since the flat prairies offer little opportunity to satisfy that instinct, they tend to make do with man-made objects, like your visitor's shiny new Buick.

(Terry Chamberlain, *The ABC's of Farming*, 1999)

GOPHER HUNTING

After the corn was planted, the younger lads were set to work snaring and shooting the gophers from the corn-fields. The prairie abounded at this time with two sorts of ground squirrel, which the settlers called "the striped gopher" and " the gray gopher." The striped gopher resembled a large chipmunk, and the gray gopher was apparently a squirrel that had taken to the fields. The "pocket gopher" was considered a sort of mole or rat and not really a gopher.

The survival of the fittest had brought about a beautiful adaptation to environment in both cases. The small one had become so delicately striped in brown and yellow, as to be well-nigh invisible in the short grass of the upland, while the gray gopher, living in and about the nooks and corners of the fields, which held over from year to year long tufts of gray and weather-beaten grass, fitted quite as closely to his background, his yellow-gray coat aiding him in his efforts to escape the eyes of the hawk and the wolf.

The little striped rogues absolutely swarmed in the wild sod immediately adjoining the new-broken fields, and were a great pest, for they developed a most annoying cleverness in finding and digging up the newly planted corn. In some subtle way they had learned that wherever two deep paths crossed, with a little mound of dirt in the centre, there sweet food was to be had and it was no uncommon thing to find a long row of sprouting kernels dug up in this manner, with most unerring precision.

It was clearly a case of inherited aptitude, for their cousins, far out on the prairie, were by no means so shrewd. Dwelling within the neighborhood of man for a few generations had been valuable. Inherited aptitude was plainly superimposed upon native shrewdness. They were a positive plague, and it became painfully necessary to wipe them out or give up the corn. It was the business of every boy in the neighborhood to wage remorseless war upon them each day in the week, from the time the corn was planted until it had grown too big to be uprooted.

So Lincoln carried a shot-gun about the field with which to slay these graceful little creatures, while Owen followed behind to cut off their tails as trophies. They were allowed two cents bounty (from their father) for every striped gopher, and three cents apiece for every gray gopher they killed. They generally made two rounds each day. They soon discovered that the little rascals were most likely to be out at about ten o'clock of each warm forenoon, and once again between four and five.

The boys went to this task with pleasure, but there was something aesthetic mingled with the delight of successful shooting. Like the angler or hunter, they enjoyed the vivid sunlight, the fresh winds, the warm earth, and especially the freedom of the hunter. Occasionally as Lincoln looked down at a poor bleeding little gopher at the door of his house, he suffered a keen twinge of remorse, and reproved himself for cruelty. However, it seemed the only way out, so he hardened himself and went on with his desolating work. He was too small to hold the gun at arm's length, but rested it on his knee or on a small stick which Owen consented to carry.

It was, after all, sad business, and often the tender, springing grass, the far-away faint and changing purple of the woods, the shimmer of the swelling prairie, leaping toward the flaming sun—all the inexpressible glow and pulse of blooming spring—witched him from his warfare. He lay prone on his back while the gophers whistled and dashed about in play, watching the hawks dipping and wheeling in the shimmering air, and listening to the quavering, wailing cry of the plovers as they settled to the earth with uplifted pointed wings. The twitter of innumerable ground sparrows passing overhead united with the sweet and thrilling signals of the meadow-lark, to complete the wondrous charm of the morning air.

Killing gophers was like fishing—an excuse for enjoying the prairie. Often on Sunday mornings, together with Milton and Rance, Owen and Lincoln sallied forth, armed with long pieces of stout twine to snare the little pests, for they were not allowed to fire a gun on Sunday. They became very expert in this business.

Having driven a gopher to his burrow, they took a little turn on the sod, in order to drag their strings taut. Then, slipping the noose well down into the hole, they retired to the end of the string to wait for the little fellow to pop his head through the noose, which he usually did after some moments of perfect silence. It is their habit to come suddenly and silently to the top of their burrows, and to cautiously and slowly lift their heads until they can fix an eye on you. You must be keen-eyed, or you will fail to observe the small head, which is almost exactly the color of the surrounding grass. If you glance away from the burrow even for a moment, you may fail to find it when you look back.

For they are not only exceedingly shrewd, but they are rare ventriloquists. After sitting a couple of minutes and seeing nothing, you may hear a low, sweet trill, like that of a sleepy bird. You cannot place it—it seems to be in the air one moment and behind you the next moment. The crafty rascal has come up at some other hole and is laughing at you.

You turn your head, "*cheep-eep*" —a slight movement and he is gone. You adjust your snare at the new burrow and again sit patiently and as still as stone for four or five minutes, perhaps ten, before you hear again that sly, sleepy trill. It sounds back of you, at first, then in front, and at last, by studying every inch of the ground before you, you detect a bright eye gleaming upon you from the burrow where your snare had been set at first. You now understand that you are dealing with "an old residenter," not a young and foolish child.

Owen often struggled for hours to snare one of these cunning old tricksters. He was accustomed to lie flat on his belly, with his feet waving in the air like small banners, his eyes fixed upon the hole, with fingers ready to twitch the string, but he generally grew impatient and looked away or moved, and so lost his chance. It required even greater patience and skill to succeed in snaring the gray gopher, who was capable of breaking the string when caught.

However, snaring was only part of the fun. When they grew tired of killing things, they could lay out full length on the warm, bright green sod, and listen to the softened sounds of the prairie, seeing the girls picking "goslins" on the sunny slopes, enjoying in sensuous drowse the clouds, the sun, and the earth, content, like the lambs or like Rover, to be left in peace in the downpour of spring sunshine. There was no grass for the wandering wind to wave, no trees to rustle, nothing to break the infinite peace which brooded over the wide prairie.

They felt, at such moments, some such pleasure as that the fisherman knows, when dropping his rod among the ferns he watches the soaring eagle high in the air, or listens to the ripple of the restless stream.

But neither the snare nor the shot-gun sufficed to keep these bright-eyed little people from eating up the seed, and Mr. Stewart went to the great length of scattering poisoned grains of corn about the field. This seemed to Lincoln a repulsive and terrible thing to do, but the father argued, "The poor beasties must give way, or you'll have no Johnny cake for your milk."

The boys soon had a box partly filled with gray gophers, which they tried hard to tame. It was supposed that the gray gopher, like the squirrel, could be made a household pet, but as a matter of fact they were particularly savage and untamable. They not only fought their captors, but they fought each other with unrelenting ferocity. There was something hard and stern, something pitiless and threatening, in their eyes. They invariably gnawed a hole through the box and escaped long before they showed the slightest affection for the boys, though they fed them on bread and milk and the choicest grains of corn.

One day Jack brought home a half-grown badger, and the boys were at once wildly excited by his snarling and hissing. He was ready to do battle at any moment; and though Owen put him in a box and fed him fat gophers and milk, and all kinds of good things, he never grew much tamer. Lincoln, as a piece of daring, sometimes stroked his flat, pointed head, but always at risk of having his fingers snapped off. He had a bad smell, also, and at last they grew tired of him, and turned him out again, on the sod. He waddled away flat in the grass, eagerly, swiftly. They followed him until he burrowed into a ridge and hid himself from sight, and never again attempted to tame one of his kind.

It was impossible not to have business with skunks, for they were thick. They were a greater terror to the boys than rattlesnakes; for aside from their nauseating odor, they were said to destroy the eyes of men by means of their terrible discharge. Nearly every dog of the neighborhood smelled of them, and they often got under the houses and barns, and rioted on good things, for no one cared to kill them there.

Lincoln, being instructed by Rance, set traps with long ropes attached, and by gently hauling them at long range, was able to get them far out on the prairie without disaster. Their discharge was clearly only a last resort, and so long as they were unharmed they were themselves harmless. They were really pretty creatures, especially the young ones, and Lincoln considered it a pity that they should smell so horribly strong.

("Snaring Gophers" from *Boy Life on the Prairie* by Hamlin Garland, 1899)

GRAIN

The main product of prairie farms. Wonderful stuff: you can eat it in 1,000 different forms, fatten up animals or birds with it and eat them, make it into beverages and get drunk on it, refine it to fuel your car, process it into chemicals, plastics, and fiber products. Or you can just watch a field of it wave in the wind and paint pictures of it or write poetry and songs about it. No wonder Western farmers love to grow it even when they have to practically give it away.

(Terry Chamberlain, *The ABC's of Farming*, 1999)

GRANARY

Farm buildings in which threshed grain is stored. The new ones are made of steel and have hopper bottoms and augers that make shoveling unnecessary. The older wooden ones required that you get into them and shovel the grain out by hand, a dusty, dirty, smelly, sweaty, back-breaking, hot, and terrible job, one of those sources of intense suffering and hardship that older and retired farmers are so proud of.

(Terry Chamberlain, *The ABC's of Farming*, 1999)

GUNNING

"You take it after a rain," said Henry . . .

Henry and I were sunning on the steps of the store. I was waiting for my wife to come along in the car and pick me up; Henry, being without attachments, was waiting for the end of time. For a brief spell we were as sensible as two cats, on the warm boards.

"You take it after a rain," said Henry, "a fox hasn't fed all night, because it's been rainin', and he'll be lookin' to feed in the morning. That's the time you got to be there with your gun."

I nodded wisely, wondering what the Meadow Brook Hunt would make of this kind of goings-on.

"I killed five foxes one fall, just half a mile from here, still-huntin'. No dog nor nuthin'. I outwitted 'em. You know where McKee's shop is, well right there, where the woods comes clean to the road in a point. I knew that's where he'd have to cross the road, to git to where the rabbits were thick. I just set there behind the wall and waited. Only you got to be mighty quiet and nice. A fox has awful good eyes."

It was the first chance Henry had ever had to tell me confidentially about himself, and it seemed significant that he had plunged without preliminaries into his triumphant chapter. From his dull galaxy of days he had picked out these five bright mornings. Every man has his memory of achievement.

It is something to have known where a fox was going to cross the road.

The burning question around here now is what I am going to do about my deer. They always speak of it as "my" deer, and it has come to seem just that. I often think of this not impossible animal, walking statelily through the forest paths and wearing a studded collar with "E. B. White, phone Waterlot 40 Ring 3" engraved on it.

"You goin' to get your deer?" I am asked by every man I meet—and they all wait for an answer. My deer-slaying program is a matter of considerable local concern, much to my surprise. It is plain that I now reside in a friendly community of killers, and that until I open fire myself they cannot call me brother.

The truth is I have never given serious thought to the question of gunning. My exploits have been few. Once I shot a woodchuck my dog had already begun to take apart; and once, in the interests of science, I erased a domestic turkey—crouching

silently on a log six feet from the bird's head, as cool as though I were aiming at my own grandmother. But by and large my hunting has been with a .22 rifle and a mechanical duck, with dusk falling in gold and purple splendor in the penny arcades along Sixth Avenue. I imagine I would feel mighty awkward discharging a gun that wasn't fastened to a counter by a small chain.

This business of going after some deer meat is a solemn matter hereabouts. My noncommittal attitude has marked me as a person of doubtful character, who will bear watching. There seems to be some question of masculinity involved: until I slay my dragon I am still in short pants, as far as my fellow-countrymen are concerned. As for my own feelings in the matter, it's not that I fear buck fever, it's more that I can't seem to work up a decent feeling of enmity toward a deer. Toward my deer, I mean. I think I'd rather catch it alive and break it to harness.

Besides, I don't really trust myself alone in the woods with a gun. The woods are changing. I see by the papers that our Eastern forests this season are full of artists engaged in making pencil sketches of suitable backgrounds for Walt Disney's proposed picture "Bambi"—which is about a deer. My eyesight isn't anything exceptional; it is quite within the bounds of probability that I would march into the woods after my deer and come home with a free-hand artist draped across my running board, a tiny crimson drop trickling from one nostril.

("Clear Days" from *One Man's Meat* by E. B. White, 1938)

HARVEST

The *Grand Finale* of the year's work, the
Ultimate Goal, the Final Crunch, the Time
of Reckoning, the Joy or Despair of the farm
community. Harvests are classified according
to yield, as follows (here using wheat as
the example):

Over 40 bushels per acre—Bumper Crop

25–40 bushels per acre—Pretty Fair Crop

15–25 bushels per acre—So-so Crop

10–15 bushels per acre—Oh-Well-Maybe-
Next-Year Crop

Under 10 bushels per acre—there are two or
three commonly used terms for this category,
but they are not suitable for printing. We want
school kids to read this, after all.

(Terry Chamberlain, *The ABC's of Farming,* 1999)

HAY

Dead grasses and other plants. You can feed it to livestock, ride on it in a wagon, use it in a parade float, or have a roll in it. The first of these uses is the most profitable, but the last one is the most fun (and, since it's just a figure of speech, you don't even have to go near the itchy stuff to do it).

(Terry Chamberlain, *The ABC's of Farming*, 1999)

HAY MOW

In winter there were no tomatoes to pick or weed, or any hay to get in, but by no means did this translate into less work to do around the place. For one thing, the cows were kept indoors and this meant they had to be fed. It also meant the manure needed to be cleaned out of their stalls twice each day. Because I had to go to school I was excused from this unglamorous job on mornings, but it was one of my chores, along with feeding the young stock, before supper.

Behind the cows' raised stalls and running the length of the tie-up was a two-foot-wide gutter about four inches deep. Each morning that gutter would be filled with steaming, soupy manure that had to be gotten rid of, and unlike Hercules we had no nearby river to divert. It always amazed me how busy the cows must have been all night to provide such a prodigious quantity. The gutter was bordered by hinged wooden scuttles that were designed to be opened, making it relatively easy to scrape the manure to the opening with a hoe, and send it plummeting into the depths of the cavernous space below. As the winter dragged on, even this enormous void would become filled with huge mounds of this composting material that grew like stalagmites up to the scuttles.

Occasionally Dad would go below and clear away some of the manure, but even in years when all this natural fertilizer had been removed and spread on the fields, the shallow end of the huge cellar would be filled to capacity. This meant that ever-longer stretches of the gutter had to be cleared by shoving a steel grain shovel along its length until you reached the first opening that still had space below. To accomplish this you needed to be physically in the gutter up against the cows' tail ends, which provided them an ideal opportunity to swat

you square in the face with a tail coated in the soupy mixture. Once the stalls and gutter were cleaned (we never called it "mucking out") we spread sawdust or shavings under the animals for a dry bed.

To produce this quantity of manure, the cows needed to eat at least an equal volume in hay, plus drink an enormous amount of water, since they were each also producing twenty-five or so quarts of milk. The watering part was not difficult because the cow barn was equipped with on-demand drinking cups, each shared by two adjacent cows. A wide, flat disk inside the steel bowl permitted water to flow in when depressed by the cow's nose. Even new cows learned the process almost instantly, and the only flaw

in the design was a tendency of the valves to sometimes stick in the open position spilling water over the rim. Most of this overflow simply ran into the boxlike manger at each cow's head, then trickled or poured down below through cracks in the wood. But it was a waste of water we could ill afford with two families and forty-five large animals depending upon a shallow spring-fed well a quarter-mile away across a snow-covered field.

Each afternoon at around four, Dad grained the milkers, while I cleaned out the barn. After supper, while Dad milked, I'd water the young stock and the horses, none of which had automatic drinking cups. Then I'd climb up into the mows, or even the scaffolds, and throw down onto the hay barn floor enough bales to feed everyone. While the cow barn kept a pretty mild temperature due to its low ceilings and the concentration of body heat in the somewhat confined space, the cavernous hay barn had no such furnace and was not much warmer than the outdoors. It also was very poorly lighted; in fact, just three defiant little light bulbs mounted beneath the fifteen-foot-high scaffolds were charged with beating back the darkness in the entire space. Very little light made it into the hay-filled mows, and less still up into the scaffolds. As I pulled down bales from their stacked tiers, carried them to the mow's edge, and tossed them down to the floor, my imagination kept speculating as to just what variety of horror, escaped from the grave, or homicidal maniac crouched, hidden in the hay that night waiting to reach out and grab me. So convincing would these images become, that I would be close to a state of full blown panic by the time I hurriedly tossed down the final bale. Often eschewing the ladder, I'd simply swing down from the eight-foot mow and land with a thud on the floor below.

Once safe in the dimly lighted bay, I'd get a hold of myself, and the grisly images would melt away. With forced composure I'd push open the door to the warm, relatively well-lighted cow barn and nonchalantly walk in.

("Winter's Promise Kept" from *Growing Up on Maple Hill Farm* by Jerry Stelmok, 2007)

HIRED MAN

An employee who once did most of the manual labor around a farm. He has largely been replaced by technology on the theory that a combine doesn't need any sleep, a tractor never talks back, and a hay baler won't get its employer's daughter pregnant. Sometimes, of course, the hired man was a girl, who might do a combination of indoor and outdoor jobs. She usually worked long, hard hours for nothing but room, board, and a pittance. However, if she was enterprising, and if the farmer had a grown son or was himself an eligible bachelor, she could often make the transition from employee to boss in one quick career move.

Now ladies, about the heading for this entry: I use it because male employees were much more common, and the phrase "hired man" was a household term like Kleenex on traditional prairie farms. I am well aware that female help was just as valuable. I am. Really. In fact, it is likely hired men were more numerous because their farm wives were able to handle all their chores better than their husbands were. Now I'm really sucking up. But that's OK, I'm used to it. (And my wife helps proofread this stuff).

(Terry Chamberlain, *The ABC's of Farming*, 1999)

HITCH

Webster's Dictionary gives the original meaning of this word as "to raise or move with a jerk" (e.g., hitching up your pants), which my wife says is probably why the word is sometimes used in place of "to marry" ("get hitched"), an act that involves moving *in* with a jerk. I try not to take offense.

But in farming this word means to hook a horse or tractor to an implement. I have had considerable experience backing a tractor up to cultivators, swathers, and other equipment. With some implements, if you are off the mark by even an inch, you must drive forward and try again. Some days I made more miles hitching up than I did in the field.

(Terry Chamberlain, *The ABC's of Farming*, 1999)

HOG

"Solomon might have done better, but I doubt it," laughed the attorney-at-law. "I was out in the country the other day on a matter of business, and while there my attention was attracted to a peculiar situation that existed among three old farmers, which promised to become serious, as they were all stubborn, not one of them being willing to admit that he was in the wrong. It was like this: One of them had planted a hill of watermelons near his line and the vine had grown over upon his neighbor's land, where it had spent its energies in developing a single huge melon. The farmer who had planted the seed claimed it, but the man upon whose ground it had grown said that it belonged to him. There had been some line fence trouble between them for years, and the melon episode only increased the bitter feeling. The old man who owned the land where the melon was threatened to sue his neighbor for trespass if he picked it, and the other swore that he would have the farmer arrested if he took the melon. Here matters rested till a hog belonging to another neighbor came along and ate the melon. At this stage of the proceedings the local minister stepped in and tried to smooth the matter over. He finally got them to agree to leave the matter to me, and 1 accepted the responsibility.

"'Now,' said I to the man whose hog had eaten the melon, 'you are clearly liable for what your hog destroyed, and I think ten cents would cover all damage done.'

"He thought this was reasonable and promptly handed the amount over to me.

"As I put the money in my pocket I said: 'Seeing that this is exactly the amount of my fee for acting as referee, I can see no need of going any further.'

"The contestants stared blankly at one another for a moment and then one of them said that he was mighty sorry that the other hog ate the melon before I came along. To tell the truth, I was sorry myself, for, according to all accounts, that melon was a buster."

("The Judgment of Solomon" from *Current Literature*, edited by Edward Jewitt Wheeler, originally printed by *Detroit Free Press*, 1901)

HOPPER BOTTOM

Time for a little quiz. Would you expect this term to refer to (a) a skin condition that makes it difficult to sit still? (b) the south end of a rabbit going north? (c) a floor shaped like an inverted cone?

The answer is (c). When used as the floor of a grain bin, with an opening at the point of the cone, the hopper bottom makes it unnecessary to shovel when emptying the bin. Which is a very, very good thing, as

you would know if you had ever shoveled out a granary.

(Terry Chamberlain, *The ABC's of Farming*, 1999)

HORSE

At one time this animal supplied most of the power for transportation, soil tillage, hay cutting, etc. around the farm. Horses were very useful creatures but had one serious drawback: they used no processed fuel, lubricants, or replacement parts, and therefore farmers were persuaded by the oil companies and machinery dealers to get rid of them.

They are still used on some ranches and in rodeo events, but industrial designers are working hard on robotic replacements. Someday soon the cowboy who rides a mount called Old Paint will have named it for its John Deere Green color.

(Terry Chamberlain, *The ABC's of Farming*, 1999)

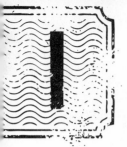

ICE SKATING

Things were quiet, serene, and peaceful out there on the little lake. There I sat, resting on the seat of my ice-fishing sled, jigging for walleyes through a hole in the ice, watching the inert flags of my tip-ups. Dusk was falling.

To the west, behind a band of tall Norway pines, an anemic winter sun was settling. Its last rays casting burnished silver, like that of polished pewter, on the snowless, frozen surface of the lake. Over on the northeast shore, where a summer cottage stands, the slanting sunbeams are reflected in brilliant gold from the dwelling's picture window.

Except for the distant whine of a chainsaw and the raucous crowing of a pair of crows heading for their night's roosting, all was still, almost a classic December "silent night" in northern Wisconsin.

The scene could have been right out of a Currier and Ives painting. Yet inside me, an unsettling instinct stirred, telling me something was amiss. What? For several fleeting moments the question gnawed at me. And then the answer dawned.

Ice skaters! That's what was missing! A young couple dressed in baggy wools of the 1920s, long red and green scarves trailing behind in the breeze, gliding gracefully over the lake. That's what the picture needed!

Old, long-muted memories began to replay in my brain. Ice skating, you see, was a big thing for my generation of youngsters. This past summer, a brother and I got to reminiscing about our lives as kids back in the late 1930s. "I remember getting a pair of skates for Christmas," Bill said. "I tried them on to make sure they were big enough. And believe me, they were! A couple sizes oversize, so I'd have room to grow into them. Mom made sure of that!"

Experiences like that well typify those times. Money was scarce, people were poor. We youngsters found our recreation in simple ways, like sledding on Deak's Hill or skating on the pond across the road.

The little puddle wasn't all that much, maybe a half acre in size, surrounded by big oaks fringing a farm field. We'd gather there after supper. Approach the site and the voices of friends, boys and girls, would grow from a distant murmur in the night air to the excited clamor of country kids having fun.

Kids of all ages and backgrounds were there. The more well-to-do were apparent by the pairs of shoe skates hanging from laces around their necks. The less-well-off were obvious by the old-fashioned clamp skates they carried.

Clamp skates were made to be fastened to the soles of your shoes. With a key, the blades would be tightened in place. In theory, the clamps were supposed to hold. But in reality, they frequently twisted loose, sending frustrated skaters spilling to the ice. Pity the youngster who tore the sole from his shoe in the process for shoes were precious and a scolding was inevitable when the unfortunate one got home.

If the night's cold warranted, wood was gathered, and a fire was built. And in its dim light, makeshift hockey games would organize. There were no storebought hockey sticks like nowadays, just sturdy crooked sticks cut from bushes and trees. The puck was just a gnarled knot to be batted around until it finally split into pieces. The older, bigger guys, the better and faster skaters, usually played hockey.

The rest of the gang was content to casually skate slowly in circles around the perimeter of the pond, laughing and teasing, with a periodic game of "crack the whip" sending a brave skater sailing at what seemed breathtaking speed across the ice.

For many years now, the little pond has been gone, filled and killed by a housing development that came in the boom following World War II. Yet I know where its waters once stood. And when I visit my home turf, especially in winter, I gaze across the rows of modern homes.

There, marked by a few aged sturdy oaks that still remain, my memory once more paints for me images of youngsters happily skating on moonlit winter evenings. For the fun of it.

("Winter Tales" from *Ya, Ya! Those Were the Days* by Bob Becker, 1993)

INVENTION

OFFICE OF ALEXANDER BOTTS,
SALES MANAGER
EARTHWORM TRACTOR COMPANY
EARTHWORM CITY, ILLINOIS

Tuesday, February 11, 1941

MR. GILBERT HENDERSON,
PRESIDENT,
EARTHWORM TRACTOR COMPANY,
EARTHWORM BRANCH OFFICE,
GRAYBAR BUILDING,
NEW YORK, N.Y.

Dear Henderson:

A controversy has recently arisen between me and Mr. H. W. Vann, our chief engineer, and I want you to use your authority as president of the company to mediate the affair in an impartial manner so as to make him do what I say. The facts are as follows:

Yesterday morning, as I was sitting in Vann's office, discussing with him the state of business in general, his secretary brought in a tall, rather attractive-looking young man who had asked for an interview. As the young man entered, he was so intent on some notes which he was making with a pencil on the back of an old envelope that he didn't seem to realize he had arrived until Vann broke in on his reverie.

"Hey, there!" said Vann. "Did you want to see me about something?"

The young man looked up somewhat blankly. "That's right," he said at length, "I did want to see you about something, didn't I?"

"Who are you?" asked Vann. "And what do you want?"

"Well," said the young man, "my name is Horace Ludlow. I live on a farm about ten miles out of town. And I thought maybe you could help me. I want to get married."

"Isn't that a question you might better take up with the young lady concerned?"

"Oh, it's all settled with her—and with me too. We both want to get married. But before we do, I want

to get some money. I want to sell one of my inventions."

"So you're an inventor?" Vann's tone was cold and suspicious.

"Yes." A dreamy, faraway look came over young Horace's face. "I've made a whole lot of inventions. Most of them, of course, don't work. But there's one that I hope will be all right. It's an apparatus for making holes in the ground."

"Holes in the ground?"

"Yes, you know—oil wells, water wells, test holes for mines and things like that. The most important feature of the machine is the business end—which I refer to technically as the Horace Ludlow Universal Self-Sharpening Automatic-Expanding High-Speed Rotary Drill Bit."

At this, Vann let out a somewhat raucous laugh.

"Maybe you think it's funny," said Horace, "but remember, they laughed at Edison too."

"This is different," said Vann. "Whatever gave you the crazy idea that a tractor company would buy a silly drill bit?"

"People often want to drill oil wells and put down test holes at inaccessible places in rough country.

So they need tractors to get there and to supply the power for the work."

"Say!" I said, entering the conversation for the first time, "there might be something in that, Vann. Maybe this thing would be a very valuable accessory for our machines."

"If it's any good," said Vann, "which I doubt."

"I could give you a demonstration out at the farm," suggested young Horace, "using my father's Earthworm tractor for power."

"Listen," said Vann, "if I investigated all the inventions that are submitted to this office, I wouldn't have time for anything else. People are always coming in here with everything from hot-air snow removers to radio-controlled plowing outfits. One guy pretty near gave the whole office a nervous breakdown by bringing in a small model of what he called a nitro-Diesel motor, with the fuel tank filled with nitroglycerin instead of fuel oil. And there was even one man with a perpetual-motion machine."

"That's interesting," said Horace. "I've been working on a sort of a perpetual-motion machine myself. If I ever get it perfected, it would be ideal for your tractors."

"In that case," said Vann, "I am afraid you are not the type of person who can be of very much help to us around here. Good morning."

"You won't even consider my invention?"

"I will not."

Slowly and dejectedly young Horace turned, opened the first door he came to, stepped into the coat closet, came out again, finally found the right door, and disappeared into the outer office.

"Just another nut," said Vann.

"I rather liked the guy," I said. "If you won't investigate his proposition, I will."

I rushed out and caught up with the young man just as he was going out the main entrance. He was naturally delighted at my interest, and a few minutes later we were heading out of town in his automobile. It was a rather decrepit vehicle, and he was such a dreamy, absent-minded driver that I almost had heart failure several times—especially as the roads were fairly icy. We arrived safely at the farm, however, and I was introduced to his father, his mother, his Aunt Emma, and the hired man—all of them obviously belonging to that group of sturdy, high-grade American yokelry which is the real backbone of the nation.

By this time it was noon, so I was invited to lunch—Horace's mother setting out as tasty a mess of vittles as I have sunk my teeth into for a long while. A delightful time was had by all.

After lunch, Horace took me out to his somewhat primitive workshop in the barn.

"These are some of my earlier efforts," he said, indicating a number of strange contraptions, "not very successful, but worthwhile because of the experience and training they gave me. Here, for instance, is a mousetrap, with an electric eye, that runs after the mouse. It works, but it's hard to control. One day it chased Aunt Emma all over the kitchen, snapping at her heels and scaring her so much that they won't let me bring it in the house anymore."

"At least," I said, "the idea is good."

By this time I was getting to like Horace very much. His engaging frankness in admitting his failures proved that he was perfectly honest and straightforward, thus lending weight to his assertion that the great drill bit was all right.

"I've really done a lot of work on that bit," he said. "It has been my main job for two years."

"Why did it take that long?"

"I experimented with dozens of different kinds of steel. I tried hundreds of different designs for the cutting elements. And I tested all of them on a lot of defective tombstones at the monument works."

"And at last you've got something that works?"

"Wait till I show you."

He led me into an adjoining shed and pointed to a sixty-horsepower Diesel Earthworm tractor hitched onto a trailer, equipped with a small folding derrick and a bewildering assortment of homemade machinery. This machinery, at first sight, looked pretty awful, being held together in true farmer fashion with haywire, binder twine and friction tape.

Horace cranked up the tractor, took the entire apparatus outside, connected up a hose to supply water, set up his little fifteen-foot derrick, up-ended a piece of pipe, inserted therein a strange-looking drill bit with a section of drill stem, and within less than ten minutes had started boring into the ground.

The drill, using almost the entire sixty horsepower of the tractor motor, whirled at a truly frightful speed. In almost no time at all, both the drill and the casing were down ten feet. After a two-minute halt to slip in a new section of casing and a new length of drill stem, the terrific whirling was resumed.

The tractor motor roared, the feed mechanism which controls the descent of the drill and the casing clanked and banged, the water pump throbbed, and a steady torrent of hot mud from the hole flowed off to one side. Horace—alert, efficient and without a trace of his former absent-minded dreaminess—controlled the entire operation with such ease and skill that I was lost in admiration. Several times, various parts of the homemade machinery fell apart, but Horace patched it up with his haywire technique so fast that hardly any time was lost.

Before long we struck limestone rock, and this slowed us up a little but not much. By the middle of the afternoon we were down over a hundred feet, and Horace called a halt, pulled up the casing, and moved the machinery over to a near-by limestone ledge. This time he drilled a hole going upward at an angle of forty-five degrees into the rock, using a core drill with a hollow center. Before long he took out a

> "I experimented with dozens of different kinds of steel. I tried hundreds of different designs for the cutting elements.

beautiful rock core—a cylinder of limestone an inch and a half in diameter and a couple of yards long.

"That shows you what I can do," he said. "I can drill holes in any direction—up, down or sidewise. I do it fast and I do it cheap. With this expansion feature, the hole is big enough so the casing follows the bit; you don't have any trouble with the sides of the hole caving in if you hit soft sand. And with these self-sharpening, high-speed steel points, you don't have to waste a lot of time and money replacing bits, and you don't need any expensive diamonds. What do you think of it?"

"Horace," I said, "your machine is a wow. And you are a mechanical genius. The only thing you lack is the salesmanship to put it across. But you do not have to worry about that anymore. I have decided to act as your manager. So all you have to do is watch my smoke. If you will drive me back to the factory, I will at once start making all the necessary arrangements—including adequate compensation for yourself—to the end that your remarkable drill rig may be put in production with the least possible delay. Following this, I confidently expect to sell hundreds of them, including, of course, the Earthworm tractors to go with them."

"Thank you, Mr. Botts," said Horace.

He drove me back to the factory, where, right away, I ran into the stone wall of Vann's invincible ignorance and stupid conservatism. He declared that no crackpot like Horace was worth even so much as two minutes of the time of a scientist such as himself. I finally withdrew, after telling him perfectly frankly I was going to appeal to you.

So now you know the entire story. And your duty is clear. You must write a letter to Vann at once, telling him the best interests of the Earthworm Tractor Company demand that he drop everything else and make the proper arrangements, so that this wonderful new drill can be put into production at once.

As soon as you mail this letter, I shall appreciate your notifying me by wire, so that I can relay the good news to Horace. It need not be a long message; the single word "yes" will be sufficient.

Yours,
ALEXANDER BOTTS
****

TELEGRAM

NEW YORK, N.Y.
FEB. 13, 1941

TO ALEXANDER BOTTS,
SALES MANAGER,
EARTHWORM TRACTOR COMPANY,
EARTHWORM CITY, ILLINOIS.

NO.

GILBERT HENDERSON
****

OTTER CREEK HOTEL
OTTER CREEK, PENNSYLVANIA

Thursday evening,
February 20, I 941

Dear Henderson:

This is to let you know that your disconcertingly negative telegram of last week has not discouraged me at all. Nor do I hold it against you. Now that I have had time to think it over, I can see that you would not care to stick out your neck by taking sides in an interdepartmental controversy—especially when the evidence is merely my word against Vann's.

However, you will be glad to know that I am now engaged in an enterprise designed to prove beyond a shadow of doubt that I am right. And, although I have been hindered by a truly hideous piece of bad luck, I still have high hopes of success. And I have reached a point where I want you to grant me a little extra authority—as will be apparent when I tell you what has happened so far.

After receiving your telegram, I immediately contacted Mr. Horace Ludlow and arranged to ship his drill rig to Pittsburgh, where it arrived last night. Horace and I arrived this morning. The young man was much excited over the trip. It seems that the parents of his fiancée, a girl called Mary Smith, live near Pittsburgh. And although Mary herself has a teaching job up in New York State, he was all in a dither at getting so close to her home—the result being that his mental processes became even more vague than anything I had previously noted. He left his watch under the pillow in the Pullman berth, his razor in the washroom and his overcoat in the taxicab. Fortunately, we were able to go back and recover all these articles. And about nine o'clock we called at the office of Mr. Henry Masterson, president of the Masterson Drilling Corporation.

This firm, one of the largest of its kind in the country, manufactures drilling equipment of all kinds, and takes on drilling contracts—not only oil wells but also diamond-core drilling for mining companies. It was my plan to put on a demonstration of Horace's machine for Mr. Masterson, with the idea that his expert opinion—if favorable, as I am sure it will be—would give you the necessary basis for going ahead and telling Vann where to get off at.

Unfortunately, Mr. Masterson was away on a trip, but his secretary said that he expected to spend the weekend at his country place, located about fifty miles north of Pittsburgh, and about ten miles from the little town of Otter Creek, where the parents of Horace's ladylove reside. I at once arranged to go there, Horace agreeing with an enthusiasm that I suspect was at least partly based on what might be called the love interest.

Our Pittsburgh dealer supplied a sixty-horsepower Diesel

Earthworm tractor and a large truck. Horace and I loaded the tractor and the drill rig on the truck, and started. About three o'clock this afternoon we arrived at Mr. Masterson's palatial country estate, where we soon found ourselves involved in a very remarkable situation.

Mr. Masterson's house is a large stone structure in a lovely open valley, with rolling fields in front and a wooded hillside rising abruptly at the rear—the entire landscape at the present time being covered with snow.

We drove our truck into the curving driveway, parked opposite the front door, rang the bell, and were admitted by the butler. He told us that Mr. Masterson was not at home, and he conducted us to the living room, where we were graciously received by Mrs. Masterson, a woman of most imposing appearance.

"Mrs. Masterson," I said, "we would like to know when your husband will arrive. We want to do some well drilling for him."

"Splendid!" she exclaimed. "My husband will not arrive until tomorrow, but that need not delay you." She then explained that her husband, although the head of the largest drilling concern in the country, had never gotten around to drilling an adequate well at his own country place. "For years," she said, "we have been using water brought by an electric pump from an old-fashioned stone-lined dug well in the side yard. This well is almost certainly polluted by surface water. It is most unsanitary. And I am delighted to learn that my husband is at last doing something about it."

I explained that this was not her husband's idea; we merely wanted to demonstrate our drill rig in the hope that he would buy it. She then asked how long it would take to drill a well. I said that it could probably be completed in a few hours. And she suggested that we start work at once.

"My husband," she said, "is arriving tomorrow with some weekend house guests—a couple of mining engineers and their wives. He is eager to make a good impression on these engineers so that he can negotiate a drilling contract with them. I am sure it would please my husband very much if you could greet him on his arrival with a beautiful new water supply."

Congratulating myself on the promising aspect of affairs, I hurried Horace outside. We set up our drill rig in the side yard between the well and the house, and Horace ran his hose line down to a near-by creek to get water. We then started operations.

After we had gone down through the snow and through about a foot of frozen soil, there was a sudden jolt which shook the entire drill rig. The bit dropped a couple of feet. And a moment later we noticed that the stream of mud pouring up out of the hole had all at once become mixed with a large quantity of dirty oil.

Horace stopped the machinery. "Holy cat!" he said. "I knew Pennsylvania was an oil region, but I never expected to strike oil only one foot below the surface."

"This is certainly going to be a happy surprise for Mr. Masterson," I said.

It soon appeared, however, that the surprise would probably not be as happy as might have been hoped. An examination of the terrain, plus a few guarded inquiries of the servants in the house, revealed that we had drilled down completely through a buried thousand-gallon steel tank which supplied fuel oil to the furnace in the house. By the time I had ascertained this fact, all of the oil had escaped from the tank and the butler reported that the furnace in the house had stopped.

"Quick, Horace!" I yelled. "There is not a moment to lose!"

I hustled him into the truck and we drove like mad into town, where I found a plumbing-and-heating contractor, who promised faithfully that he would bring out a new tank, install it on the surface of the ground outside the house, fill it with oil, connect it to the furnace, and start the heat going once more. As he had to go to another town to get the tank, he thought it would take at least until midnight.

Horace and I then hurried back to the Masterson country place, where we found that the situation was even worse than we had expected. By this time the sun had set and a cold wind had come up. Outdoors, the temperature was dropping toward zero. Inside, the living-room thermometer stood at forty-five degrees Fahrenheit. And that was not all.

The butler informed us that Mrs. Masterson, feeling a bit chilly, had started to take a hot shower in her luxurious bathroom, and that the flow of water had abruptly changed to furnace oil, which so thoroughly smeared the poor lady that it took her personal maid half an hour to get her cleaned up again. Upon hearing this, Horace and I at once rushed out with a flashlight and inspected the old stone-lined well. It was only too clear what had happened—the oil which had run out of the tank had seeped down into the well, and the source of the water supply was completely ruined.

"We've certainly tried hard enough," said Horace, "to make a fine impression on these people, but, somehow, it doesn't seem to me we are doing so good."

"By a strange coincidence," I said, "that same thought had just occurred to me. But we must not lose hope. It is now absolutely essential that we drill a new well as fast as we can. And it might be wise to shift our operations away from this area of oil-soaked ground."

Horace promptly agreed, and we moved the drill rig to the other side of the house.

"Do you think, Horace," I asked, "that you can handle this drilling job without my help?"

"Certainly"

"Are you sure you won't lapse into one of your absent-minded fits and forget what you are supposed to be doing?"

"Absolutely not," said Horace, with deep sincerity. "It's true that I sometimes get absent-minded about ordinary affairs, but that is because my whole mind is so completely occupied with my inventions. I'm never absent-minded when I'm working with my drill."

"All right, Horace," I said. "I will leave you to handle the mechanical side here, while I devote myself to the human angle—meaning Mrs. Masterson."

Having arranged this division of labor, I went to the house and started working on the old lady in a really big way. At first, she was inclined to be pretty nasty, but I produced such a remarkable flow of excuses, words of sympathy and encouraging promises that she could not help but be impressed. I told her that the whole trouble was caused by the carelessness of the people who had buried that tank in the wrong place and then failed to mark its location.

"But what can I do?" she wailed. "Am I to entertain my husband's distinguished guests like Eskimos in an igloo? Can I ask them to bathe in this noxious liquid which now comes out of the faucets and shower baths?"

"Absolutely not," I said. "I have already made all necessary arrangements so that you will have a beautiful new water supply and plenty of steam heat by tomorrow morning. It is a lucky thing for you, Mrs. Masterson, that an efficient executive like myself happened to be on hand when this accident occurred."

I then told her that it would be foolish for her to endanger her health by staying in a cold house overnight, and I advised that she let me conduct her to the hotel ten miles distant, in the town of Otter Creek.

After considerable persuasion, she agreed to this. She summoned her chauffeur and car. And we both drove there to the hotel, where I have been utilizing my expense account by distributing lavish tips in all directions, and thus making sure she receives the very best service which the limited facilities of the hotel are capable of rendering.

As Mrs. Masterson is the type that always wants to be the center of attention, these activities have made a considerable impression upon her. She is actually beginning to have a high opinion of my ability. And she has assured me that she will try to interest her husband in my proposition.

Everything is thus going at least as well as could be expected. I am sure to make a reasonably good impression on Mr. Masterson when he arrives tomorrow. And, after he has seen what Horace's drill can do, it is highly probable that he will order a considerable number, as well as the tractors to go with them.

And this makes it necessary for me to know exactly where I stand. I will, therefore, send this letter at once by air mail, special delivery, so that you will receive it in New York tomorrow morning. And I want you to wire me at once whether the Earthworm Tractor Company will be ready to start prompt production of these drills.

Yours sincerely,
ALEXANDER BOTTS
****

TELEGRAM

NEW YORK, N.Y.
FEB. 21, 1941

TO ALEXANDER BOTTS
OTTER CREEK HOTEL, OTTER CREEK, PA.

REGRET YOU HAVE SO OUTRAGEOUSLY ANNOYED HOUSEHOLD OF HENRY MASTER-SON, WHO HAPPENS TO BE AN OLD FRIEND OF MINE. HOWEVER, HAVING GONE THIS FAR, YOU MAY AS WELL CONTINUE. I HAVE COMPLETE CONFIDENCE IN MASTERSON'S JUDGMENT. IF HE APPROVES DRILL, YOU MAY BUY RIGHTS FROM HORACE LUDLOW, TEN THOUSAND DOLLARS. YOU MAY ALSO GIVE LUDLOW ONE-YEAR CONTRACT, THREE THOUSAND DOLLARS, IN OUR ENGINEERING DEPARTMENT, WHERE HIS HELP MAY BE NEEDED IN ADAPTING INVENTION TO OUR PRODUCTION. IF YOU FAIL TO GET MASTERSON'S APPROVAL, YOU WILL DROP WHOLE MATTER AT ONCE, AND REFRAIN FROM BOTHERING ME WITH IT AGAIN. THIS IS FINAL.

GILBERT HENDERSON
****

OTTER CREEK, PENNSYLVANIA,
Friday morning, February 21, 1941

Dear Henderson:

Your wire arrived just after another incredible piece of bad luck had caused Mr. Masterson to kick me off his place and forbid me to return—thus making further negotiations impossible. This means that by your flat refusal to consider Horace's invention without the approval of Mr. Masterson you have sounded the death knell of all my hopes.

Furthermore, you have made the disaster even harder to bear by injecting into your message a truly brilliant, but now impossible, idea which has my most enthusiastic approval—namely, the beautiful plan for putting Horace into our engineering department over what would almost certainly be the insanely violent objections of the head of that department, Mr. H. W. Vann.

In expressing my approval of the above plan, I do not want you to make the mistake of thinking that I am actuated by any vindictive or childish desire to get even with old Vann. On the contrary, I am thinking only of his own best interests, and of how much good it would do the old buzzard to bring his semifossilized brain into close, though unwilling, contact with Horace's brilliantly creative and totally uninhibited intellect.

However, I fear that all this is now a mere pipe dream; knowing your stubborn nature, I have little hope—especially after the unfortunate events of this morning—of getting your approval on this deal.

Such being the case, I would not even write you this letter, except that ordinary courtesy demands that I let you know what has been going on. And it may somewhat relieve my feelings to pour out my troubles onto a piece of paper.

When I arose this morning, everything seemed auspicious. A brief note, left by the plumber at 2 a.m., announced that the furnace was running. Mrs. Masterson and I had a very pleasant breakfast together. And, immediately afterward, Mr. Masterson himself came in with his two distinguished guests and their wives.

He had made an early start from wherever he had spent the night, and had stopped in at the hotel to telephone his wife that he would arrive earlier than expected. He was naturally astonished and annoyed at his wife's account of the intricate disaster of the day before. But he was at least partly reassured by her glowing account of how nobly I had come to the rescue. He promptly put in a call for his country house to learn the true condition of affairs, but the telephone line had just gone dead—as sometimes happens in rural regions—so we had to drive out to the house without any knowledge of what awaited us.

We made the trip with Mr. Masterson and me riding in his car, and Mrs. Masterson, the two guests and their wives riding in Mrs. Masterson's car. During the course of the drive, I gave Mr. Masterson a glowing account of Horace's outfit, which he received, I am compelled to admit, with a certain amount of hard-boiled skepticism. When we arrived, Mr. Masterson and I walked around to the side yard, while the rest of the company went into the house. The large truck was gone and there was no sign of Horace. But the drill rig and the tractor were exactly where I had left them the night before.

As Mr. Masterson's eye lit upon Horace's homemade machinery, with all its haywire and friction-tape trimmings, he let out a loud and somewhat vulgar horse laugh.

"So this," he said derisively, "is the wonderful machine you think you are going to sell to me!"

"Wait till you see what it can do," I said. I pointed underneath, to direct Mr. Masterson's attention to the top of the well casing. "Look," I said—and then realized, to my indescribable horror, that there was nothing to look at. There was no well casing, no well, no nothing, except the blank surface of the snow, as pure and unsullied as it had been the night before. It was all too plain that the drilling operations had never even started.

In a wild panic, I looked around for Horace. Horace was not there. My eye caught sight of a piece of paper on the seat of the tractor. It was a note: "Dear Mr. Botts: I just called up Mr. and Mrs. Smith, the parents of my fiancée, in Otter Creek. I had merely expected to give them my cordial greetings. But they told me that Mary, instead of being up in New York State, as I had supposed, has unexpectedly come home to spend the weekend. As this is too good a chance to miss, I have taken the truck and gone to see her. Horace."

As I read these words, I realized—alas, too late—that I never should have trusted anyone as intellectually unstable as Horace. The mere fact that his absorption in his invention made him forget the ordinary affairs of life should have put me on my guard. I should have remembered that there is a primordial, biological urge which is more powerful than all else in life, and that the irresistible call of his mate would inevitably cause Horace to forget his invention as completely as the call of his invention had

previously caused him to forget his watch, razor and overcoat.

Having analyzed the situation in this keen manner, I turned to Mr.

> As I read these words, I realized—alas, too late—that I never should have trusted anyone as intellectually unstable as Horace.

Masterson and started a flow of excuses, which I hoped would be at least vaguely plausible. "Apparently," I said, "the inventor and operator of this drill rig was called away by important business last night before he had a chance to do anything."

"What! This miraculous well, that you told me would be all finished, has not even been started?"

"That seems to be the story," I said sadly. "But there is really nothing to worry about. If you will have your chauffeur drive me to town, I will try to find Horace and our truck, so I can bring him out here to give you a real demonstration of this remarkable machine."

"I will be glad to send you to town," said Mr. Masterson coldly, "so that you can get your truck and remove this aggregation of junk from my property. But you don't need to bother about any demonstration. I can tell, just by looking at this hick machinery, that it is nothing I would be interested in. Besides, you've done enough damage around here already."

He called his chauffeur, directed that I be taken to Otter Creek, and disappeared into the house.

When we arrived in town, I picked up your wire at the hotel and then, after a few inquiries, located the Smith home. The big truck which l had borrowed from the Pittsburgh dealer was parked out in front. But

> I can tell, just by looking at this hick machinery, that it is nothing I would be interested in.

when I applied at the front door, I was told by Mrs. Smith—Mary's mother—that Horace was not there.

"He was here earlier," she explained, "but he and Mary have gone off on an all-day skiing expedition in the hills. They took their lunch with them."

"It's a wonder," I said, "that Horace didn't forget the lunch."

"He did," said Mrs. Smith, "but Mary remembered, and sent him back for it."

"You don't know where they went?"

"No," she said. And then, noticing my disappointment, and being, to all appearances, a kindly

soul, she suggested that I come in and wait.

"It's a cold day," she said. "Perhaps they'll come back sooner than they planned."

As I had nothing better to do, I accepted Mrs. Smith's invitation to come in, and further imposed upon her to give me some paper and a pencil. So, for the past hour, I have been seated in the Smiths' comfortable living room writing this letter to you.

When Horace arrives I will tell him exactly what I think of him, and then drag him back to the Masterson place in the forlorn hope that I may be able to persuade Mr. Masterson to look at a demonstration. Probably, considering the old guy's state of mind, this will now be impossible. But I can try. And, at least, I can give myself the grim pleasure of handing that fatheaded Horace a piece of my mind.

LATER, 8 P.M.

A few minutes after I had written the above, Horace and Mary arrived back at the house, demanding something to eat. It seems that Horace, in his usual scatterbrained manner, had contrived in some way to lose the box containing their lunch. As the two young people came in, flushed and happy from their skiing, they made what would have been a very pretty picture of young love, if I had been in any shape to appreciate it—which I was not. I at once launched forth in such a steady stream of denunciation that it was pretty near fifteen minutes before Horace could get in a word edgewise. But when he did, he had an explanation which changed the whole aspect of everything.

"I'm sorry you've had all this worry," he said. "I was so anxious to see Mary that I guess I forgot to put the whole story in that note. But I didn't mean to let you down."

"Then why didn't you drill that well the way you promised?"

"Because, after you left, I decided we had picked the wrong place to drill. I decided there was no sense in having the well deep down in the ground, where the water would have to be pumped up at considerable expense."

"Where else can you put a well except down in the ground? Up in the treetops, maybe?"

"No. I took the drill rig a little way up that slope behind the house, and drilled sidewise into the hill. About midnight, when I had gone in a hundred and fifty feet, I struck some nice water-bearing sand that delivered eight or ten gallons to the minute. So I brought the drill rig back to the side yard and had the plumber run a pipe from the well down to the house. They can bury it later. And, in the meantime, it's covered with gunny sacks so it won't freeze as long as the water keeps running. We let all the faucets run until dawn, so as to flush the oil out of the pipes. And now they have a much better water supply than ever before—pure and abundant, and delivered by gravity, without any expense for pumping."

Before I could recover from this news, Mr. Masterson, highly excited, came bursting in upon us.

"I tried to telephone you, Mr. Botts," he said, "but the line is still out. I want to thank you for the new water supply. With the house in good running order, I have been able to have a very pleasant conference with my mining friends, and they have agreed to give me a very good drilling contract. But the main thing I am after is to find out more about that drill. If it really did what it seems to have done, it must be worth investigating."

"Mr. Masterson," I said, "we are at your service."

We at once drove out to his place, and spent the rest of the day drilling test holes and explaining the fine points of the apparatus. At the end of the afternoon, Mr. Masterson decided that Horace's homemade machinery is pretty sad, but the drill bit is such a honey that he has decided to use it in a really big way.

He is going to set up a subsidiary, to be known as The Gravity-Flow Side-Hill Well-Drilling Corporation, with a slogan which I myself made up: Let Sir Isaac Newton Tote Your Water. He plans to send hundreds of drill rigs into all parts of the country where there are farmhouses and country dwellings located so that Horace's side-hill drilling technique can be used.

In carrying out his plans, Mr. Masterson prefers to make the drill bits in his own plant, so Horace—with my approval—has sold him the rights. This will be all right for us, as I slipped a clause into the agreement providing that Earthworm tractors are to be used exclusively for power. And it is all right for Horace, as he now has ten thousand dollars to get married on.

I trust you will approve my reasons for disregarding that part of your telegram relative to buying the drill ourselves. And I am happy to announce that I have carried out the rest of your instructions to the letter. As Horace feels that he has completed the really important work on his drill, and as he is anxious to go on to new and finer things, I have signed him up to work on his perpetual-motion machine, in our engineering department—thus, even if the machine is as impractical as the pursuit-model mousetrap, insuring that old Vann will receive a much-needed and highly beneficial mental upheaval.

Yours,
ALEXANDER BOTTS

("They Laughed at Edison, Too" from *Botts in War, Botts in Peace* by William Hazlett Upson, 1933)

INVITATION

I've had a bright cheerful winter. (?) I had the neuralgia for six weeks, and I've been to a funeral or two, and I almost attended a wedding. The reason that I didn't was that I was not invited. And ever since the wedding I've been worrying myself thin trying to study out the reason that I wasn't invited.

At first I thought it was my black cashmere; and I had a great mind to hang it in the garret and let the mice devour it root and branch; but then I thought maybe it was not the cashmere, and probably I had better keep it.

Then I thought it was because I was so homely. I thought perhaps Nellie was ashamed to have her St. Louis and Chicago friends see me. And I had half a mind to buy a box of pink whiting and a Saratoga wane and make myself beautiful, but I heard that the St. Louis and Chicago ladies who attended the wedding were very homely, and I didn't buy the face powder. Then I thought that it was because Nellie knew I was too poor to give her a wedding present, but I won't permit myself to think that Nellie is mercenary. If she had been she would not have married a poor young man "for love" when she might have had a rich one for the asking—only she did not need to do the asking—the rich young man did that. So it can't be on account of the wedding present.

Then I thought it might be my manners. Perhaps I did not bow quite low enough. And I've practiced an hour every morning before tile glass, and now I'm ready to challenge Queen Victoria to a bowing match, You just stand with your feet "so" and hold both arms flat against your sides "so," and bend your whole body all at once, "so," and that is all there is of it. Anyone can do it properly with a little practice.

Nellie was my daughter's music teacher—and she was a good teacher—and a good girl every way. She came once a week and gave the lesson and ate dinner here, and I liked her and she liked me, and when she was getting ready to marry I knew about everything. I furnished the honey and turkeys, and I felt sure I would be invited to the wedding.

I ironed the wrinkles out of my black cashmere, and sponged the shoulders to take off the shine, and wet my black lace tie in coffee and pressed it between two papers, and I put my front hair up in crimping pins and expected she would send me cards as she did the others. She sent out three hundred invitations. But about a week before the wedding she kissed me and told me she would like to invite me to the wedding, but that there were so many that she was obliged to invite that she couldn't have me. And she said she was sorry she couldn't invite me, and that she expected she

would think of me more than of any one that would be at the wedding. And she said she knew that I knew how it was, and would not think hard. And I don't. Not if thinking hard means that I am mad, for I am not mad, not at all; but when Nellie told me "not to come to the wedding" my heart went down a couple of inches, and it is there yet, and it don't beat right; I fear it is dislocated.

I don't care anything about going to weddings and dinners and parties generally. I don't think it is

> Of course I knew that "want of room" was not the true reason. There were sixty at the wedding and two more could not have made much difference.

"good form" for a woman that has only one dress, and that one a black cashmere, to go out too often. Three or four times a year is about enough, and three out of the four times should be funeral occasions; because people with eyes dimmed with tears can't see very well what you have on.

But I wanted to go to Nellie's wedding for several reasons: First, I liked her and was glad that she was happy, and I knew she would be dressed nice and look lovely and I wanted to see her; and secondly, I wanted to see a real stylish wedding so that I could marry my Heroines off properly in the stories I write; and thirdly, I knew that all the folks thought I was going to the wedding, and I was sorry to disappoint them.

There is just one more *perhaps*, and that is that Nellie thought if we were invited—for of course John would go with me—we would go to the expense of a present for her, and as she knew how poor we were she

would save us that much, and she was right in thinking that, if she did think it, for I had put away the five dollars that John had given me to buy a pair of new shoes—consecrated as it were—to buy Nellie a wedding present, and I wore a pair of John's old shoes for every day; of course they were sizes and sizes too big for me, but I rather enjoyed the sacrifice, for I liked Nellie very much.

Of course I knew that "want of room" was not the true reason. There were sixty at the wedding and two more could not have made much difference. I feel satisfied that the walls wouldn't have been pushed outward, nor the tables broken in the rush on my account.

They had a splendid time. Ruby velvet and California grapes, Elizabethian collars and scalloped oysters, bananas and a long train, oranges and kisses, ice cream and the "Wedding March." Everything passed off lovely, and they had lots of silverware given them, most enough to set up housekeeping, if it hadn't been nearly all pickle castors and cake baskets. And I wrote as good an account of the wedding as I could, and sent it to the county papers, and I don't feel hard. But my heart goes on beating strangely in a new place, and I can scarcely sleep for asking myself why I was not invited to the wedding.

("Why I Was Not Invited to the Wedding" by Rose Park, from *Farm Journal*, 1886)

JACK

Defined in Webster as "a male ass." Before jumping to any unjustified conclusions see jenny.

(Terry Chamberlain, *The ABC's of Farming*, 1999)

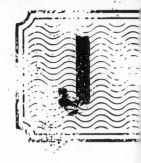

JENNY

Webster's dictionary defines this as "a female ass." But before you go telling your wife she's getting a little wide in the jenny I should tell you we're referring here to a beast of burden, a donkey. The male is called a **jack** or, naturally, a "jackass." These animals are sometimes kept with other livestock on farms and ranches where their sharp hooves, feisty natures, and god-awful braying keeps predators away.

(Terry Chamberlain, *The ABC's of Farming*, 1999)

JUNK

With the present mania for recycling, "getting rid of" may soon be an idiom gone from the language. Certainly getting rid of anything down on the farm these days is next to impossible.

For years now Paul has been wanting to burn the kettle house, a little vine-covered shack in the backyard, containing a great kettle built into a brick fire pot used once for rendering lard and making apple butter.

"Don't you dare touch that!" I say. "It's a period piece—irreplaceable!" And besides, I need it. It's crammed with old newspapers and pop bottles and flower pots and push lawn mowers and dozens of other things awaiting recycling.

Forty feet south of the kettle house is the ice house crowded with antique tools and household implements and Great-great-grandfather Leimbach's gilt-framed portrait. The seed house, forty feet to the north, houses a wealth of old doors and windows and lumber and porch swings and butter churns and discarded appliances "somebody might need sometime."

The horse barn, in addition to motorcycles and bicycles, shelters old harnesses and horse collars and wagon wheels.

That's just the beginning. There's also the granary, the chicken coop, the hay barn, and the "big barn"; then there's Newberry's barn (when you buy a neighbor's farm his fields and buildings traditionally carry his name ad infinitum); Newberry's milk house, and Newberry's toolshed. And every weathered building has its cache of farm treasures.

For a hundred years the Leimbachs have prevailed on this site, enlarging, expanding, acquiring, with neither a sale nor a fire. The accumulation is overwhelming.

Every time I get ready to do a good cleaning job, some yahoo comes around blabbing, "Don't throw THAT away! They're paying fabulous prices for that stuff." Where, I ask, are all these people paying "fabulous prices" for barn siding, mason jars, old bottles, rusty nails, wavy window panes, hand-hewn beams, and—are you ready for this one?—worn and faded blue denim?

Yup! I was just fixin to go down cellar and make a clean sweep of those dusty old overall jackets I inherited when we bought the Newberry place, and then I read it right there in *Time*: Saks Fifth Avenue was selling old denim jackets for twenty-six bucks! And bikinis made of old denim go for twenty. Wow! If Nelson Newberry thought his overall jackets might be resurrected as bikinis, he'd have himself reincarnated!

Odd as it seems, there's justice in placing such value on genuinely faded blue denim. (It seems they try to simulate the faded effect, but imitations don't command the price of the real McCoy.) In order to achieve the desired quality, blue denim needs to do a lot of bending in the sun and whipping in the wind. It needs to be dunked in farm ponds and ground into the slag of playgrounds. It needs to fall from horses or motorcycles or bicycles a few dozen times, and be forgotten on a fence post for a while. It should kick around in a dusty pickup truck a couple of weeks. Most of all it needs to be soaked repeatedly in sweat. It has to lie in dirty laundry piles on damp cellar floors and hang for long spells on clotheslines. It needs to be shortened and lengthened again and mildewed in the mending, nursed back to health with patches.

Then, and only then, does a garment of blue denim have integrity. And believe me, it's worth more than any city slicker's money can pay.

I wonder idly, while I'm pondering the new values, if there's any market for a retread farmer's wife in her late forties who can bake bread in an old black stove, make apple butter in one of those old kettles, can tomatoes (she raised herself) in those old mason jars, make butter in a stomp churn, and manufacture faded blue denim as a matter of course.

("One Man's Junk" from *All My Meadows* by Patricia Penton Leimbach, 1975)

KILOGRAM

A foolish and unnecessary unit of weight, more than a pound and less than a bushel (good, honest measures both), but don't ask me how much.

(Terry Chamberlain, *The ABC's of Farming*, 1999)

KILOMETER

A foolish and unnecessary unit of distance, shorter than a mile (which prairie people understand better, those my age anyway—did anyone ever ask you what kind of kilometrage your truck gets?).

(Terry Chamberlain, *The ABC's of Farming*, 1999)

K

KITCHEN HELP

In a farm family without girls, each boy in turn helped in the house. Because I was the youngest, I worked with Mother longer than any of my brothers. There weren't any younger sons to take over and free me to work in the fields with Father.

At threshing time, until I was about twelve, my work had to do with meals. Mother made her plans—getting ready for as many as twenty-five men—and I

helped her put them into action. I carried extra water, brought in fresh vegetables from the garden, carried canned fruit up from the cellar, sliced loaf after loaf of the bread she had been up half the night to make. I peeled great pans of potatoes from the bin in the cellar, or dug new ones from the potato field. I got all the extra leaves from the dark closet at the foot of the stairs and soon the dining-room table stretched almost from wall to wall, lined with chairs from all over the house.

I set up buckets of water, washbowls, and great stacks of towels on the outdoor work stand, under the dinner bell. I made certain the stock tank was filled with water for the horses from the bundle wagons.

The roar of the threshing rig and the rattle of the wagons were constant reminders of men building up a hunger. Finally, the table was set, extra dishes stacked and ready for the men who couldn't fit at the first table. Pots bubbled on the wood

range and good smells began to come from the steamy kitchen.

Then I began going back and forth between Father and Mother. The conversation would go like this, with a lot of running in between:

"Mother wants to know when you'll be ready?"

"When will she be ready?"

"She says the potatoes need forty-five minutes."

Father might call to the man on the last bundle wagon in line. "Hey, how many loads left out there?" He'd get his answer and turn back to me.

"We got this field about whipped. Then we have to move across the road. Ask her if we could eat early?"

"But she says the potatoes need forty-five minutes."

"Ask her about that."

"He says could they eat early?"

"Well. Maybe I can cut the potatoes up smaller. Tell him twenty minutes."

"She says twenty minutes. And she wants to know if they'll be eating here for supper."

"I don't know yet."

"She said if you said that to ask you when you will know."

With the exact time set, Mother shifted her pots and pans, making sure everything came out even. And Father knew when to keep the empty wagons from going out for another load.

With the men beginning to look at their watches more often and measuring the height of the sun, the tractor would slow, the great belt slapping, and the hum of the threshing machine would slowly die.

In the strange warm quiet, after hours of steady sound, the men came to the yard, flapping chaff and dust from clothes and hats. They smelled of horses, grease, and grain dust, clothes stained with sweat and salt. Their straw hats made a pile on the grass. Once a puppy chewed some of them up while everyone was eating.

Four at a time, the men went to the washbowls, splashing and snorting like walruses, then rearing up, eyes full of soap, to feel for a towel. Every year, at least once, someone would hand a groping man a grease-filled rag brought in from the machines. The half-blind person would mop himself, not knowing anything was wrong until his face

was black and a roar of laughter surrounded him.

Then to the house. Big, heavy bowls began to move around the table, forks spearing meat, potatoes, vegetables—sometimes a fork coming across from the other side of the table. One person was always the butt of all the jokes about eating too much.

"By God, George" (or "Tom," or "Spike," or "Dingy"), "we've been talking about you. What we decided is we ain't going to change work with you anymore. Nothing personal, mind you. Just can't afford it, you eating ten times what the rest of us do."

"He could bring his own dinner."

"Hell, to do that he'd have to bring two wagons."

George would go on shoveling, talking through the food. "You're right. I *do* eat ten times as much as anybody else. No argument about that. Figure I got it coming, seeing as I work *twenty* times harder."

A hoot of laughter. The bowls made a second round. George speared a potato, popped the whole thing into his mouth and couldn't talk, eyes bulging as if he might explode. Still working on the potato he filled his plate with dessert, taking pie, cake, Jell-O, and cookies.

The chairs scraped back from the first table. The men went out to the yard, sprawling under the maple tree, to light pipes and hand-rolled cigarettes or take a chew from a plug of tobacco.

The second shift came in, heavy eaters sometimes taking a quick look into the kitchen to make sure there was plenty of food. I scurried from kitchen to dining room with more bowls of hot food, more bread, more coffee. I refilled the sugar bowl, put it down in front of a fat man, and waited while he put half the bowl over freshly sliced tomatoes and the other half into his coffee, running it over into the saucer. With the cup in one hand, he lifted the saucer and drank with a loud, vibrating slurp. Each time, someone at the table would rise to the occasion, frowning, looking under the table and saying, "Damnation, sure sounds like there's pigs and a slop trough in here somewhere."

The fat man grinned, handed me the empty sugar bowl, and went on eating. I kept circling the table, grabbing the bowls and platters as they emptied. I carried more cream and milk from the cellar, the pitchers steaming as they came up into the hot summer day.

> Still working on the potato he filled his plate with dessert, taking pie, cake, Jell-O, and cookies.

Finally, with the food almost gone, the tractor started up, calling the men back to work. Mother and I sat down at the great long table, not talking, sobered by a mountain of dirty dishes waiting and another meal to be ready in five hours.

Father joined us sometimes for a consultation. Would the threshing be finished today? That might mean supper should be earlier than usual or later. Did we need anything from town?

When a job was going to be finished during the day, the women got nervous. Would the men eat at this job or move on to the next one, thresh an hour, and eat there? The women needed a definite answer. The men hedged. A tractor could break down, some wet bundles plug the machine; the last load slide off a wagon and have to be pitched back on.

In a situation like that, my liaison trips between Father and Mother seemed like every five minutes and the telephone rang with questions from a woman who might,

> **It wasn't talked about much, but there were farms where the men tried to avoid eating.**

or might not, have to feed twenty-five men two hours from now.

It wasn't talked about much, but there were farms where the men tried to avoid eating. They might quit a little early and decide everybody should go home to eat. They might decide to eat early at the present job.

I remember eating once at a house with no screens on the windows. The flies were a constant hum over the table. We ate with one hand and waved flies away with the other. Ben Twining had brought some repair parts for the tractor from Gays Mills. He made the mistake of staying for supper. When it came time for dessert, he reached out for a pie, saying, "I think I'll have some of that raisin pie."

A swarm of flies rose as his hand came near. "Oh," he said, "I guess that's custard pie."

("Rites of Passage" from *The Land Remembers* by Ben Logan, 1975)

LAGOON

If this word conjures up for you a picture of blue water, sailboats, and swaying palm trees, you're not a rural prairie resident. Here the term refers to a large excavation used to collect sewage effluent from a farmyard, village, or town. You wouldn't want to boat, much less swim, in it. However, a teaching colleague of mine, during one of his first skydiving experiences, was unable to maneuver his parachute skillfully enough to avoid splashing down in the middle of a large sewer lagoon in central Alberta. A true story, I swear.

(Terry Chamberlain, *The ABC's of Farming*, 1999)

LAMBING

Long before my farmer father had cows or cornfields, he was a shepherd. Last March marked his fortieth lambing season. The sense of anniversary was monkey-wrenched during the first week when, as he climbed aboard a tractor (something he has done almost daily during those decades), the knee of his trailing leg emitted a celeriac crunch, which, as it turned out, was the sound of his meniscus dismantling. He was instantly hobbled with pain, unable to bear weight on that leg, and confined to the recliner. We kids—all grown up now—took turns staying at the farm to help out.

Lambing season amounts to a month of insufficient catnaps. You tromp to the sheep shed every couple of hours, around the clock, for four weeks straight until the last ewe delivers. Each time you enter the shed you're looking for a sheep giving signs of imminent birth. She may be pawing the straw, walking in circles, or simply looking distracted. An ewe experiencing the early twinges of labor will sequester herself along a wall or in a corner. At the commencement of a contraction, the otherwise placid animal will extend her neck, raise her head, roll back her upper lip, and wrinkle her nose. A laboring ewe will grunt softly, as if she is being nudged in the belly (I hear a chorus of female voices: *As she is, Einstein!*). Another means of early detection is to put out fresh hay. As her compatriots rush the feeders like woolly pigs, watch for the ewe who remains apart—she's next.

Midwifery-wise, your basic job is to stay out of the way. Observe from a quiet remove and let nature take its course. Recede. Wait.

From my largely oblivious childhood perspective, Dad's sheep were a sideline, whereas cows required our daily attention. When you weren't working with the cows, you were working on chores predicated on cows. Sheep, on the other hand, spent most of the year as distant gray lumps in the outermost pastures, forgotten until the occasional faint bleat floated in from the back forty. In the warmer months, they required little more than watering. If they were close by, we dragged out the green garden hose. If they were in outlying pastures, we transported the water in old milk cans. In the deeper parts of winter, we would take them hay daily, busting bales over the snow. A few times a year there would be worming sessions during which we also gave vaccinations and trimmed hooves. The summer worming sessions always took on a rodeo feel, as we would quite literally shepherd the sheep from one pasture to another, sometimes detouring unexpectedly down the county road; all those frantic hooves on the asphalt set up a scuffy little clatter.

In the early part of the year, however, the sheep begin to wedge their way back into the schedule until they dominate. In February, Dad sets up the pens and feeders and gathers the flock to be shorn, after which—having lost their winter coats—they take up permanent residence in the lambing shed until spring when the grass returns.

Dad frequently refers to himself as a "dumb sheep farmer," but he loves his "woolies," as he calls them. Once when someone suggested that sheep were not so bright, he said, "Y'know how you make a cow? Inflate a sheep, paint it black and white, add two faucets, and remove its brain." He was gentle with all of his animals, but I suspect the sheep speak to him on a level the cows never did. This may be tied to his faith and the presence of sheep in the Bible, something which I have never inquired about but should put on the list of Before It's Too Late. What I do know is the cows are gone, and the sheep remain, and someone must watch over them. Tonight it's me.

When the alarm sounds at 2:00 a.m. (rousing by habit and intuition, Dad rarely requires the uncouth tool), every lazy bone in my body—to say nothing of my cotton-bound brain—assumes a specific gravity designed to drive me deeper abed. I summon the strength to rise only by conjuring the fantasy of how sweet it will feel to drift off upon my return. By the time I am dressed and downstairs, I am reanimating my childhood. On weekend nights, we kids were allowed to rise and accompany Mom or Dad on midnight maternity rounds. There was always a feeling of anticipation coming down to the dark kitchen and bundling up for the trek to the barn. Beyond the weak pool of the yardlight, the farm was socked in darkness. Wisconsin's March is highly variable. Sometimes a soft wind was soughing in the pines, shushing through the needles and pushing the scent of melt. Sometimes the night was clear and deep-frozen. Sometimes snow was coming down. One night when big flakes were lazing past the yardlight like feathers from a burst pillow, I went to check the sheep with Mom. While she held the iron gate open, I stepped through and the top of my head brushed the underside of her outstretched arm. "My goodness," she said. "Pretty soon you won't fit under there!" I felt eight feet tall and strode the rest of the path with shoulders squared. When I married two years ago, I was given a daughter named Amy who is now just six years old but growing fast. The top of her head has already reached my sternum, and the day when she won't fit beneath my arm is fast approaching. This is her first lambing season, and I was happy yesterday when she walked with me to the barn, and we found a sheep ready to deliver. I told her she could name the lamb.

The lambs are named alphabetically. The practice dates back to my childhood and was always a fun game. I remember long-gone fuzzballs named Herkimer and Knucklehead and Lillelukelani. Adherence to the alphabetical constraints was jovially strict and resulted in fuzzy little creatures named X-ray and Zapata. The ledger of record was a clipboard hung on a nail. The pencil dangled on a string. The system remains unchanged.

In the barn, Amy was eager and attentive, watching closely and asking questions as the lamb emerged. It was stillborn. She cried a little, and we talked about it. Two hours later, she returned, this time to see twin lambs arrive alive. As they shook themselves and tottered to life, Amy smiled and chattered brightly. While I have attempted a career out of overthinking things, I suspect her smile was all the wider in light of her recently acquired prior knowledge.

I love the sheep barn at night. The animals are settled, resting like woolly boulders with their legs folded and hooves tucked beneath their bodies. If you stand in the quiet, you will hear them chewing their cuds. The sound of human mastication drives me nuts in a split second, but for some reason, the sound of sheep chewing in the nocturnal quiet calms me. An animal in distress does not work its cud, and all that muffled molar work—with regular pauses to swallow one bolus and raise another—sends a subliminal message of contentment. When I was young, I would climb the haystack into the rafters, curl up, and simply listen.

Tonight I hear an infantile bleat before I reach the barn, and when I straddle the fence and cross to the straw, I find a young ewe lying on her side and straining. There is a fresh-born lamb beside her, and as I approach, she presses out another. It arrives in a slithery amniotic gush and plops wetly to the straw. Encircling its nose with my fingers, I milk its nostrils and mouth clear of fluid, then stand back to watch its ribs bow in and out as the first hacking breaths transpire. By the time it shakes its ears loose (this always reminds me of an accelerated version of the emergent butterfly uncrinkling its wet wings after escaping the chrysalis), I am experiencing the standard moment of marvel at how the whole deal works. The ewe has turned, snuffling and chuckling as she licks the amniotic fluid away, roughing and fluffing the tight wool curls so they can air-dry. As usual, the other sheep ignore the goings-on, with the occasional exception of the yearling ewes. Having never given birth, they sometimes sniff the lambs or the hind end of the laboring ewe curiously, their ears cocked forward in a mixture of curiosity and alarm.

Dad keeps a baby food jar filled with iodine in the barn, and I retrieve it now, removing the cap and lifting each lamb so I can thread the umbilicus into the iodine. I do it how I remember seeing Dad do it, clapping the jar tightly against the lamb's belly, then tipping it back so the umbilicus gets a good soak. The lamb is left with a circular orange stain on its abdomen. The practice prevents navel ill. In a week or so, the umbilicus will turn to jerky and eventually drop unnoticed to the straw.

By the time I have finished, the ewe has gone to pushing again. I ease around behind her. I'm hoping to see a soft pair of hoof tips cradling a little lamb snoot. The hooves are there, sure enough, but they are dewclaws-up and there is no snoot. Bad sign. These are the back legs. Breech delivery. I hustle back to the house and wake Mom. Dad has always shouldered the bulk of the lambing chores but defers to my mother for tricky deliveries. A registered nurse, she comes armed with delivery room experience and delicate hands. Dad's hands are not overlarge, but they have a sausage-y thickness brought on by manual labor and are therefore poorly suited for navigating obstetrical tangles.

I get back to the barn before Mom and find the ewe panting and the lamb half out—its head, shoulders, and front legs are still lodged in the birth canal. It appears there is no time to wait, so I grab the lamb and pull it the rest of the way out. Its head is still inside the amniotic sac. I clear the nostrils and mouth, but there is no breath. I give a couple of pushes on the ribs and dangle the lamb by its back legs, which looks drastic, but it allows fluid to drain from the air passages. When I place the lamb on the straw, its flanks flutter, and then I hear the familiar crackle of air working into the lungs. Shoot, the little feller's off and running. Mom arrives. Minutes later the lamb gives a high-pitched bleat, and I am just plumb happy.

We stand and observe, let the new family get to know one another. Mom kneels behind the sheep and checks inside to rule out quadruplets. Nothing. The ewe's long push is over. Using another trick my father taught me, I guide the sheep to the pen by dangling the third lamb in my hands while slowly backing across the barn and into the small square pen. It takes a while. The mother wants to dart back and forth between lambs, so I carry two and Mom the other. Soon they are ensconced, the two oldest lambs already stumbling about in their jabby-stabby knock-kneed way. The breech lamb is worn out. After watching the first two lambs suckle, we try to help him latch on, but he's tuckered. Dad says the emerging thinking is that immediate nursing isn't as necessary as previously thought, so we'll leave and let the family settle. Over the course of the coming day, we'll keep an eye on the little guy and make sure he learns how to get his dinner. Mom jots the ewe's ear tag number and the sex of each lamb on the clipboard, but we leave the name spaces blank. Amy can name them in the morning.

We return to the house. The frozen air is bell-jar still. The sky is deep black; the stars press down brilliantly all around. At the age of forty-one, walking beside my mother, I feel young and old at once. I am reminded that we are not beneath the stars, but among them.

When I was a young boy and accompanied Dad to do the checks, once the lambs were dipped and penned and the clipboard filled, and we were back in the house, he would disappear into the cellar and come back up with a Mason jar of canned dewberries. We'd share a bowl of the sweet berries, the dark red juice in the bowl reminding me of the iodine in the baby food jar.

Tonight there are no dewberries. Mom is off to bed, and I cross to the kitchen sink where I begin to scrub my hands. I am soaping up when I realize my wedding ring is missing. It must have come off during the delivery when my hands were slick with amniotic fluid. I grab a flashlight, retrace my steps, and spend a good hour diligently searching the straw. Nothing. A week later, I return with a metal detector and try again. Still nothing. Spring arrives. Dad's knee heals, the sheep return to the far pastures (accompanied now by galumphing, growing lambs), and it comes time to clean the barn. I drive to the farm and make one more pass with the metal detector. A rusty nail, a rusty hinge, and nothing more. Dad moves in with the skid steer and begins loading out the manure.

Married for over a year, and already I've lost my wedding ring. Some wise guy asks me if I checked inside the ewe. Well, no. But perhaps this year we can expect a little miracle lamb—born with a golden band around one ear. I've notified my father and put him on watch. His knee is holding up, and this year it will be him out there around the clock. Forty-two years a father, forty-one years a shepherd, and always, his eye on the flock.

("My Father's Flock" by Michael Perry)

LAND

They paused on the last ridge of the pasture, overlooking the house and the windmill and the stables that marked the site of John Bergson's homestead. On every side the brown waves of the earth rolled away to meet the sky.

"Lou and Oscar can't see those things," said Alexandra suddenly. "Suppose I do will my land to their children, what difference will that make? The land belongs to the future, Carl; that's the way it seems to me. How many of the names on the county clerk's plat will be there in fifty years. I might as well try to will the sunset over there to my brother's children. We come and go, but the land is always here. And the people who love it and understand it are the people who own it—for a little while."

("The Land Belongs to the Future" from *O Pioneers!* by Willa Cather, 1913)

LANGUAGE

I find that, whether I will or no, my speech is gradually changing, to conform to the language of the country. The tongue spoken here in Maine is as different from the tongue spoken in New York as Dutch is from German. Part of this difference is in the meaning of words, part in the pronunciation, part in the grammar. But the difference is great. Sometimes when a child is talking it is all one can do to translate until one has mastered the language. Our boy came home from school the first day and said the school was peachy but he couldn't understand what anybody was saying. This lasted only a couple of days.

For the word "all" you use the phrase "the whole of." You ask, "Is that the whole of it?" And whole is pronounced hull. Is that the hull of it? It sounds as though you might mean a ship.

For lift, the word is heft. You heft a thing to see how much it weighs. When you are holding a wedge for somebody to tap with a hammer, you say: "Tunk it a little." I've never heard the word tap used. It is always tunk.

Baster (pronounced bayster) is a popular word with boys. All the kids use it. He's an old baster, they say, when they pull an eel out of an eel trap. It probably derives from bastard, but it sounds quite proper and innocent when you hear it, and rather descriptive. I regard lots of things now (and some people) as old basters.

A person who is sensitive to cold is spleeny. We have never put a heater in our car, for fear we might get spleeny. When a pasture is sparse and isn't providing enough feed for the stock, you say the pasture is pretty snug. And a man who walks and talks slowly or lazily is called mod'rate. He's a powerful mod'rate man, you say.

When you're prying something with a pole and put a rock under the pole as a fulcrum, the rock is called a bait. Few people use the word "difference." When they want to say it makes no difference, they say it doesn't make any odds.

If you have enough wood for winter but not enough to carry you beyond that, you need wood "to spring out on." And when a ewe shows an udder, she "bags out." Ewe is pronounced yo by old-timers like my friend Dameron.

This ewe and yo business had me licked at first. It seemed an affectation to say yo when I was talking about a female sheep. But that was when I was still thinking of them as yews. After a while I thought of them as yos, and then it seemed perfectly all right. In fact, yo is a better-sounding word, all in all, than yew. For a while I tried to pronounce it half way between yew and yo. This proved fatal. A man has to make up his mind and then go boldly ahead. A ewe can't stand an umlaut any more than she can a terrier.

Hunting or shooting is called gunning. Tamarack is always hackmatack. Tackle is pronounced taykle. You rig a block and taykle.

If one of your sheep is tamer than the others, and the others follow her, you say she will "toll" the others in. The chopped clams that you spread upon the waters to keep the mackerel schooling around your boat are called toll bait. Or chum bait. A windy day is a "rough" day, whether you are on land or sea. Mild weather is "soft." And there is a distinction between weather overhead and weather underfoot. Lots of times, in spring, when the ground is muddy, you will have a "nice day overhead."

Manure is dressing, not manure. I think, although I'm not sure, that manure is considered a nasty word, not fit for polite company. The word dung is used some but not as much as dressing. But a manure fork is always a dung fork.

Wood that hasn't properly seasoned is dozy. The lunch hour is one's nooning. A small cove full of mud and eelgrass is a gunkhole. When a pullet slips off and lays in the blackberry bushes she "steals a nest away." If you get through the winter without dying or starving you "wintered well."

Persons who are not native to this locality are "from away." We are from away ourselves, and always will be, even if we live here the rest of our lives. You've got to be born here—otherwise you're from away.

People get born, but lambs and calves get dropped. This is literally true of course. The lamb actually does get dropped. (It doesn't hurt it any—or at any rate it never complains.) When a sow has little ones, she "pigs." Mine pigged on a Sunday morning, the ol' baster.

The road is often called "the tar." And road is pronounced ro-ud. The other day I heard someone called President Roosevelt a "war mongrel." Statute is called statue. Lawyers are busy studying the statues. Library is liberry. Chimney is chimley.

Fish weir is pronounced fish ware. Right now they're not getting anything in the wares.

Hoist is pronounced hist. I heard a tall story the other day about a man who was histed up on the end of a derrick boom while his companions accused him of making free with another man's wife. "Come on, confess!" they shouted. "Isn't it true you went with her all last year?" For a while he swung at the end of the boom and denied the charges. But he got tired finally. "You did, didn't you?" they persisted. "Well, once, boys," he replied. "Now hist me down."

The most difficult sound is the "a." I've been in Maine, off and on, all my life, but I still have to pause sometimes when somebody asks me something with an "a" in it. The other day a friend met me in front of the store, and asked, "How's the famine comin' along?" I had to think fast before I got the word "farming" out of his famine.

The word dear is pronounced dee-ah. Yet the word deer is pronounced deer. All children are called dee-ah, by men and women alike. Workmen often call each other dee-ah while on the job.

The final "y" of a word becomes "ay." Our boy used to call our dog Freddie. Now he calls him Fredday. Sometimes he calls him Fredday dee-ah; other times he calls him Fredday you ol' baster.

Country talk is alive and accurate, and contains more pictures and images than city talk. It usually has an unmistakable sincerity that gives it distinction. I think there is less talking merely for the sound that it makes. At any rate, I seldom tire of listening to even the most commonplace stuff, directly and sincerely spoken; and I still recall with dread the feeling that occasionally used to come over me at parties in town when the air was crowded with loud intellectual formations—the feeling that there wasn't a remark in the room that couldn't be brought down with a common pin.

("Maine Speech" from *One Man's Meat* by E. B. White, 1938)

LEISURE

In these days of relatively easy access to high-tech communications and travel, farm families can do and engage in most of the same leisure pursuits as anyone else. However, there are some activities which seem to predominate: hunting and fishing are popular because, I think, like farming they offer the illusion of getting something tangible—the basic need for food—for nothing, directly from nature. And there are other pastimes—golf, for example—that don't catch on to any great extent; after all, what do you really get to show for hours of traipsing around a fancy pasture where you might as well have been knocking horse turds into gopher holes with a pitchfork handle? Curling, on the other hand, is fairly popular, perhaps because wielding a broom (as you would when sweeping out a grain bin) lends a feeling of doing something practical and at least you earn a row of metal numbers if you work at it.

(Terry Chamberlain, *The ABC's of Farming*, 1999)

MACHINERY GRAVEYARD

Every farm has one of these. When an implement is no longer worth repairing it is dumped in the Machinery Graveyard where it begins a series of status changes. For the first few years it is *Salvage Material*, which means you might be able to use some of the parts on other equipment. When it has become too obsolete for that it is called *Scrap Metal*, which means you intend to sell it by the pound for the iron or steel in it. But since you often never get around to that it becomes just plain *Junk*. Many years later, when the original owner is long dead, his family becomes quite nostalgic about it; they call it *Memorabilia*, and talk about restoring it. But as soon as a lot of *other* people get interested and it looks like it might fetch a buck or two it becomes an *Antique*.

(Terry Chamberlain, *The ABC's of Farming*, 1999)

MANURE

Ranching and farming are occupations constantly concerned with animal manure. Its collection and dispersal are important springtime duties. "Money-in-the-bank" is an oft-repeated slogan. This natural fertilizer will make the grass green and the alfalfa grow, and you can sell any overabundance to city gardeners by calling it "steer manure."

Throughout the winter, from the cow barn, the pig shed, the chicken house, and the sheep shed, the stuff has been regularly scooped up and tossed onto an ever-growing pile. The cow barn even has a special window out of which to pitch manure. By spring, the heap reaches as high as the windowsill. The roosters enjoy climbing to the peak of manure for a good crow and pigs will scale the summit to jump through the open window into the barn to steal grain. The piles down by the pig sheds and the sheep shed have also reached impressive dimensions. All winter you've been wheel-barrowing the stuff onto the heaps. It is now time to utilize all this home manufactured fertilizer.

To the tune of terrifically clever remarks, your husband and Number One son fill the manure spreader one shovelful at a time. If you're lucky enough to have a front loader for the tractor, the job can be accomplished in no time. Number One son will miss a meal just to get to scoop manure.

A manure spreader is a long, usually green, box affair on wheels. Situated at the back end of the thing is a large, spiked, horizontal cylinder thing that looks like a huge bristled hair curler. Somehow this whole contraption turns when the spreader is hitched to the tractor and certain gears are engaged.

Try to arrange it so your husband will "let" you drive the manure spreader even if you have to hitch up the loaded spreader yourself. (As a good Country Woman, you learn to hitch up and operate all the farm equipment. WARNING: Take Care! All ranch and farm machinery is stealthily hostile to women and will pinch, bruise, and bash.)

Begin at the lower corner of the hay meadow and line out the tractor with the manure spreader following faithfully behind. Reach down, pull that short-handled knob to half position, and commence spreading. Which means that as the hair curler turns on a steel track arrangement, the heaped manure is combed off the end of the spreader. The manure doesn't merely drop quietly to the ground, though. With joyful abandon, small flakes and globules of the stuff fly up and up into the air to rain back to earth. Most of the material flies straight up and you've driven ahead before it has a chance to fall back on you. But there are always occasional flying curds that seek you out, especially if you've just washed your hair. (If the wind is blowing, reconsider spreading for that day.) A wide-brimmed straw hat, leather driving gloves, overalls, and denim jacket is the ensemble of choice for this operation. Somehow the combination of fresh sunny air, the buzz of the tractor, and the excitement of the flying fertilizer arouses your urge to sing. Hymns and spirituals lend themselves particularly well, so as you sweep around the meadow, let go with a hearty "R-o-c-k-of-A-a-a-ges-s-s. . . . "

Through the winter, the cattle have been pastured and fed on some of the hay meadows. Cattle are roving creatures and have done a good job depositing their droppings at random all over the fields. Before the spring thaw, feeding the cattle demands skill, a sturdy vehicle, and a sound body. Both body and vehicle must withstand the spine cracking, teeth rattling, jarring, and thumping, which occur as you bounce over terrain littered with frozen cow pies. In winter, a fresh dropped cow pie turns to instant cement, which miraculously softens as the weather warms.

The problem now becomes one of dispersion. A cow pie that just sits there in its own juices eventually dries to a pancake, which smothers the grass under it. So one fine, warm spring day your man will ask, "Do you have time to harrow?" (As a good Country Woman, you always have time for a harrowing experience.)

Harrows come in a variety of styles. A favorite instrument is that contraption of steel, grill-like arrangements alternating with hard-wood poles. The whole looks like a jail house's barred windows laid flat on the ground and linked together by a system of chains. (Harrows can be home-built out of random pieces of iron pipe, wagon spokes, old tires, and old hot-water radiators. Country Men have been known to spend whole days happily knitting all this together.)

Garb yourself in denim jacket, grab your straw hat, and wear leather gloves. No special requirements for coveralls or overalls. Regular jeans and natural cushioning will do. Mount the tractor steed and charge the field. (Your thoughtful husband has hitched the harrow to the tractor for you.) Begin at the fence corner and drive over the field in ever diminishing circles. The harrow bounces along behind, crashing into the cow piles, mashing and mauling them into acceptable sprinkles of manure. While harrowing, the Country Woman is completely free of the house for a time. As you watch the harrow chew away at the cow pies, the sun warms your back and a beautiful, peaceful chunk of time happens to you. Sometimes you think you'd like to write a book—if you ever get time.

("Manure" from *The Ranch Woman's Manual* by Gwen Petersen, 1976)

MANURE SPREADER

On garden plots this is a man or woman with a wheelbarrow and spade; on small farms it is a guy or girl with a wagon and pitchfork; on large farms it is a mechanically activated machine; in our local bar it is my brother-in-law.

(Terry Chamberlain, *The ABC's of Farming*, 1999)

MAPLE SYRUP

Maple Hill was aptly named because of the abundance of sugar maples, both in the woodlots and along stretches of road. This was especially true between our farm and the Longels', as well as in our yard, which supported several mature trees with heavy spreading limbs and healthy crowns. These regal maples were perfect for a syrup operation, but that was yet another seasonal venture that we never had the time or energy to take full advantage of.

After the winter dormancy, the sugar-rich sap stored in the tree's roots over the winter begins to rise up into the tree once daytime temperatures climb high enough—a few degrees above freezing for several days. These conditions can arise as early as late February, but on average the prime sap-running season encompasses two or three weeks in March. During the season, this lifeblood of the tree rises up inside the bundles of hollow phloem located just beneath the rough bark, on its way to each branching twig in the tree's crown where it will nourish an awakening bud. When the nighttime

M

temperature drops below freezing the internal pressure is eased and some of this sap flows back down into the roots, only to be sent back up the next warm day. It is this pumping action that accounts for the relatively long sapping season, when the sweet, slightly sticky fluid can be interrupted during its passage and diverted into receptacles, or in the case of big operations, hose networks. Metal or plastic spiles are inserted into the cambium of the tree and, at least in the days of my youth, buckets, cans, or jugs hung beneath the spiles to catch the steady drips of sap.

Although most years we tapped a tree or two just for this sweet tonic, there was one season when we went at it a bit more seriously. On a day selected for its warm temperatures, Dad would drill into the furrowed gray bark with an auger bit in a brace, angling the hole slightly upward. Two or so inches of penetration was sufficient, and the clumpy sawdust, wet with sap and extruded by the auger, was an indicator that the season had indeed started. Lacking genuine sap buckets, which are tall and narrow and equipped with lids to keep out snow and rain, we used a variety of collection containers, including a few two-quart mason jars.

When there was a strong flow of sap these needed to be emptied two or more times during the day, and if Dad was too busy and we kids were at school, Mother would empty the contents into a bucket and add the take to the variety of pots and pans on the wood end-heater on the kitchen range, where the refining began. This reduction process required a significant amount of energy to complete, when you consider the ratio of raw sap to finished syrup runs about forty to one.

With the sap bubbling slowly on the stovetop pans, the kitchen would fill with a lovely sweet aroma. Partially reduced sap would be combined with similar batches to be reduced still further, and in the evening Dad might finish up a batch in a pan on one of the range's propane burners for added control. The results of this great maple syrup venture were a few quarts of delicious but commercially imperfect syrup, and the walls adjacent to the stove stripped clean of their wallpaper by the rising steam.

But it was the maple sap itself that we really loved and continued collecting in small quantities. It was a treat to go outside and lift a frosty jar of nearly frozen sap from a spile and enjoy a deep draft of this distinctive life-affirming tonic. It is the taste of springtime itself, and if not a proven elixir, it's the best medicine I know to cleanse the bitter taste of winter from one's palate and spirit.

("Spring's Fickle Dance" from *Growing Up on Maple Hill Farm* by Jerry Stelmok, 2007)

MEADOW

Like a pasture, but classier. Pastures are used to graze animals, but meadows are used for lovers in movies to run across in slow motion, accompanied by romantic music, into each other's arms. Never try that in a pasture, not if you know what a cow pie is.

(Terry Chamberlain, *The ABC's of Farming*, 1999)

MILK

Product of dairy cows. It is sold as Whole Milk (snow-white, smooth, delicious), fat-reduced (1% or 2%), or Skim Milk (think, pale, bluish, sickly looking). Guess which form is considered best for your health?

(Terry Chamberlain, *The ABC's of Farming*, 1999)

MILL

The old red mill in Wild Rose, Wisconsin, stands next to the dam that holds back Pine River and forms the millpond. Water tumbles over the spillway and twists through eastern Waushara County on its way to Lake Winnebago. The mill was built in 1873, the same year the village of Wild Rose was organized. Farmers in this part of the Midwest grew wheat, and this mill, like many water-powered mills, ground the tan kernels into flour. By the late 1870s, farmers discovered that they could no longer grow wheat profitably. This old mill and hundreds like it in the upper Midwest shifted from producing flour to grinding grist (ground grain) for dairy cattle.

Farmers regularly gathered at the old mill, once or twice a week to have their grist ground. The mill was a place for swapping stories, starting gossip, and discussing the ups and downs of farming. I accompanied my father to the mill many times, often on a Saturday when I was home from school. When the morning chores were done, we'd gather up an armful of gunny bags—burlap sacks, to be more formal—and head for the corncrib. I'd hold the sack open while Pa used a big scoop fork to shovel in the yellow cobs. I had to hold the sack just right to keep it open and keep the corn from spilling on the floor. We'd fill sack after sack, tying each one with a shank of binder twine. We'd use a miller's

knot on the twine so that it would come untied with a quick tug.

When we had scooped full a half dozen sacks with corn, we'd move to the granary, where we filled several grain bags with oats. The cotton grain bags were longer than gunny sacks and more closely knit than the coarse burlap. Once more I'd hold the sacks open while Pa scooped the grain from the oat bins with a grain shovel.

Pa would start the old four-door 1936 Plymouth and drive it to the granary. He'd pull out the backseat and lean it against a grain bin. Then we'd stuff the sacks of oats and corn into the back of the car, and we'd be off to town—the back tires of the Plymouth halfway flat from the load. The snow would be melting, for it was March, and the country road would be muddy in the low places. Pa would gun the engine, and we'd slide through the mud; with all the weight in the car, the back wheels seldom slipped.

At the mill, we'd take our turn to unload our sacks of corn and oats. While we waited, we'd talk with the farmers already in line. Several of our neighbors would be there—Bill Miller, Andrew Nelson, Arlin Handrich—as well as farmers from the other side of town, people who Pa knew, but I didn't.

For me, the mill was a mysterious, exciting place. Water powered its mechanical parts, the inside of the building was filled with pulleys and belts, and the entire structure shook a little as the grinding mechanism operated. The maple wood floor was smooth from the hundreds of sacks of grain pulled across it over the years.

When our turn came, Pa would lift the sacks out of the back of the Plymouth and hoist them, one after the other, onto the mill platform. The miller, who in those days was Rodney Murty, would help dump the sacks into little square holes located on the mill floor. The grain rattled down a metal tube to the grinding wheels. An enclosed wooden chute about four inches square ran from the basement to the second floor of the mill; when the grinding was completed, the grist made its way to the top of the building by means of little cups fastened to a belt running inside this chute.

After a few minutes, we'd hang our sacks on the end of a little chute, and the sacks would be filled with the warm, sweet-smelling grist. When a sack was filled, we'd tie it shut and drag it across the floor to where it was weighed. (The miller was paid according to the pounds of grist ground.) After the weighing, we'd lift and shove the sacks back into the Plymouth. The entire grinding process took a little more than half an hour.

Having the grain ground was not the only reason for coming to the mill. The stories and the visiting also attracted farmers to the mill, but none would say that was the reason. To a person, these farmers were storytellers, surpassed in ability only by the miller himself.

Rodney Murty often told the story of when the previous miller, Ed Hoaglin, brought electricity to Wild Rose. Hoaglin had built a little brick building alongside the mill and installed a water-powered electric generator in 1908. When the generator was installed, the homes and businesses in the village of Wild Rose had electricity. That one convenience—a few electric bulbs—created a tremendous gulf between the village and country people.

When the mill started generating electricity, Murty was Hoaglin's assistant. Murty helped string electric wires throughout the village, and nearly everyone replaced their kerosene lamps with electric bulbs. Villagers soon moved beyond electric bulbs to washing machines with electric motors and even electric irons. Because the mill was busy grinding grain all through the day, the electric generator was not turned on until after five o'clock in the afternoon, when the grinding shut down. Promptly at eleven each evening, the miller blinked the lights, three times, pulled the switch, and shut off the generator. He said he had to build up a head of water in the millpond for the next day's grinding. Thus the electricity was on for only about six hours each day. Village women hurriedly washed clothes and ironed during the evenings.

As Murty told the story, a group of women marched to the mill one day at noon and asked to speak to Mr. Hoaglin. He went outside to talk with them, having no idea why a group of village women were visiting the mill, which was clearly a man's domain.

"We want the electricity on at noon," the leader of the women said.

"Whatever for?" Hoaglin asked. "It's broad daylight at noon. "

"It's not for the light."

"For what then?"

"We want to iron clothes."

"Iron clothes?" the incredulous miller asked.

"Yes, iron clothes. We know you shut down milling during the noon lunch hour and we thought you could turn on the electricity then."

After considerable discussion, the women of the village got their way. It's difficult to turn down a group of women when they are united in what they want and determined not to return to their homes until they get the decision they want. One could imagine that every day all the women in Wild Rose frantically ironing from twelve until one, when the electricity would be turned off until five o'clock that afternoon.

Today the mill stands quietly on the banks of the Wild Rose millpond. It is a private home. Water tumbles over the dam's spillway, and the little electric generator building is still there. The memories return as I stand and watch and listen to the soothing sound of the water make its way to Lake Winnebago and on to Green Bay and Lake Michigan.

("The Mill" from *Living a Country Year* by Jerry Apps, 2007)

MIXED FARMING

Raising both crops and livestock instead of specializing in one or the other. Specialization is like putting all your eggs in one basket, leaving you vulnerable to market downturns, say many agricultural experts. Mixed farming, on the other hand, makes it possible to go broke two different ways at the same time.

(Terry Chamberlain, *The ABC's of Farming*, 1999)

MULE

The mule is haf hoss, and haf Jackass, and then kums tu a full stop, natur diskovering her mistake. Tha weigh more, akordin tu their heft, than enny other kreetur, except a crowbar. Tha kant hear enny quicker, nor further than the boss, yet their ears are big enuff for snow shoes. You kan trust them with enny one whose life aint worth enny more than the mules. The only wa tu keep them into a paster, is tu turn them into a medder jineing, and let them jump out. Tha are reddy for use, just as soon as they will du tu abuse. Tha haint got enny friends, and will live on huckel berry brush, with an ockasional chanse at Kanada thissels. Tha are a modern invenshun, i dont think the Bible deludes tu them at tall. Tha sel for more money than enny other domestik animile. Yu kant tell their age by looking into their mouth, enny more than you kould a Mexican cannons. Tha never hav no dissease that a good club wont heal. If tha ever die tha must kum rite tu life agin, for i never herd nobody sa "ded mule." Tha are like sum men, very korrupt at harte; ive known them tu be good mules for 6 months, just tu git a good chanse to kick sumbody. I never owned one, nor never mean to, unless there is a United Staits law passed, requiring it. The only reason why tha are pashunt, is bekause tha are ashamed ov themselfs. I have seen eddikated mules in a sirkus. Tha kould kick, and bite, tremenjis. I would not sa what I am forced tu sa again the mule, if his birth want an outrage, and man want tu blame for it. Enny man who is willing tu drive a mule, ought to be exempt by law from running for the legislatur. Tha are the strongest creeturs on earth, and heaviest, ackording tu their sise; I herd tell ov one who fell oph from the tow path, on the Eri kanawl, and sunk as soon as hs touched bottom, but he kept rite on towing the boat tu the nex stashun, breathing thru his ears, which stuck out ov the water about 2 feet 6 inches; i did'nt see this did, but an auctioneer told me ov it, and i never knew an auctioneer tu lie unless it was absolutely convenient.

("Josh Billings on the Mule" from *Josh Billings, Hiz Sayings* by Josh Billings, aka Henry Wheeler Shaw, 1866)

NEIGHBOR

Prairie farm communities are nothing if not neighborly. Your neighbors are almost always friendly and willing to lend a hand. There is one drawback, however, that might bother city-bred folk, and that is that your neighbors often make it their business to make your business their business. This does not bother people with rural backgrounds; we know this habit has nothing to do with nosiness, it is just that everyone *cares* about everyone else. And they are absolutely ingenious in finding out all about

you. They always seem to know what I am doing, for instance, and can distribute that knowledge with amazing speed. In fact, on one occasion I have discovered via the grapevine that I am doing something before I actually start doing it. I found this a bit disconcerting but it was even more unsettling to find out they were right every time; what they said I was doing I was soon doing. It's scary as hell.

(Terry Chamberlain, *The ABC's of Farming*, 1999)

NEXT YEAR

A traditional article of faith and perennial source of strength on the prairie farm. It is a season of perfect weather conditions that produce an unprecedented bumper crop simultaneous with rapidly expanding market, record high prices for all commodities, and low prices for input costs. You say you have never seen that? Weren't you listening? I said it won't happen until **next year**.

(Terry Chamberlain, *The ABC's of Farming*, 1999)

NOISE

There is lots of noise in the tractor business. The tractors make a big noise. The tractor salesmen and service men make more. But the biggest and noisiest noise I heard in all the time I worked for the Farmers'

Friend Tractor Company came from a bird who owned one of the tractors—Jim Swigley, the demon of the Mississippi swamps.

It was one sleepy, peaceful Sunday morning. Little Sam Simpson and I had just got back from demonstrating a couple of ten-ton Earthworm Tractors that the company was trying to sell to the Park Commission up in Chicago, and we had stopped around at the factory to see if there was any mail for us. It being Sunday, everything was pretty quiet. We found we had no mail, and we were starting home, when we heard a noise from the front office and looked in to see what it was.

Now, the front office was where the president of the works used to hang out, and it sure was a swell dump. A big mahogany desk all polished up as handsome as any bar you ever run acrost in the old days. Big expensive chairs. Swell wall-paper, swell woodwork, and on the floor an elegant oriental rug as soft and beautiful as the cushions in a Pullman. Then at one end of the room was a genuine oil painting that they said was the pride of the president's heart. It showed an army model Earthworm tractor, with a funny little guy with a beard in the driver's seat, and underneath the picture was a sign that said, "His Majesty, the King of England, in his Earthworm Tractor." And then under that it said: "There is but one

Earthworm. The Farmers' Friend Tractor Company builds it."

On week days when the president was using this office, I used to be scared of the place, on account of the president being such a big bug, and the office such an elegant joint. But this Sunday when I stuck my snoot in the door, I had to laugh, because there was old Bill Johnson, and Luke Torkle, and another bird that had on a red necktie—all of them nothing but service men like Sam and me. And

> "So this bird he opens his big mouth, and calls me a poor ham, and he says, 'I asked for a mechanic, and they sent me a damn' fool.'"

they was lolling around in the fancy upholstered chairs, and chewing tobacco, and resting their thumbs in the armholes of their vests, and using the big brass spittoons and swapping yarns.

So Sam and I went in and sat down, too. And just about this time Jim Swigley was getting off the train down at the station and heading out toward the factory. But we didn't know it, so we just sat there unsuspecting, and listened to the bird with the red necktie. I forget his name, but he had a loud voice.

"Speaking of hard-boiled hombres," he said, "I've met a lot of 'em since I been a service man for this company. I've met tough ones. And I've met 'em as mean and ornery as they make 'em. But them birds don't put no muffler on me. I talk to 'em. I tell 'em. The tougher they come, the better I like 'em. I remember a tough Swede up in Duluth—"

"That's me, too," said Luke Torkle. "There can't none of them birds get funny with me. I'm a peaceful guy, but if they think they can impose on me, they got a surprise on the way. I remember one guy out in Kansas by the name of Wilkins that tried to get hard-boiled to me. Had a daughter by the name of Mildred. Good-looking girl, too—"

"Never mind the girl," said old Bill Johnson. "What about the tough guy?"

"Well, you see, this bird owned an old-style Model forty-five Tractor that needed new bearings in the transmission, and they sent me out to do the job. And this was one of them old, old tractors that come out before the days of Hyatts and Timkens. All the bearings was babbitt, and had to be repoured.

"We had a mean time. This bird Wilkins was too cheap to get a house for the machine, and he had it right out in the middle of the prairie, with sand blowing around, and the sun just a-burning and a-blazing—you know how the sun is in Kansas—and not a tree or a speck of shade in miles. And no tools to work with.

"It took me a day and a half to get the thing torn down and the old babbitt chiseled out of the bearings. Which got old Wilkins sore, because he was in a hurry to get started again. All the time I was working he was crabbing about how much expense the tractor was, and how much money he was losing by being idle. But finally we got all the shafting back in the transmission case, and blocked up in place. And that took a lot more time, because you have to get each shaft exactly in the middle of what is going to be the bearing, and you have to have every gear meshed right to a hair with every other gear. And each bearing has to be dammed up with mud. Then you melt up the babbitt metal and pour it in around the shaft and the mud keeps it from running away, and when it cools, there you have your bearing."

"We know how to babbitt a transmission," said old Bill Johnson, kind of weary. "Tell us about the tough guy."

"Well, as I was saying, this Wilkins was sore already about the length of time it was taking. But I didn't say nothing. I got the fire going, and melted up a ladle full of babbitt, and I was just pouring it into the front bearing when my foot slipped."

"All right," said Bill. "Go on. We're listening."

"My foot slipped, and I fell over against the tractor and knocked all that shafting for a goal. And the babbitt went all over this Wilkins's shoes. Nice new shoes they was, too, that he had told me cost him $4.98, F.O.B. Sears Roebuck.

"So this bird he opens his big mouth, and calls me a poor ham, and he says, 'I asked for a mechanic, and they sent me a damn' fool.'

"Well, sir, I run that old feller around and around that tractor for half an hour, hitting at him with the babbitt ladle, and—"

"Couldn't you find nothing heavier," said Bill, "than a babbitt ladle?"

"It didn't need to be heavy. It was red-hot. And besides I was throwing bolts and nuts and washers and spark plugs and everything else I could pick up. Till finally he just begged for mercy, and I let him be. I remember there was loose tractor parts all over that quarter section. But that was the way to handle him. Me and him was the best of friends after that. He seen he couldn't scare me, and he respected me. I made him chase around in the hot sun and pick up all them stray parts. That's the way to treat these mean babies. Show 'em you ain't afraid of 'em and they'll eat out of your hand."

Luke quit talking and leaned back in the fancy upholstered chair, and lit a cigarette, and looked around at us. And about this time,

Jim Swigley must have been halfway up from the station. But we didn't know it.

"Yes, sir," said the bird with the red necktie—I forget his name, but he had a loud voice. "That's the way to treat these ornery brutes. I know. I've met 'em. And they don't put no muffler on me. I remember a big mutt of a Swede up in Duluth—" . . .

"Oh, look!" said Luke Torkle.

We looked, and the door had opened a little and a great big mean, ugly face was looking in at us. You've heard about "a skin you love to touch." Well, this could have been advertised as "a face you want to hit." It had about three days' growth of whiskers on it, besides a lot of dirt and grease, and an ugly look.

"Where is the president of this works?" it said, and its voice reminded you of feeding time in the lion house at the zoo.

"I don't know," said old Bill.

The owner of the face came in. He was built something like these pictures you see of gorillas. He wasn't more than twice as big as Jack Dempsey, I should say, or this Wild Bull of the Pampas. But he looked wilder. He had on old greasy clothes, a coat like one of those Army trench coats, and big leather boots. One pants leg tucked in a boot and the other out. And if a whale had feet, that would be about the size of this gent's feet. He had engine grease on him, and a lot of mud like he had just come out of the swamps—which we found out later he had.

In his hand was something heavy that he set down kerplunk on the handsome rug. I looked at it and saw it was a cylinder off a tractor. It wasn't wrapped up nor nothing. He had been carrying it in a shawl strap. I think that's what you call it—a couple of straps with a handle. Apparently he had just taken it off of the machine, and here he had dragged it in without washing it off, or cleaning it at all. It was all over oil, and right away as soon as it got in the warm room, the oil begun to drip down and make little puddles on the thousand-dollar rug.

I was going to put the gorilla wise to these puddles, but I looked him over again, and I thought maybe I wouldn't, either. Even the bird with the red necktie wasn't saying anything.

"I want to see the president of this works," said the gorilla. He scowled at us like he expected us to say something, but we didn't say nothing, so he went on. "My name is Jim Swigley, and I come all the way from Mississippi. I called up your president from the railroad station. I told him to come over here, and I told him to be damn quick about it."

"Oh!" said Bill. "So he's coming over?"

"He'd better. I told him if he didn't, I'd go up to his house and shoot him out." He opened his coat, and underneath were two revolvers stuck into the top of his trousers, a big one and one not so big.

"The little one is for squirrels and rabbits," he said. "And if any of you crooks tries to get funny, maybe you'll find out what the other one is for." The guy with the red necktie got him a chair and he sat down. He leaned back, and just as he was hoisting his big muddy feet up on the top of the desk, the door opened and in walked Mr. L. L. Mansfield, President and General Manager of the Farmers' Friend Tractor Company, makers of Earthworm Tractors—"There is but one Earthworm. The Farmers' Friend Tractor Company builds it."

Now, L. L. Mansfield was a dignified old gent, and used to being treated very respectful indeed. When he seen this old gorilla in his best chair, scratching up the polish on his desk with them big boots, I thought he was going to blow out a fuse right off.

But the gorilla didn't give him no chance.

"You come right in and sit down and listen to what I got to say and keep your mouth shut until I'm through."

The president began to get red in the face, and took a big breath like he had a lot to say. And I guess he had. But before he said it, he began to notice the size of this brute and the artillery he carried, and finally he sat down.

"What do you wish?" he asked.

"I got one of your tractors. I bought it three months ago. It's no good. It never was no good. And it never will be no good. It's nothing but a bunch of junk. I've written you three letters, and I got no satisfaction. I've seen your little salesman you sent down there, this little George Sherwood, and I couldn't get no satisfaction out of him. I finally run him off the place with my shotgun. And now I've come up here all the way from Mississippi, and by Gosh and just as sure as my name is Jim Swigley, I'll get satisfaction out of you, or I'll wreck your factory."

He took out the largest of the two guns and hit the desk a crack with the handle. "Yes, sir, I'll wreck the joint." And he hit the desk again. Every time he hit, it made a big dent. I could see the president looking at them dents, and it didn't seem to me he was pleased.

Swigley pointed across the room with his gun. "See that cylinder?" he said.

We all looked and the president give a little jump. He seen the cylinder all right, and he also seen what it was doing to the rug. Swigley dragged his feet off the desk, gouging big grooves in the polished surface with his hob nails.

"Come over here," he said, "and don't sit there looking like a fool. Come here." The president went over. "Run your hand over that,"— and he made the president feel of the inside. "Scored up. Worn out. Ruined. And why?"

"Probably insufficient lubrication."

"What? What? What?"

"Well—of course—"

"Yes, I guess you better say 'well,' and hum and haw. And don't let me hear any more about 'insufficient lubrication.' That's all you birds know: 'Insufficient lubrication.' Makes me sick. Why, I change the oil every day. In the crankcase and transmission both, and all the bearings in all the rollers and everywhere else. I have three men doing nothing else but oil that machine. And here you say I don't lubricate it. Call me a liar, will you?" He stuck his face about an inch from the president's. "Call me a liar, will you?"

"No, indeed, sir, you misunderstand me. I have no doubt that your care of this machine is excellent. I was just wondering—"

"Wondering, was you? Well, you don't have to wonder no more. I'll tell you. Your machine is no good— rotten. It's junk. You claim to build a tractor. And you have the nerve to sell it to honest people. You ought to be in jail. That tractor ain't built, it's just throwed together. You get a lot of stove iron from some junk yard, throw it together, ship it out, and swindle somebody into paying real United States money for it. Then you say you 'wonder' what's the matter with it. You 'wonder' why it starts to fall apart right away."

Bang, went the butt of the gun on the desk.

"And you have the nerve to tell me it's insufficient lubrication." Bang on the desk again. "That's all you know. And look here." He reached down in his pocket, brought up a lot of oily fragments, and slapped them on the desk. Four or five little steel balls went rolling off in different directions. "That's a ball bearing from what you call your transmission. Look at it! Been used three weeks and simply fallen apart, burnt up, come to pieces, gone to hell, rotten, rotten. Not lubricated? Why, man, look at it! It's just dripping with oil right now." Yes, it was dripping all right, all over the desk.

"And look here." He went down in his pockets again, brought up a double handful of old broken washers, castings, bushings, and other junk, and rolled and dragged them around over the shiny mahogany. "All of them defective material. Rotten, busted up, full of sand holes and air holes, no good, no account, no use."

The president started to say something, but he didn't get no chance.

"Wait a minute, wait a minute!" Bang went the butt on the desk. "I'll tell you what I'm going to do. And I want to tell you I mean what I say. My name is Jim Swigley, and I always do what I say I will. I come from the Yazoo Delta. I come from

Bluefield, the Queen City of the Delta. I come from a real he-man country. Down there we shoot a man for pulling off anything so low down as what you pulled off on me when you sold me that bunch of junk. But I'll go easy with you. I'll give you one more chance.

"I came all the way up here to have this out with you people. I came all the way from Mississippi, and I won't go back until you make it right. I brought part of the stuff with me. Look it over. It's defective. Anybody can see that. Cheap stuff, full of flaws, low quality, no good, rotten—rotten! All right, I want you to come right down into your place where you keep your spare parts, and get out this order for me. And I want you to send it down to the station right off in your truck so I can see it is shipped myself. I won't stand for no foolishness!'

"Is there much material you will need?" said the president politely.

"Oh, not a great deal." He took out a dirty hunk of paper and began to read. "Four cylinders, four cylinder heads, four cylinder-head gaskets, eight valves, eight valve springs, eight valve-spring keepers, sixteen split collars, one crank shaft, eight connecting-rod bushing halves, eight laminated shims, four pistons, twelve rings, four piston pins, four piston-pin bushings, one motor-oil pump complete, one—"

"Is there much more?" said the president.

"No, that's all for the motor except a fan belt and upper and lower radiator hose, and points for the magneto. Then I want a complete set of clutch discs—the others

> "I came all the way up here to have this out with you people. I came all the way from Mississippi, and I won't go back until you make it right.

simply wore out in no time at all— and one bevel pinion, one bevel gear, two final drive pinions, and all them roller bearings in the transmission, with washers, and some more little junk. Here's the list. Oh, yes, and pins and bushings for the track."

The president looked at Swigley. He looked at us. Finally he seemed to get an idea.

"Our service engineer is the man who passes on these matters," he said. "I will refer the question to him at the earliest possible moment."

"I want action. And I want it now, see?"

"Unfortunately our service engineer is at present out of town; however—"

"Say, can that stuff! You heard what I said the first time I said it. You're the president of this works, ain't you? You can give me satisfaction if you want to. All right,

will you do it? Or will I wreck the joint?"

The president looked sort of helpless for a minute, and then hit on another idea. "I can assure you, Mr. Swigley," he said, "that it is our earnest desire to be perfectly fair with all our customers. And now that I see what an urgent case this is, I believe we can take some action at once. Fortunately, we have with us several of our expert mechanics, and we can get their opinion on this material." So he calls over the guy with the red necktie. I forget his name, but he had a loud voice.

"What is your opinion as to this cylinder?"

The guy with the red necktie stepped up and took a long look at the cylinder, and felt of it, and looked wise, and then took a sort of side squint at Jim Swigley and the two guns.

"I think," he said—and his voice was soft and gentle—"that this cylinder is defective. Yes, poor material. The—the heat treatment must 'a' been wrong, or something. Oh, yes, very defective. Probably the defectivest cylinder I ever run across, sir."

The guy with the red necktie sort of sidled off back into the corner of the room, and it may have been imagination, but it seemed to me that the president give him a kind of a dirty look.

"Well, Johnson," said the president, "What do you think? And you, Torkle?"

Bill and Luke stepped up, looking straight at the cylinder, and sidewise at the artillery.

"Better give him a free replacement," said Bill.

"Yes, sir," said Luke, "I think so, too."

The president scowled for a minute, and then decided to make the best of it. "Let me see your list," he said.

Jim handed it over. The president began to read it. Nobody said a word, and the room was very quiet.

All at once Sammy Simpson's weak little voice piped up. "Oh, look! Oh, look!"

We turned around, and there was Sammy rubbing away at the top of the cylinder with his handkerchief. Sammy was such a quiet, insignificant little toad that we had forgotten he was there.

"Who are you?" asked the president.

"Sam Simpson."

"You work for the company?"

"I've been a service man for two years."

"Well, you must do your work pretty quietly; I don't seem to remember you at all. What is it you want?"

"Look," said Sam. We gathered around the cylinder, and on the smooth machined top was stamped, "R.M. Co. 1917."

"You have another tractor besides the one you bought from us, haven't you, Mr. Swigley?" said Sam.

"Yes," said Jim, "but—" He stopped.

"Sure," said Sam. "During the first war the Army needed more Earthworm Tractors than we could make. So several automobile companies were licensed to manufacture them from our designs. And after the war, when the Army had more tractors than it could use, it transferred a lot of them to the state and county road commissions. This cylinder is from a tractor made by the Rex Motor Company in 1917. You probably got it from the Mississippi State Highway commission."

"You're a liar," shouted Swigley. "I got it from the county."

"All right," said Sammy politely, "you got it from the county. And it's seven years old. This company never

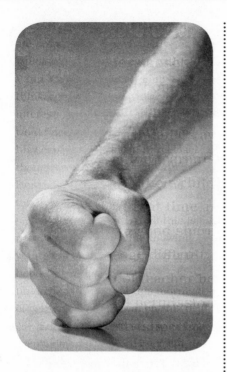

made it or had anything to do with making it. And you want us to give you free repairs for it. Is that right?"

Swigley came across the room a-snarling and a-growling. "Don't get funny with me, young feller," he said. "I'd shoot you as quick as I would a rabbit."

"No, you wouldn't," said Sammy, "because you got too much sense. It wouldn't do you no good, and they would put you in jail and probably hang you later on. You wouldn't want them to do that. You don't want to shoot me—and you know it, and I know it. So why discuss it? Let's take another look at this cylinder."

We gathered around to get another squint at the letters, and all at once the door banged, and we looked up, and the demon of the swamps was gone. Sneaked out on us, by Gosh.

For a minute nobody said a word.

Then the president took out his watch. "Must be going," he said. "Due at the country club an hour ago." He hurried out.

The bird with the red necktie took a big breath. I forget his name, but he had a loud voice. "These hard-boiled sons of guns can't fool me," he said. "I could see through this one right from the start."

"Me too," said old Bill Johnson.

"I knew he was a fake," said Luke Torkle, "even before we found the mark on the cylinder. I've met a lot of these hard-boiled birds, and they can't slip nothing over on me."

Sammy took me by the arm and we started home. As we went down the hall, we could hear the guy with the red necktie: "Well, sir, when it comes to handling tough customers, there is nobody can beat me. They never try to get fresh with me more than once. I remember a hard-boiled Swede up in Duluth—" But we didn't wait to hear any more.

There is lots of noise in the tractor business.

("Noise" from "Hello, Mr. Henderson" by William Hazlett Upson, 1924)

OATS

A grain, a little taller than wheat, with long, slim kernels and loosely structured seed heads. Oats comes in various forms, such as the plain kind that is fed to horses and the rolled kind that is fed to sullen children who would rather have Sugary-Sweet Krunchos. There is also the wild kind that nobody likes, though it is sometimes fun to sow them (but not to harvest them).

(Terry Chamberlain, *The ABC's of Farming*, 1999)

OUTHOUSE

It seems only natural that throughout history we have created many a name for the "unmentionable" that was the common privy. Polite euphemism, humorous slang, and derogatory pun all have seen service in describing this delicate subject. Here's a handy glossary to privy parlance.

Outhouse or **Backhouse**: As the privy was often set away from the house, it was commonly known as the **Outhouse**, just as working buildings on a farm other than the barn are termed "outbuildings." **Backhouse** also referred to its location out back.

Private Place or **Privy**: The outhouse was known among the more prudish as the **Private Place**. From this term came the common slang, **Privy**. The term **Biffy** is believed to be a down-home derivative of **Privy**.

Necessary House or **Nessy**: The name describes simply and succinctly the service the outhouse provided. **Nessy** was a shortened version of the term. **Chapel of Ease** and **Comfort Station** played on the privy's function. **Shithouse** was a crude but straightforward evocation of the outhouse's purpose.

Loo: This common name has a long heritage. **Loo** is a widely used English and American colloquialism for a privy, but is believed to originate from the old French warning call, "Gardez l'eau!"— "Watch out for the water!"—that was shouted out when dumping cooking slops or chamber pots from an upper-floor window into an open street sewer. Those days are thankfully gone, but the word lives on.

Latrine: *Latrina* was the Latin term for a toilet facility; the term was Anglicized as **Latrine**.

Uncle John or **Aunt Sue**: Polite euphemisms for the outhouse, as in "I'm going to visit Uncle John." Any relative's name could be used. The phrase could also double as caustic commentary on said relative's character. The **John** was likely a shortened version of the phrase **Uncle John**.

Woodpile or **Rosebush**: When in polite company, it was often preferable to say you were on your way to the woodpile or the rosebush instead of announcing that the privy was your destination. The downside to this show of good manners was that you needed to return with an armload of wood or a bouquet of flowers.

Sears Booth: Chicago mail-order monolith Sears, Roebuck & Company was famous for its thick catalog that did double duty as toilet paper in the privy; **Sears Booth** paid homage to the company's years of faithful service.

Reading Room or **Library**: With the Sears catalog handy, the privy was often dubbed the **Reading Room**. Many folk kept other reading material at hand—from books of trivia to volumes of the encyclopedia—so you could edify your mind while in the **Library**.

Throne Room: A fine descriptive phrase for the royal room where one sits in state on the throne. Naturally, this phrase may incorporate none-too-subtle commentary on the current ruler.

White House or **House of Parliament**: The otherwise unblemished name of the privy was sometimes taken in vain by disgruntled voters, who would announce their trip to the outhouse as "I'm going to send a letter to the White House." In Canada, messages were addressed to the **House of Parliament**.

Eleanor: During the Great Depression, President Franklin Delano Roosevelt's Work Projects Administration sought to offer jobs and promote rural sanitation by building outhouses. Three-man teams would spend some twenty hours erecting a privy; the WPA labor was free, but farm families paid for the materials at a cost of about $17 per outhouse. And these were glorious privies, with cast cement floors and fancy ventilation shafts. Many politicos saw the WPA outhouse project as a wasteful boondoggle, and as a dig against the president, scornfully took to calling the privies **Eleanors**. Some folk also termed them **Roosevelt Monuments**.

Chic Sale: Charles "Chic" Sale was a 1920s vaudeville actor and comedian who penned a book entitled *The Specialist* based on one of his stage routines about a carpenter named Lem Putt who specialized in building privies. In fact, the book struck such a chord with people that it worked its way into popular jargon: Some folk began calling an outhouse not a "Lem Putt" but a **Chic Sale**—to the author's everlasting consternation.

("An Outhouse by Any Other Name: A Glossary of Privy Parlance" by Michael Dregni, from Ode to the Outhouse by Roger Welsch)

PART

This is a very comprehensive word; there are many different kinds of parts. We are talking here about mechanical parts for tractors, balers, and other farm machinery; they differ from other parts in several unique ways:

1. They cost about the same, ounce for ounce, as processed uranium. If you were to build a combine from separately purchased dealer's parts it would cost about the same as the space shuttle Columbia.

2. You need lots of them. Farmers, or their spouses, spend hundreds of hours per year chasing up and down the roads from farm to town and town to town searching for coarse-threaded thingamajigs, double-flanged doohickies, and the like.

3. They fail when you need them, seeding and harvest time in particular.

4. The one you need right now is seldom in stock, at least not in your province.

5. The one you need right now and isn't in stock will, once you no longer need it, be found lying around everywhere by the case lot.

(Terry Chamberlain,
The ABC's of Farming, 1999)

PICKUP

In the city this word refers to a spontaneous date negotiated at a bar, but in the farm country it refers to something equally exciting and sexy: a small (one-half or three-quarter-ton) truck. They are used to commute to and from fields and town, to transport goods and equipment, and, most of all, as status symbols. The rural prairie male loves his wife, his kids, and his pickup truck, not necessarily in that order. He and his cronies discuss the relative merits of their pickups endlessly, and each is as fanatically devoted to his particular brand as the PLO is to Palestine. To a confirmed Dodge devotee like my brother the owners of Fords and Chevies are poor, misguided, weak-minded losers, more to be pitied than condemned for their unfortunate choices. And the feeling is mutual. (You will notice that the smaller Asian versions are not mentioned here; rural prairie folk do not classify them as trucks but as pitiful, underpowered things not worthy of the name.)

(Terry Chamberlain, *The ABC's of Farming*, 1999)

PLOW

Implement with a big blade for tilling soil. Now they are pulled by tractors, but once farmers walked behind them just three or four feet in back of a team of oxen or horses—a lousy job, considering the deplorable bathroom etiquette of those animals, not to mention the monotony of the view in front of you. Then there is the *breaking plow*, which is not, as you urbanites may think, an implement in need of repair, but one used to turn over uncultivated soil for the first time.

(Terry Chamberlain, *The ABC's of Farming*, 1999)

PORCH SITTING

September should be devoted to sitting on the porch, looking out through the long shade to the warm place in the sun where summer was. The weeds are blossoming there now. The crabgrass is feathering, and the smartweed is a pink blush among the clover. (Frost will rake the weeds and the clover will triumph.) In the fencerows the foxtail is waving. There's hardly a farmer around who appreciates the graceful sway of this noxious weed. (Though I did read once of a farmer who makes foxtail hay. Three cheers!)

It's a nice porch, tucked under the roof, quite a bit more than a stoop but yet not a veranda. Paul thought we should push out the wall and absorb the

space into the kitchen, but I protested. "It belongs to the architecture, and if your great-grandmother could afford a porch, so can I."

There are tintypes in an antique cigar box here of overweight ladies in long heavy skirts, dark shawls, and bonnets, sitting, like figures in a wax museum, upon this same porch. Or is it the same? The pillars rotted away and were replaced; the floor, likewise. The clapboard has a saw curve like the original, but it is of vinyl-coated steel. God and new tenants make all things new.

The rocking chair belongs. I rescued it from the woodshed years ago, sanded and painted it, and found a craftsman to weave a seat. I like to think it's the same chair those old wives sat on for the photo, though they obscured it with their bulk.

Sit on the porch and enjoy the courageous flowers. They weren't planted till July. (Three nested clay pots sit on the well stone even yet.) And they persisted through puppies and summer heat and gross neglect. We are on the same schedule, the flowers and I. Now that I have time to sit, they are ready with their flourishes.

Enjoy the fresh paint on the porch floor, the only tangible

evidence of summer accomplishment. Not much, but rejoice. It involved a lot of deliberation with the guy at the hardware store. Rejoice in hardware clerks who know what they're selling, what you want to buy. "I want a blue porch paint."

"Got a nice one here—Amish Blue."

"Uhhh . . . nice, but a little dark."

"How about if I leave out one part of black? Can always add it if you don't like it." It was perfect.

"We'll call it 'Almost Amish,' " he said. "I'll mark the formula on the can."

Sit on the porch and peel apples and know that this is a timeless pursuit, linking you to three generations of Leimbach women and farm women of all time. Heidi ambles up and crowds close to me, jealous of every porch minute not devoted to her. Her wagging tail beats rhythmically on the siding, fanning mud against the white, matching the "Heidi tracks" on the blue. This is her porch, after all, and I'm invading the watchdog corner.

Sit on the porch and enjoy the smell of applesauce wafting through the open kitchen window. I bought the apples yesterday from an Amish lady down south of Apple Creek. A sign said, "Apples." And up at the end of the long driveway, in the cellar of her house set into the hill, she poured them into a sack.

The apples were disappointing, but the Amish lady was worth the price of the fruit. She was big, robust, and barefoot, with a pretty, peaceful face. She wore a white bonnet, a long burgundy pleated skirt, and a black blouse held together as is customary with straight pins. Two little carbon copies—also barefoot, long-skirted, white-bonneted—clustered about her skirts. Two older girls wandered down a path fringed with purple asters to share summer secrets in the woods. From an upstairs window yet another pair of girls gazed furtively down upon this intruder from the outside world.

She apologized for the gnarled and wormy little Melbas, "All I have left." (Her wealth lay in daughters.)

"Never mind, I'll take them." We talked then of the universal farm subject. "Did ya get some rain?"

"Nice rain. Needed it."

"Sure did." I turned my car around on the steep hillside and drove off, curving past the front porch.

It was not Amish Blue, nor much sat upon, I judged. But I had relieved her of those apples. Maybe today she too sits on her porch, watching the butterflies sip nectar from the purple asters.

("Porch Sitting" from *Harvest of Bittersweet* by Patricia Penton Leimbach, 1987)

POULTRY

Birds raised on farms for food or eggs. Most common are chickens; they are raised in specialized operations, either for eggs or meat. The chickens themselves, of course, prefer the egg farm as a residence over the one designed to supply drumsticks, nuggets, fingers, and McChicken sandwiches.

Turkeys are given no such choice; fortunately this doesn't bother them as a turkey has approximately the same IQ as a carrot. The farmer treats these birds like royalty, giving them the finest food and living quarters available. As a result the turkey becomes unbearably conceited and struts around as though he owns the place, not realizing that the rent comes due and the lease ends at either Thanksgiving or Christmas.

Geese and ducks are not big items on the prairies, but there are enough—considering their intelligence levels (about the same as turkeys')—to put smiles on the faces of the local fox and coyote population.

(Terry Chamberlain, *The ABC's of Farming*, 1999)

During summers on the North Dakota prairie, we were often forewarned of bad weather because we could see it pile up far off on the horizon, sometimes early in the day, through wavy sheets of heat. And so most farmers in those days kept one eye cocked toward the horizon with a mind as to what the weather might allow them to do—or not to do—that workday.

But Gordie, the farmer I worked for, was no ordinary farmer. He owned a gift of gab, as well as the local sales barn (which, rumor had it, he had won in a high-stakes poker game in the back room of a local bar), and farming wasn't his highest priority. This was why he needed a hired hand, and eventually I filled that bill between my junior and senior years of high school. I had just turned seventeen.

Unfortunately, I was no normal hired hand. I knew as much about agriculture as you might expect from a farming-area city kid who had picked rock, hauled bales, and once or twice butchered chickens and pigs. This might not have been a problem, except that Gordie was seldom around to help me or direct me or give me advice.

On that fateful morning, Gordie had already hopped into his pickup and was hightailing it out of the yard ahead of a plume of dust when I flagged him down and asked him what he wanted me to do.

"Oh yeah," he said, removing his co-op hat and scratching his white scalp. "Well, why don't you take the B and the hayrack and load them bales from that field I showed you yesterday? That should do you most of the day." He glanced at the sky. "Might rain," he said, and then he floored it and was gone, hidden in a cloud of dust before I could yell that I'd not only never driven the Allis-Chalmers B before, but I'd never driven a tractor before. And I'd only driven a car once or twice.

If you were a steady and dependable kid, the people in my small town would assume that you could handle pretty much anything, which is why I routinely collected bills for Sayler Bros. Hardware, pedaling around town with a couple thousand in cash stuffed in my back pocket every month, ran the projector at the Dakota Theatre five nights a week, and delivered all the newspapers in town.

And that was why Gordie figured I could handle a tractor without too much trouble—which proved to be true, at least at the outset. Soon I was proudly standing on the tractor platform getting a feeling for the steering as the little beast bounced over the prairie roads toward my date with destiny, trailing a clattering flatbed hayrack behind. Duck soup, I figured, as I spotted a pair of tractor-sized boulders—you wouldn't want to crash into them with a vehicle—that signaled the entrance to a steep, sloping path choked with stinkweed. I negotiated the narrow way between the boulders to the nearly invisible path, and nearly killed the little tractor before I goosed the Allis B up the long steep hill on top of which storm clouds seemed to be piling.

But the day was young, the clouds far away, and I was weaving the lies I would tell my friends about what size tractor Gordie had let me drive my second day at work—maybe a brand-new 5010 John Deere that had just come out, and the factory had asked him to test (he'd tested several products prior to their coming onto the market, although no tractors) or a Minneapolis Moline G-VI. I certainly didn't want to tell my friends that the first tractor I'd ever driven was a dinky little Allis B, and this was definitely a dinky one. It was the first Allis B of late-1930s vintage, and seemed not

much bigger than a go-cart to a kid who wanted to drive a big tractor. My friends would make fun of me all winter if they ever found out.

The air was soupy, and the sweat bees swarmed and bumped into my bare back as I pulled off into an alfalfa field. At first I wasn't sure it was the right field, but then I saw the bales. They were small and square because Gordie was too busy to adjust his baler. He said they were the perfect size for one person to haul.

That was true, I discovered as I idled the B beside a group of bales, tossed them onto the hayrack, climbed up, and hoisted them to their proper positions on the rack, and then drove on to the next group. I felt like a real farmer.

I filled the bottom row, and then most of the second, third, and fourth rows, leaving an area to toss the bales, and a path for me to climb up the rows. Time flew by. Clouds had blotted out the sun long before, and a cool breeze had thankfully sprung up. I had nearly filled all the rows when I paused for a minute to glance at the sky. Instead of puffy clouds or long gentle white ones, the sky had turned variously gun-metal gray, angry black, and purple as a bruised grape.

While I had worked, the anvil-topped black clouds had clawed miles up into the atmosphere, until now they towered menacingly over me, their hulking weight pressing down ominously, dwarfing the hayrack and the Allis and me. All I could say was, "Uh oh." I felt alone and tiny and insignificant.

A white zigzag of lightning sizzled across the sky, followed instantly by a clap of thunder that nearly startled me off the edge of the hayrack. I tried to calmly finish pushing the last bales of the load into their slots as a cold wind surged and the first fat raindrops plopped in the dust and plinked on the Allis.

I scrambled down, climbed onto the cabless tractor, and slowly turned it around, puttering toward the prairie path and home. I knew I was in for a little blow. Had I been wiser or more experienced, I would simply have crawled under the hayrack and waited for it to pass. But Gordie had said something about not wanting those bales to get wet, and, well, I simply didn't know what I was doing.

A hundred yards of driving and the deluge from the skies opened, drenching me instantly in ice-cold rain, and blotting out the landscape around me. I could have been in a blizzard, for all I could see. I was all alone with the gray hissing rain, howling wind, and crackling thunder. I trembled at every flash and noise, and when the hail began pummeling me, I shoved the Allis into high, and decided to outrun the storm.

For a few moments, it was actually fun. To control my terror, I whooped and yelled as though I was on an old-time cattle drive trying to keep the beasts together during the storm. Had anyone seen me, my white-knuckled hands knotted around the steering wheel, black hair streaming behind, teeth gritted, and a maniacal look in my eyes as the rain cascaded around me and pellets of snow-white hail bounced off the hood of the orange Allis, they would have thought me insane. If you have ever been caught unprotected in the open during a prairie storm, you'll know that I probably was, a little bit.

Finally, with whips of white lightning and growls of thunder reverberating around me, I came to my senses. Ozone burned my nostrils as I bounced along the path. I peered behind me into the stinging rain and saw that bales were beginning to jar loose.

But before I could slow, the earth seemed to give way. The front edge of the tractor, the back wheels, and suddenly the entire hayrack was slanting downward and gaining speed. The hill!

I'd forgotten about that long and steep hill I'd climbed up to get to the alfalfa field. There was one other little knell of warning in my brain, but before I could capture it, my attention was pulled back to the tractor.

I was going too fast. I had to slow down. Bales had begun to bounce off the side of the hayrack, disappearing into the torrents of rain and hail. I shoved in the clutch, and tried to downshift. But it wouldn't slip into another gear. Now I was in neutral, and if I had not already been sopping wet, I would have been covered in sweat, because I knew I was in big trouble. The unfettered tractor and hayrack and I picked up amazing speed, plunging wildly down the hill, clanging and clattering and crashing into dips and ruts in the road. I was tossed every which way. My teeth ached from the jarring. Fenceposts were a blur. Bales shot by me on both sides, ejected from the rack. Half the time I was in the air, tethered to the machine only by my death grip on the steering wheel.

I had to stop. So I jammed on the brakes. The rear wheels of the Allis locked, and began skidding. I glanced behind me, and the hairs on the nape of my neck prickled. The hayrack had turned almost sideways, and was skidding recklessly towards me, the hitch bent at a "V" where it was attached to the Allis. I felt the front wheels of the Allis lift off the ground. Half the bales were gone, and the others were jouncing around in the rack, seeking an exit.

Lightning smashed into the field not a dozen feet away. The clap of thunder was deafening. The tractor skidded sideways, front wheels in the air like a rearing pony, back wheels gouging out great gouts of wet black dirt and spewing it off to the side.

Then I remembered what my subconscious had been trying to warn me about: the boulders at the entryway to the road I was now careening down. In my mind's eye I could see the tractor piling up against one of the boulders, followed by the hayrack slamming into it, pulverizing the little Allis and me.

I could feel the force of the hayrack behind me, controlling me, and instinctively I knew that in seconds the drama would be over: I would soon tip over, or be tossed off and ground under, or smashed into the rock.

So I did the only thing I could do: I released the brakes. For a moment the small tractor and hayrack and I continued sliding sideways down the hill toward the rocks. Then slowly the rear tractor wheels gained purchase, the front end touched earth, and the tractor found the road. In short order, the hayrack followed as though nothing untoward had happened.

There was but one thing to do now, and I did it. I grasped the steering wheel, gritted my teeth, and rode the clattering beast down the rest of the hill. Now I knew how Pecos Bill of myth felt when he rode a tornado.

With breathtaking speed, the huge boulders loomed up out of the mist, and then I shot the gap between them—one wheel of the hayrack scraping past—and I darted across the main road (if another vehicle had been coming, I would have been in pieces small enough for soup, for sure). I drove onto another grassy road on the other side. I bounced and jounced and rattled, until with judicious use of the brakes, I calmed the beast clown, slowed it, and stopped.

And there I sat, trembling, sucking air, and blowing as hard as a horse that had been ill-used, while the wind roared and the rain washed over my face and the occasional hailstone rapped me on the head. I just sat while lightning crackled overhead and thunder boomed, until I stopped shaking.

Shortly, the worst of the storm blew over. I turned the tractor around and slowly headed between the rocks and back up the hill. Only a few bales remained in the rack. The rest were strewn up and clown the hill, and on either side, like casualties of a great war.

The storm clouds blew away, the sun peeped out, and I began picking up the bales and carting them back to the hayrack one by one, until I had it filled.

At supper, Gordie smiled mischievously and asked how my first tractor ride had gone.

"Um, pretty good," I lied. "Except the storm slowed me down a little bit."

"What about that hill?
Any trouble?"

"Not really," I lied again. "A little tricky, maybe."

"Good, good," he said. "I came home that way, and saw that somebody else had some trouble on that hill," he said, "judging by how the road was tore up."

I inhaled some soup into the wrong pipe, and spluttered and coughed for a while. When I regained my voice I said, "That is a tricky hill. But other than that, my first day on a tractor was duck soup."

("Duck Soup" by Bill Vossler, from *This Old Tractor*, 1998)

PRECIPITATION

H²O from the clouds, the most sought-after and at the same time the most feared of natural phenomena. *Rain* is the most valued kind, except when it comes at harvest time. *Snow* is good—a provider of spring moisture reserve— except when it stays too late or comes to early (much like visiting relatives). *Hail* is bad, except when you have a very poor crop in the field and lots of crop insurance. Then it is known fondly in farm country as the Great White Combine in the Sky; a combine which requires no fuel, replacement parts, or operating time.

(Terry Chamberlain, *The ABC's of Farming*, 1999)

PRESSURE COOKER

Toward the end of June when the cougar episode had cooled somewhat, Bob and I made several early morning pilgrimages to the abandoned farm and picked five gallons of wild blackberries—and the canning season was on. How I dreaded it! Jelly, jam, preserves, canned raspberries, blackcaps, peas, spinach, beans, beets, carrots, blackberries, loganberries, wild blackberries, wild raspberries, applesauce, tomatoes, peaches, pears, plums, chickens, venison, beef, clams, salmon, rhubarb, cherries, corn, pickles and prunes. By fall the pantry shelves would groan and creak under nature's bounty and the bitter thing was that we wouldn't be able to eat one tenth of it. Canning is a mental quirk just like any form of hoarding. First you plant too much of everything in the garden; then you waste hours and hours in the boiling sun cultivating; then you buy a pressure cooker and can too much of everything so that it won't be wasted.

Frankly I don't like home-canned anything, and I spent all of my spare time reading up on botulism. Bob, on the other hand, was in the thing heart and soul. He stepped into the pantry, which was larger than most kitchens, and exhibited pure joy at the row on row of shining jars. And I couldn't even crack his complacency when I told him that, although the Hicks were at the time using year before last's canned beef, they were busily preparing to can another one hundred and fifty quarts. Women in that country were judged not by their bulging sweaters, but by their bulging pantries. Husbands unashamedly threw open their pantry doors and dared you to have more of anything.

I reminded Bob, as I began hauling out jars, lids, sugar and the pressure cooker, that the blackberries of the summer before tasted like little nodules of worsted and we still had twenty-five quarts. But he was adamant and so "Heigh-ho and away we go"—the summer canning was on.

I crouched beneath the weight of an insupportable burden every time I went out to the garden. Never have I come face to face with such productivity. Pea vines pregnant with bulging pods; bean poles staggering under big beans, middle-sized beans, little beans and more blossoms; carrots with bare shoulders thrust above the ground to show me they were ready; succulent summer squash and zucchini where it seemed only a matter of an hour ago there were blossoms; and I picked a water bucket full of cherries from *one* lower branch of the old-fashioned late cherry tree that shaded the kitchen.

There was more of everything than we could ever use or preserve and no way to absorb the excess. I tried sending vegetables to our families, but the freight rates and ferry fares and time involved (plus the fact that Seattle has superb waterfront vegetable markets) made this seem rather senseless. I sent great baskets of produce to the Kettles, but with Paw on the road every day imploring the farmers to give him anything they couldn't use, even they had too much. I picked peas and took a shopping bag full to Mrs. Kettle, and was embarrassed and annoyed to find two bushel baskets of them sitting on the back porch, covered with swarms of little flies and obviously rotting. There was no market for this excess since the market gardeners supplied the neighboring towns. I became so conscience stricken by the waste that of my own volition I canned seventy-five quarts of string beans and too late noticed that the new farm journal carried a hair-raising account of the deaths from botulism from eating home-canned string beans.

Birdie Hicks took all the blue ribbons at the county fair for canning. She evidently stayed up all night during the summer and early fall to can, for she would come to call on me at seven-fifteen, crisp and combed and tell me—as her sharp eyes noted that I still had the breakfast dishes and the housework to do, the baby to bathe and feed and my floor to scrub before I could get at my canning—that she had just finished canning thirty-six quarts of corn on the cob, twenty-five quarts of tomatoes, eighty-two quarts of string beans and a five-gallon crock of dill pickles. She canned her peaches in perfect halves, stacked in the jars like the pictures in the canning book. They were perfectly beautiful, but tasted like glue. She canned her tomatoes whole and they came out of the jars firm and pretty but tasted like nothing. Mother had taught me to put a couple of pits and a little brown sugar with my peaches; plenty of clove, onion and finely chopped celery with tomatoes—and anyway, I like the flavor of open-kettle canned fruit and tomatoes.

By the end of the summer the pullets were laying and Bob was culling the flocks. With no encouragement from me, he decided that, as chicken prices were way down, I should can the culled hens. It appeared to my warped mind that Bob went miles and miles out of his way to figure out things for me to put in jars; that he actively resented a single moment of my time which was not spent eye to pressure gauge,

ear to steam cock; that he was forever coming staggering into the kitchen under a bushel basket of something for me to can. My first reaction was homicide, then suicide, and at last tearful resignation.

When he brought in the first three culled hens, I acidly remarked that it wasn't only the cooker which operated under pressure.

No answer.

Later, because of my remark, he said that I did it on purpose. I didn't, I swear, but I did feel that God had at last taken pity on me—for the pressure cooker blew up. It was the happiest day of my life, though I might have been killed. A bolt was blown clear through the kitchen door, the walls were dotted with bits of wing and giblet, the floor was swimming in gravy, and the thick cast aluminum lid broke in two and hit the ceiling with such force it left two half moon marks above Stove. I was lyrical with joy. I didn't know how it happened and I cared less. I was free! *Free!* F-R-E-E! After supper as I went humming about the house picking pieces of chicken off the picture frames and from the mirror in the bedroom, Bob eyed me speculatively. Then he picked up the Sears, Roebuck catalogue and began looking for a bigger, quicker and sturdier variety of pressure cooker.

("That Infernal Machine, the Pressure Cooker" from *The Egg and I* by Betty MacDonald, 1945)

PROCRASTINATION

Today I should carry the pumpkins and squash from the back porch to the attic. The nights are too frosty to leave them outdoors any longer. And as long as I am making some trips to the attic I should also take up the boat cushions and the charts and the stuff from the galley and also a fishing rod that belongs up in the attic. Today I should finish filling in the trench we dug for the water pipe and should haul two loads of beach gravel from the Naskeag bar to spread on top of the clay fill. And I should stop in and pay the Reverend Mr. Smith for the gravel I got a month or two ago and ask him if he has seen a bear.

I ought to finish husking the corn and wheel the old stalks out and dump them on the compost pile, and while I am out there I should take a fork and pitch over the weeds that were thrown at the edge of the field last August and rake the little windfalls from under the apple tree and pitch them on to the heap too. I ought to go down to the shore at dead low water and hook on to the mooring with a chain and make the chain fast to the float, so that the tide will pick up the mooring rock and I can tow the whole thing ashore six hours later. I ought to knock the wedges out from the frames of the pier, put a line on the frames, and tow them in on the high water. First, though, I would have to find a line long enough to tie every frame. If I'm to do any work at the shore I ought first to put a cement patch on the leak in my right boot. After the frames are on the beach another fellow and myself ought to carry them up and stack them. And there is probably enough rockweed on the beach now so that I ought to bring up a load or two for the sheep shed. I ought to find out who it is that is shooting coot down in the cove today, just to satisfy my own curiosity. He was out before daybreak with his decoys, but I do not think he has got any birds.

I ought to take up the wire fence round the chicken range today, roll it up in bundles, tie them with six-thread, and store them at the edge of the woods. Then I ought to move the range houses off the field and into the corner of the woods and set them up on blocks for the winter, but I ought to sweep them out first and clean the roosts with a wire brush. It would be a good idea to have a putty knife in my pocket, for scraping. I ought to add a bag of phosphate to the piles of hen dressing that have accumulated under the range houses and spread the mixture on the field, to get it ready for plowing. And I ought to decide whether to plow just the range itself or to turn over a little more on the eastern end. On my way in from the range I ought to stop at

the henhouse long enough to climb up and saw off an overhanging branch from the apple tree—it might tear the paper roof in the first big wind storm. I shall have to get a ladder of course and a saw.

Today I certainly ought to go over to the mill and get four twelve-inch boards, twelve feet long and half an inch thick, to use in building three new hoppers for dry mash feeding to my pullets. They are now laying seventy-eight per cent and giving me about eighty dozen eggs a week. I should also get one board that would be an inch thick, for the end pieces and for making the ends of the reels. I shouldn't need anything for the stands because I have enough stuff round the place to build the stands— which I had better make twenty-three inches high from floor to perch. If I were to make them less than that, the birds on the floor would pick at the vents of the birds feeding.

I ought to get some shingle nails and some spikes while I am at it, as we are out of those things. And I ought to sharpen the blade of my plane if I am going to build some hoppers. I ought to take the cutting-off saw and have it filed, as long as I am going over to the mill anyway. On the way back I ought to stop in at Frank Hamilton's house and put in my application for government lime and super, because I shall be passing his house and might just as well take advantage of it. Frank will ask me to sit down and talk a while, I imagine.

It is high time I raked up the bayberry brush which has been lying in the pasture since the August mowing. This would be a good chance to burn it today because we have had a rain and it is safe to burn. But before burning it I ought to find out whether it is really better for the pasture to burn stuff like that or to let it rot for dressing. I suppose there is so much wood in it it wouldn't rot up quickly and should be burned. Besides, I was once told in high-school chemistry that no energy is ever lost to the world, and presumably the ashes from the fires will strengthen my pasture in their own way.

I ought to take the buck lamb out of the flock of lambs today, before he gets to work on the ewe lambs, because I don't want them to get bred. I don't know just where to put him, but I ought to decide that today, and put him there. I should send away today for some phenothiazine so that I can drench my sheep next week. It would probably be a good idea to try phenothiazine this time instead of copper sulphate, which just gets the stomach worms and doesn't touch the nodular worms or the large-mouth bowel worms. And I ought to close the big doors on the north side of the barn cellar and board them up and bank them, so that the place won't be draughty down there at night when the sheep come in, as they are beginning to do. I have been thinking I ought to enlarge the south door so that I won't lose any lambs next spring from the ewes jamming through the narrow single opening, and this would be the time to do that.

Today I ought to start rebuilding the racks in the sheep shed, to fix them so the sheep can't pull hay out and waste it. There is a way to do this and I know the way. So I am all set. Also I ought to fix up the pigpen down there in the barn cellar too and sweeten it up with a coat of whitening so that I can get the pig indoors, because the nights are pretty cold now. The trough will probably not have to be rebuilt this year because last year I put a zinc binding all around the edges of it. (But if I *shouldn't* get round to fixing up the pen I should at least carry a forkful of straw down to the house where the pig now is—I should at least do that.)

This would be a good day to put in a new light in the window in the woodshed, and also there is one broken in the shop and one in the henhouse, so the sensible thing would be to do them all at once, as long as I have the putty all worked up and the glass cutter out. I ought to hook up the stove in the shop today, and get it ready for winter use. And I ought to run up the road and see Bert and find out why he hasn't delivered the cord of slabwood he said he was going to bring me. At any rate, I ought to make a place in the cellar for it today, which will mean cleaning house down there a little and neating up, and finding a better place to keep my flats and fillers for my egg cases. Incidentally, I ought to collect eggs right now so there won't be any breakage in the nests.

It just occurred to me that if I'm going to the mill today I ought to measure the truck and figure out what I shall need in the way of hardwood boards to build a set of sideboards and a headboard and a tail board for my stakes. I ought to bring these boards back with me along with the pine for the hoppers. I shall need two bolts for the ends of each sideboard, and one bolt for the cleat in the middle, and two bolts for the ends of each of the head- and tail boards, and there will be three each of them, so that makes fifty-four bolts I shall need, and the stakes are about an inch and a half through and the boards will be three-quarters, so that makes two inches and a quarter, and allow another half inch for washer and nut. About a three-inch bolt would do it. I better get them today.

Another thing I ought to do is take that grass seed that the mice have been getting into in the barn and store it in a wash boiler or some pails or something. I ought to set some mousetraps tonight, I mustn't forget. I ought to set one upstairs, I guess, in the little northeast chamber where the pipe comes

through from the set tubs in the back kitchen, because this is the Mouse Fifth Avenue, and it would be a good chance for a kill. I ought to gather together some old clothes and stuff for the rummage sale to raise money to buy books for the town library, and I ought to rake the barnyard and wheel the dressing down into the barn cellar where it will be out of the weather, because there is a lot of good dressing there right now. I ought to note down on the calendar in my room that I saw the ewe named Galbreath go to buck day before yesterday, so I can have her lambing date. Hers will be the first lamb next spring, and it will be twins because she is a twinner. Which reminds me I ought to write Mike Galbreath a letter. I have been owing him one since before Roosevelt was elected for the third term. I certainly should do that, it has been such a long time. I should do it today while it is in my mind.

One thing I ought to do today is to take a small Stillson wrench and go down cellar and tighten the packing nut on the water pump so it won't drip. I could do that when I am down there making a place for the slabwood—it would save steps to combine the two things. I also ought to stir the litter in the hen pen in the barn where the Barred Rocks are, and in the henhouse where the crossbred birds are; and then fill some bushel baskets with shavings and add them to the litter in the places where it needs deepening. The dropping boards under the broody coops need cleaning and I should do that at the same time, since I will be out there anyway. As far as litter is concerned, a man could take and rake the lawn under the maples where there is such an accumulation of leaves and add these dry leaves to the litter in the houses for the birds to scratch around in. Anything to keep their minds occupied in healthy channels.

Today I intend to pull the young alders in the field on the north side, as they are beginning to get ahead of me. I must do that today, probably later on this afternoon. A bush hook would be a good tool for that. I should also clean up the remaining garden trash and add it to the compost, saving out whatever the sheep might eat, and should remove the pipe from the well under the apple tree and store it down below in the barn.

I also think I had better call up a buyer and get rid of my ten old hens, since we have canned all we are going to need. After the hens are gone I shall no longer need the borrowed range house that they are living in, and I can get two long poles, lash them on behind the truck, and load the house on and drag it up to Kenneth's house. But it will be necessary to take an ax and flatten the ends of the poles so they won't dig into the highway, although the tar is so cold now they probably wouldn't dig in much anyway. Still, the thing to do is do it right.

Another thing I should try to manage to do today is to earmark the two pure-bred lambs. That will be easy enough—it just means finding the ear tags that I put away in a drawer or some place last spring and finding the special pliers that you have to use in squeezing a tag into a sheep's ear. I think I know where those pliers are, I think they are right in my cabinet next to that jar of rubber cement. I shall have to get the lambs up, but they will come without much trouble now because they are hungry. I *could* take the buck away at the same time if I could think of a place to put him.

Today I want to get word to Walter about the plowing of the garden pieces, and I had also better arrange down cellar about a bin for the roots, because on account of the extra amount of potatoes we have it will mean a little rearranging down there in order to get everything in. But I can do that when I am down tightening the nut on the pump. I ought to take the car into the village today to get an inspection sticker put on it; however, on second thought if I am going to the mill I guess it would be better to go in the truck and have a sticker put on that while I am seeing about the lumber, and then I can bring the boards back with me. But I mustn't be away at low water, otherwise I won't be able to hook on to the mooring.

Tomorrow is Tuesday and the egg truck will be coming through in the morning to pick up my cases, so I must finish grading and packing the eggs today—I have about fifty dozen packed and only ten to go to make up the two cases. Then I must nail up the cases and make out the tags and tack them on and lug the cases over to the cellar door, ready to be taken out in the morning, as the expressman is apt to get here early. I've also got to write a letter today to a publisher who wrote me asking what happened to the book manuscript I was supposed to turn in a year ago last spring, and I also should take the green chair in the living room to Eliot Sweet so that he can put in some little buttons that keep coming out all the time. I can throw the chair into the truck and drop it by his shop on my way to town. If I am going to take the squashes and pumpkins up to the attic I had better take the old blankets that we have been covering them with nights and hang them on the line to dry. I also ought to nail a pole up somewhere in the barn to hang grain sacks on so the rats won't be able to get at them and gnaw holes in them; empty sacks are worth ten cents for the heavy ones and five cents for the cotton ones, and they mount up quite fast and run into money. I mustn't forget to do that today—it won't take but a minute.

I've got to think about getting a birthday present for my wife today, but I can't think of anything. Her birthday is past anyway. There were things going on here at the time and I didn't get around to getting her a present but I haven't forgotten about it. Possibly when I am in the village I can find something.

If I'm going to rebuild the racks for the sheep it would be a good idea to have the mill rip out a lot of two-inch slats for me while I am there, as I shall need some stuff like that. I ought to make a list, I guess. And I mustn't forget shingle nails and the spikes. There is a place on the bottom step of the stairs going down into the woodshed where the crocus sack that I nailed on to the step as a foot-wiper is torn off, and somebody might catch his foot in that and take a fall. I certainly should fix that today before someone has a nasty fall. The best thing would be to rip the old sack off and tack a new one on. A man should have some roofing nails if he is going to make a neat job of tacking a sack on to a step. I think I may have some but I'd better look. I can look when I go out to get the Stillson wrench that I shall need when I go down to tighten the packing nut on the pump, and if I haven't any I can get some when I go to town.

I've been spending a lot of time here typing, and I see it is four o'clock already and almost dark, so I had better get going. Specially since I ought to get a haircut while I am at it.

("Memorandum" from *One Man's Meat* by E. B. White, 1938)

QUALIFICATIONS

Not everyone can or should be a farmer. Many people who like plants and animals think that means they should take up farming, when what it really means is that they should get a couple of goldfish and some petunias. School counselors should encourage would-be farmers to consider whether they have the "right stuff," which includes the following:

1.   EDUCATION AND BACKGROUND. The best background, of course, is to have a father who farms and who is also rich, very old, and has no other offspring. As for education, courses in finance, chemistry, global marketing, veterinary medicine, mechanics, plumbing, and about 150 other trades and professions would be appropriate, but no one lives long enough to do more than scratch the surface. Expect to learn these things on the job. Schools of agriculture are fine places, but most of the graduates seem to find they can make more money selling herbicides or farm computer systems than farming.

2.   PHYSICAL ATTRIBUTES. At one time physical strength and endurance were important, but in these days of advanced technology if you are strong enough to push a hydraulic lever, can see and hear fairly well, and appear likely to live long enough to pay off your mortgage, that will do.

3. PSYCHOLOGICAL TRAITS.

(a) *Intelligence.* Indeed farmers and ranchers must be able to outsmart gophers, bugs, weeds, fungi, and financial institutions, and be able to read, write, and calculate. However, too much intelligence may be counterproductive; after all, who would keep struggling with the vicissitudes of drought, flood, hail, frost, plagues of insects, plant and animal diseases, unpredictable markets, cost-price squeezes, and the like if they had every one of their marbles?

(b) *Tenacity.* Considering the inevitable setbacks associated with farming, this is perhaps the most necessary quality of all. It is sometimes called persistence, constancy, determination, perseverance, or strength of will.

I call it stubbornness. Government planners and agricultural strategists (who often find famers unwilling to adopt immediately their brilliant schemes) call it pigheadedness, and they don't admire it one damn bit.

(c) *Independence.* Farmers know that no matter how much aid and advice you can get from government agencies, agricultural organizations, and commercial services you must eventually make your own decisions. You can't always follow the directions of others, especially when they often conflict. Most farmers I know have discovered that, and as a result won't listen to anybody most of the time, not even to each other, and certainly not to the government. Again, this is

not stubbornness, they insist, only independent thinking. Which is a good thing, right?

(d) *Enterprise and initiative.* The true farmer or rancher is an entrepreneur, a French word meaning you have the gambling disease but are too chicken to bet everything on the roulette wheel and therefore prefer a method where, if you're going to go broke, you can do it more gradually. Also the government does not provide aid packages for professional five-card stud players who fall on hard times.

(e) *Emotional stability.* If you're the type who cringes when you see a hail cloud approaching, turns pale when the price of wheat or cattle dips, feels a cold chill when a weird sound develops in your tractor transmission, or is appalled when you see your year-end financial statement, then welcome to the club; you're an average farmer and a normal human being. However, if you keep on doing that, season after season, year after year, in spite of those nervous reactions, well, you just might have what it takes to be a success in this unpredictable business. Or you need professional help.

(f) *Self-control.* All the negative emotions mentioned in the previous paragraph come to every farmer at one time or another. The secret is not to panic but to be able coolly to assess the situation, search diligently for rational solutions, and act accordingly. But this kind of restraint can be carried too far as well. If you find yourself calmly smiling as clouds of grasshoppers descend on your wheat, laughing when you hear the price of hogs has plunged again just as yours are ready for market, or whistling cheerfully as you repair the same mechanical malfunction for the eighth time without throwing a single wrench or uttering one word of profanity, look out. The boys in white will soon be at your house making soothing comments as they lead you away. Sometimes a little tantrum clears your head and leaves you feeling refreshed.

By now you have probably concluded that only Superman has all the qualities mentioned above in abundance, and he is too busy saving the planet and chasing Lois Lane around the house to farm. If, however, you're a young man or woman with your heart set on farming, and you don't have every one of the qualifications mentioned above, don't despair. Six out of eight isn't bad; just make sure one of them is stubbornness—well, okay, let's call it perseverance.

(Terry Chamberlain, *The ABC's of Farming*, 1999)

QUILTING

Of all the Elwell family Aunt Mehetabel was certainly the most unimportant member. It was in the New England days, when an unmarried woman was an old maid at twenty, at forty every one's servant, and at sixty had gone through so much discipline that she could need no more in the next world. Aunt Mehetabel was sixty-eight.

She had never for a moment known the pleasure of being important to anyone. Not that she was useless in her brother's family; she was expected, as a matter of course, to take upon herself the most tedious and uninteresting part of the household labors. On Mondays she accepted as her share the washing of the men's shirts, heavy with sweat and stiff with dirt from the fields and from their own hard-working bodies. Tuesday she never dreamed of being allowed to iron anything pretty or even interesting, like the baby's white dresses, or the fancy aprons of her young lady nieces. She stood all day pressing out a tiresome, monotonous succession of dish-cloths and towels and sheets.

In preserving-time she was allowed to have none of the pleasant responsibility of deciding when the fruit had cooked long enough, nor did she share in the little excitement of pouring the sweet-smelling stuff into the stone jars. She sat in a corner with the children and stoned cherries incessantly, or hulled strawberries until her fingers were dyed red to the bone.

The Elwells were not consciously unkind to their aunt, they were even in a vague way fond of her; but she was so utterly insignificant a figure in their lives that they bestowed no thought whatever on her. Aunt Mehetabel did not resent this treatment; she took it quite as unconsciously as they gave it. It was to be expected when one was an old-maid dependent in a busy family. She gathered what crumbs of comfort she could from their occasional careless kindnesses and tried to hide the hurt which even yet pierced her at her brother's rough joking. In the winter when they all sat before the big hearth, roasted

apples, drank mulled cider, and teased the girls about their beaux and the boys about their sweethearts, she shrank into a dusky corner with her knitting, happy if the evening passed without her brother saying, with a crude sarcasm, "Ask your aunt Mehetabel about the beaux that used to come a-sparkin' her!" or, "Mehetabel, how was't when you was in love with Abel Cummings." As a matter of fact she had been the same at twenty as at sixty, a quiet, mouselike little creature, too timid and shy for anyone to notice, or to raise her eyes for a moment and wish for a life of her own.

Her sister-in-law, a big hearty housewife, who ruled indoors with as autocratic a sway as did her husband on the farm, was rather

kind in an absent, off-hand way to the shrunken little old woman, and it was through her that Mehetabel was able to enjoy the one pleasure of her life. Even as a girl she had been clever with her needle in the way of patching bedquilts. More than that she could never learn to do. The garments which she made for herself were the most lamentable affairs, and she was humbly grateful for any help in the bewildering business of putting them together. But in patchwork she enjoyed a mild, tepid importance. She could really do that as well as anyone else. During years of devotion to this one art she had accumulated a considerable store of quilting patterns. Sometimes the neighbors would send over and ask "Miss Mehetabel" for such and such a design. It was with an agreeable flutter at being able to help someone that she went to the dresser, in her bare little room under the eaves, and extracted from her crowded portfolio the pattern desired.

She never knew how her great idea came to her. Sometimes she thought she must have dreamed it, sometimes she even wondered reverently, in the phraseology of the weekly prayer-meeting, if it had not been "sent" to her. She never admitted to herself that she could have thought of it without other help; it was too great, too ambitious, too lofty a project for her humble mind to have conceived. Even when she finished drawing the design with her own fingers, she gazed at it incredulously, not daring to believe that it could indeed be her handiwork. At first it seemed to her only like a lovely but quite unreal dream. She did not think of putting it into execution—so elaborate, so complicated, so beautifully difficult a pattern could be only for the angels in heaven to quilt. But so curiously does familiarity accustom us even to very wonderful things, that as she lived with this astonishing creation of her mind, the longing grew stronger and stronger to give it material life with her nimble old fingers.

She gasped at her daring when this idea first swept over her and put it away as one does a sinfully selfish notion, but she kept coming back to it again and again. Finally she said compromisingly to herself that she would make one "square," just one part of her design, to see how it would look. Accustomed to the most complete dependence on her brother and his wife, she dared not do even this without asking Sophia's permission. With a heart full of hope and fear thumping furiously against her old ribs, she approached the mistress of the house on churning-day, knowing with the innocent guile of a child that the country woman was apt to be in a good temper while working over the fragrant butter in the cool cellar.

Sophia listened absently to her sister-in-law's halting, hesitating petition. "Why yes, Mehetabel," she said, leaning far down into the huge churn for the last golden morsels— "why yes, start another quilt if you want to. I've got a lot of pieces from the spring sewing that will work in real good." Mehetabel tried honestly to make her see that this would be no common quilt, but her limited vocabulary and her emotion stood between her and expression. At last Sophia said, with a kindly impatience: "Oh, there! Don't bother me. I never could keep track of your quiltin' patterns anyhow. I don't care what pattern you go by."

With this overwhelmingly, although unconsciously, generous permission Mehetabel rushed back up the steep attic stairs to her room, and in a joyful agitation began preparations for the work of her life. It was even better than she hoped. By some heaven-sent inspiration she had invented a pattern beyond which no patchwork quilt could go.

She had but little time from her incessant round of household drudgery for this new and absorbing occupation, and she did not dare sit up late at night lest she burn too much candle. It was weeks before the little square began to take on a finished look, to show the pattern. Then Mehetabel was in a fever of impatience to bring it to completion. She was too conscientious to shirk even the smallest part of her share of the work of the house, but she rushed through it with a speed which left her panting as she climbed to the little room. This seemed like a radiant spot to her as she bent over the innumerable scraps of cloth which already in her imagination ranged themselves in the infinitely diverse pattern of her masterpiece. Finally she could wait no longer and one evening ventured

> Mehetabel tried honestly to make her see that this would be no common quilt, but her limited vocabulary and her emotion stood between her and expression.

to bring her work down beside the fire where the family sat, hoping that some good fortune would give her a place near the tallow candles on the mantelpiece. She was on the last corner of the square, and her needle flew in and out with inconceivable rapidity. No one noticed her, a fact which filled her with relief, and by bedtime she had but a few more stitches to add.

As she stood up with the others, the square fluttered out of her trembling old hands and fell on the table. Sophia glanced at it carelessly. "Is that the new quilt you're beginning on?" she asked with a yawn. Up to that moment Mehetabel had labored in the purest spirit of disinterested devotion to an ideal, but as Sophia held her work

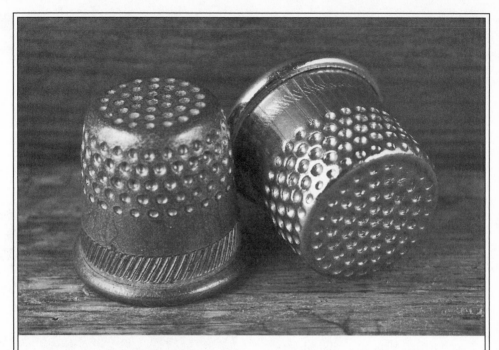

towards the candle to examine it, and exclaimed in amazement and admiration, she felt an astonished joy to know that her creation would stand the test of publicity.

"Land sake!" ejaculated her sister-in-law, looking at the many-colored square. "Why, Mehetabel Elwell, where'd you git that pattern?"

"I made it up," said Mehetabel, quietly, but with unutterable pride.

"No!" exclaimed Sophia, incredulously. "*Did you!* Why, I never see such a pattern in my life. Girls, come here and see what your aunt Mehetabel is doing."

The three tall daughters turned back reluctantly from the stairs. "I don't seem to take much interest in patchwork," said one, listlessly.

"No, nor I neither!" answered Sophia; "but a stone image would take an interest in this pattern. Honest, Mehetabel, did you think of it yourself? And how under the sun and stars did you ever git your courage up to start in a-making it? Land! Look at all those tiny squinchy little seams! Why, the wrong side ain't a thing *but* seams!"

The girls echoed their mother's exclamations, and Mr. Elwell himself came over to see what they were discussing. "Well, I declare!" he said, looking at his sister with eyes more approving than she could ever remember. "That beats old Mis' Wightman's quilt that got the blue ribbon so many times at the county fair."

Mehetabel's heart swelled within her, and tears of joy moistened her old eyes as she lay that night in her narrow, hard bed, too proud and excited to sleep. The next day her sister-in-law amazed her by taking the huge pan of potatoes out of her lap and setting one of the younger children to peeling them. "Don't you want to go on with that quiltin' pattern?" she said; "I'd kind o'like to see how you're gain' to make the grape-vine design come out on the corner."

At the end of the summer the family interest had risen so high that Mehetabel was given a little stand in the sitting-room where she could keep her pieces, and work in odd minutes. She almost wept over such kindness, and resolved firmly not to take advantage of it by neglecting her work, which she performed with a fierce thoroughness. But the whole atmosphere of her world was changed. Things had a meaning now. Through the longest task of washing milk-pans there rose the rainbow of promise of her variegated work. She took her place by the little table and put the thimble on her knotted, hard finger with the solemnity of a priestess performing a sacred rite.

She was even able to bear with some degree of dignity the extreme honor of having the minister and the minister's wife comment admiringly on her great project. The family felt quite proud of Aunt Mehetabel as Minister Bowman had said it was work as fine as any he had ever seen, "and he didn't know but finer!" The remark was repeated verbatim to the neighbors in the following weeks when they dropped in and

examined in a perverse silence some astonishingly difficult *tour de force* which Mehetabel had just finished.

The family especially plumed themselves on the slow progress of the quilt. "Mehetabel has been to work on that corner for six weeks, come Tuesday, and she ain't half done yet," they explained to visitors. They fell out of the way of always expecting her to be the one to run on errands, even for the children. "Don't bother your aunt Mehetabel," Sophia would call. "Can't you see she's got to a ticklish place on the quilt?"

The old woman sat up straighter and looked the world in the face. She was a part of it at last. She joined in the conversation and her remarks were listened to. The children were even told to mind her when she asked them to do some service for her, although this she did but seldom, the habit of self-effacement being too strong.

One day some strangers from the next town drove up and asked if they could inspect the wonderful quilt which they had heard of, even down in their end of the valley. After that such visitations were not uncommon, making the Elwells' house a notable object. Mehetabel's quilt came to be one of the town sights and no one was allowed to leave the town without having paid tribute to its worth. The Elwells saw to it that their aunt was better dressed than she had ever been before, and one of the girls made her a pretty little cap to wear on her thin white hair.

A year went by and a quarter of the quilt was finished; a second year passed and half was done. The third year Mehetabel had pneumonia and lay ill for weeks and weeks, overcome with terror lest she die before her work was completed. A fourth year and one could really see the grandeur of the whole design; and in September of the fifth year, the entire family watching her with eager and admiring eyes, Mehetabel quilted the last stitches in her creation. The girls held it up by the four corners, and they all looked at it in a solemn silence. Then Mr. Elwell smote one horny hand within the other and exclaimed: "By ginger! That's go in' to the county fair!"

Mehetabel blushed a deep red at this. It was a thought which had occurred to her in a bold moment, but she had not dared to entertain it. The family acclaimed the idea, and one of the boys was forthwith dispatched to the house of the neighbor who was chairman of the committee for their village. He returned with radiant face. "Of course he'll take it. Like's not it may git a prize, so he says; but he's got to have it right off because all the things are going' to-morrow morning."

Even in her swelling pride Mehetabel felt a pang of separation as the bulky package was carried out of the house. As the days went on she felt absolutely lost without her work. For years it had been her one preoccupation, and she could not bear even to look at the little stand, now quite bare of the litter of scraps which had lain on it so long. One of the neighbors, who took the long journey to the fair, reported that the quilt was hung in a place of honor in a glass case in "Agricultural Hall." But that meant little to Mehetabel's utter ignorance of all that lay outside of her brother's home. The family noticed the old woman's depression, and one day Sophia said kindly, "You feel sort o' lost without the quilt, don't you, Mehetabel?"

"They took it away so quick!" she said, wistfully; "I hadn't hardly had one real good look at it myself."

Mr. Elwell made no comment, but a day or two later he asked his sister how early she could get up in the morning.

"I dun'no'. Why?" she asked.

"Well, Thomas Ralston has got to drive clear to West Oldton to see a lawyer there, and that is four miles beyond the fair. He says if you can git up so's to leave here at four in the morning he'll drive you over to the fair, leave you there for the day, and bring you back again at night."

Mehetabel looked at him with incredulity. It was as though someone had offered her a ride in a golden chariot up to the gates of Heaven. "Why, you can't *mean* it!" she cried, paling with the intensity of her emotion. Her brother laughed a little uneasily. Even to his careless indifference this joy was a revelation of the narrowness of her life in his home. "Oh, 'tain't so much to go to the fair. Yes, I mean it. Go git your things ready, for he wants to start tomorrow morning."

All that night a trembling, excited old woman lay and stared at the rafters. She, who had never been more than six miles from home in her life, was going to drive thirty miles away—it was like going to another world. She who had never seen anything more exciting than a church supper was to see the county fair. To Mehetabel it was like making the tour of the world. She had never dreamed of doing it. She could not at all imagine what it would be like.

Nor did the exhortations of the family, as they bade good-by to her, throw any light on her confusion. They had all been at least once to the scene of gayety she was to visit, and as she tried to eat her breakfast they called out conflicting advice to her till her head whirled. Sophia told her to be sure and see the display of preserves. Her brother said not to miss inspecting the stock, her nieces said the fancy work was the only thing worth looking at, and her nephews said she must bring them home an account of the races. The buggy drove up to the door, she was helped in, and her wraps tucked about her. They all stood together and waved good-by to her as she drove out of the yard. She waved back, but she scarcely saw them. On her return home that evening she was very pale, and so tired and stiff that her brother had to lift her out bodily, but her lips were set in a blissful smile. They crowded around her with thronging questions, until Sophia pushed them all aside,

> She who had never seen anything more exciting than a church supper was to see the county fair.

telling them Aunt Mehetabel was too tired to speak until she had had her supper. This was eaten in an enforced silence on the part of the children, and then the old woman was helped into an easy chair before the fire. They gathered about her, eager for news of the great world, and Sophia said, "Now come, Mehetabel, tell us all about it!"

Mehetabel drew a long breath. "It was just perfect!" she said, "finer even than I thought. They've got it hanging up in the very middle of a sort o' closet made of glass, and one of the lower corners is ripped and turned back so's to show the seams on the wrong side."

"What?" asked Sophia, a little blankly.

"Why, the quilt!" said Mehetabel in surprise. "There are a whole lot of other ones in that room, but not one that can hold a candle to it, if I do say it who shouldn't. I heard lots of people say the same thing. You ought to have heard what the women said about that corner, Sophia. They said—well, I'd be ashamed to *tell* you what they said. I declare if I wouldn't!"

Mr. Elwell asked, "What did you think of that big ox we've heard so much about?"

"I didn't look at the stock," returned his sister, indifferently. "That set of pieces you give me, Maria, from your red waist, come out just lovely!" she assured one of her nieces. "I heard one woman say you could 'most smell the red silk roses."

"Did any of the horses in our town race?" asked young Thomas.

"I didn't see the races."

"How about the preserves?" asked Sophia.

"I didn't see the preserves," said Mehetabel, calmly. "You see, I went right to the room where the quilt was, and then I didn't want to leave it. It had been so long since I'd seen it, I had to look at it first real good myself, and then I looked at the others to see if there was any that could come up to it. And then the people begun comin' in and I got so

> "You see, I went right to the room where the quilt was, and then I didn't want to leave it."

interested in hearin' what they had to say I couldn't think of goin' anywheres else. I ate my lunch right there too, and I'm as glad as can be I did, too; for what do you think?"—she gazed about her with kindling eyes—"while I stood there with a sandwich in one hand didn't the head of the hull concern come in and open the glass door and pin 'First Prize' right in the middle of the quilt!"

There was a stir of congratulation and proud exclamation. Then Sophia returned again to the attack. "Didn't you go to see anything else," she queried.

"Why, no," said Mehetabel. "Only the quilt. Why should I?"

She fell into a reverie where she saw again the glorious creation of her hand and brain hanging before all the world with the mark of highest approval on it. She longed to make her listeners see the splendid vision with her. She struggled for words; she reached blindly after unknown superlatives. "I tell you it looked like—" she said, and paused, hesitating. Vague recollections of hymn-book phraseology came into her mind, the only form of literary expression she knew; but they were dismissed as being sacrilegious, and also not sufficiently forcible. Finally, "I tell you it looked real *well*!" she assured them, and sat staring into the fire, on her tired old face the supreme content of an artist who has realized his ideal.

("The Bedquilt" by Dorothy Canfield, *Harper's Monthly Magazine*, 1906)

RANCH

Unit of grazing land on which, traditionally,
herds of cattle, horses, or sheep are raised.
However, with the livestock diversification of
recent years you may now find ranches devoted
to bison, wild boar, fallow deer, llamas, ostriches,
and the like. And since the men who herd cattle
are called cowboys (not bullboys or steerboys) it
follows from the same logic that those who herd
fallow deer are called doeboys, those who herd
wild boar are called sowboys, and those who
herd Guinea fowl are called henboys. Soon
there'll be sowboy hats and henboy boots and
Western songs like "Trail of the Lonesome
Henboy" and "Give Me a Home Where the
Ostriches Roam." No doubt Roy Rogers and Tex
Ritter are spinning in their graves.

(Terry Chamberlain, *The ABC's of Farming*, 1999)

RAT CATCHING

One winter when I was older and sleeping with Allison in that same room, we both awoke to hear something falling and bumping down the stairs outside our door. While we lay holding our breaths, we heard Mother get up to investigate. She found a cob of popcorn on the steps and realized that a rat had stolen it from our supply in a box under Allison's bed. She came up to tell us, knowing that we were probably rigidly awake.

"Be sure your door is shut," she told us, "so the rat can't get back in." Then she went out and brought in the cat from the woodshed. Carrots, a golden-orange knobby animal, was a stray that originally came to our house seeking a place to have kittens, and birthed her litter of six orange-and-whites in a nest of chips in our woodshed. She was no welfare case, it turned out, though she did drink some warm milk we gave her that first morning we found her. She proved to be a phenomenal rat catcher, able to climb the walls of our barn to catch large shrieking rats trying to escape Solomon's stick as he poked it in our corn crib. Carrots would kill one rat, drop it and catch another, until rat corpses littered the barn floor. She was petted and made much over for this, and accepted hands on her prominent backbone with stoic patience, then licked smooth all the fur rumpled by praise.

My mother put her in the upstairs hall that night and she immediately understood why she was there; the smell of rat set her whiskers twitching. She settled down, watchful and alert, her instinct telling her that sooner or later a rat would appear. Then Allison and I went to sleep. Later we were aroused by vigorous gnawing sounds under the floorboards.

"That rat is coming up through the floor!" Allison said, sitting up in the cold air.

"Let's get Carrots," I said. She slid out and lit the lamp, shivering. I followed her, and all our stirring silenced the gnawing. Allison turned the doorknob, and Carrots must have been pressed against it on the other side listening to rat sounds, for she pushed into the room and started sniffing along the floor.

"I guess we scared him away," Allison said, standing uncertainly and chilled in her nightgown. Since we were both cold, we left Carrots on patrol, blew out the light and went back to bed. Sometime in the night the gnawing began again and Allison and I both were immediately awake, listening for the momentary meeting of cat with rat. But the floorboard proved too thick and the gnawing went on and on and on. Finally we slept anyway. At daylight Carrots, her front paws neatly tucked under her, sat, still waiting. The rat, though, apparently discouraged by its all-night work, was no longer heard from. Carrots was put back outside temporarily; my mother knew enough about rodent habits to say, "He'll be back tonight to try again."

Sure enough. This time Carrots was installed in our room before we went to bed. All was quiet, and Allison and I believed the rat had taken himself elsewhere in defeat. We were curled in deep slumber when a loud thump and a piercing squeal brought us upright. More thumps, a growl and a scuffle. My sister said, "I'm afraid to get out of bed; I might step on it." Then my mother opened the door, holding a lamp. In its light we saw Carrots gripping the neck of a rat nearly her size, its hind legs kicking, its hairless tail thrashing. She paid us no attention but set the rat down, holding it with her claws so she could get a better grip with her teeth. This time she bit down, bones snapped and the rat was immediately still. Carrots dropped him, pawed at him to be sure he was dead, and then went to Mother and rubbed around her ankles.

"You're a wonderful kitty," my mother told her, and we got out of bed to join in the praises and to pet old Carrots's bony back. She knew she had done her job well and accepted her due. She never gave the rat another look, and my mother took her downstairs to feed her milk and find some tidbit for a reward. Carrots returned to the woodshed peaceable and content. When I went out to see her in the morning she yawned in my face, blinking her golden eyes, then smoothed a wrinkle in her fur, turned over and went back to sleep.

("Places" from *Once There Was a Farm . . .* by Virginia Bell Dabney, 1990)

REAL ESTATE

I can't say I blamed the children for not wanting to do chores with me on that February morning after the storm. The cold nibbled at my feet as I left the sheepskin rug beside the bed. When I tried to get the kids up, they only made comfortable little moans and curled deeper into the covers.

Downstairs, the waterpipes were frozen and the discouraged day struggled through the snow-smothered windows. A county snowplow down the road kept losing its roar in the drifts.

When the children finally got down into the kitchen that morning, their protests came near to mutiny.

"This is pure Siberia!" said our 12-year-old Sydney. "We *work* like Siberia and it *looks* like Siberia!"

His younger sister started in. "Other people just have to worry about getting to the bus. But not us! We have to feed pigs and cows and silly old hens that don't even bother to lay eggs."

I thought that was being pretty mean to the old man, and I said so. "All you have to do is to feed the chickens, Miss Huffy!" I said. "Now let's get your mitts on!"

So amidst tears that nearly froze to their cheeks, they went to the barn with me that awful morning. There were three of them: Marielle of the chickens, Sydney of Siberia, and the one whom we call Chief Big Fellow because he's a head taller than I am.

We kicked our way through the drifts, shoveled out the barn doors and somehow got the job done. But when we were trying to follow our own step marks back to the house again for breakfast, and I had supposed the rebellion to be over, the Big Fellow began to talk.

"Pretty stupid to go through all this agony when you could have a nice comfortable job in the city. Or do you like all this extra worry and no cash?"

That was the unkindest cut of all. Because the truth is, we never do seem to have as much money as our neighbors.

At first I thought it was because our operations were so small. We had only a small flock of hens, a couple of Springer spaniel females, a few cows and a garden that kept us eating. But now we had hens by the hundreds and dozens of Springers and a big herd of cattle. Besides pigs, sheep, ducks, geese, goats, turkeys, Persian cats, chinchillas and even rabbits and hamsters in season. Some of these made our living; some were mostly for fun. Yet we never showed much of a profit.

I had never claimed our farm was altogether practical. But until that morning I wouldn't have believed my family could be so unforgiving about it. It was my wife who shook me hardest.

"Why couldn't we be happy with just a nice home?" she asked. "Why don't we sell the farm?"

I pushed my breakfast aside and put on my cap and windbreaker.

"We could keep our house, darling," she went on, "but we could get a real good price for the farm now. And your friends in town have been after you a dozen times to work for them."

I didn't listen. She followed me to the door. "What do you get out of all that slaving?"

It was a question to which I gave a lot of thought that morning.

Before noon that day, a real estate man rapped on the barn door.

"I don't thank my wife for this," I told him, as he looked for a clean place to sit. "She could at least have given me a little time to think it over."

The real estate agent was a gay, sharp little fellow. "Take all the time you want," he said. "Only remember that nine years ago you bought your 40 acres for only $1,000."

It annoyed me to discover how much he knew about my private affairs. "When I want to sell, I'll let you know."

"We're offering $500 an acre. Cash!"

I took a step toward the door, but he stayed where he was. "Let's look at it this way," he said. "You're the last farmer left. City people are coming in so fast it's only a matter of time before you'll have to quit."

"I was here first."

"They can pass laws and tax you out." He edged in closer. "You know as well as I do that the only way to make money out of farming these days is to sell your farm for more than you paid for it. All that stuff about the joys of country life! Why I've got half a hundred farms aching to be sold!"

"I'll think it over," I promised.

We had lamb stew that night for supper, a meal my wife always makes when she wants to sign the peace. So I had to postpone giving her the scolding she deserved for putting the real estate agent on my trail. Besides, I hadn't quite decided the right reply to her question.

What *did* I get out of my farm?

I took the question with me to the barn that night. Well, one thing sure, I got a lot of work out of it. Other men on my road get up to catch the eight o'clock bus. I start the chores at six. For them the work day ends with supper (they call it dinner). For me there's an hour or more of work in the barn.

I know what it's like to get up every two hours on a frosty March night to search the sheep yard for new lambs. Or to wait up through the cold dark hours to watch a sow on the brink of maternity.

And with the work comes muss. In the summer the big lawns all down our road are neat and well-barbered. We have no lawn, only a huge rambling yard where the dogs dig, the geese squat and the children build feed-bag tents. Where on wash day the rooster proclaims himself cock of the walk from the clothes pole, and the pigs have made their own farm pond and the pony scratches his rump on a trellis once intended for roses.

Nor is the muss confined to the stables and the yard. We go into the house with animal husbandry still stuck to our boots and our pants cuffs full of chaff. And in the kitchen there is all too often an orphan lamb to dart out from his nook behind the stove and cast aspersions on the wife's clean floor. Or a runt pig, or chilled chicks.

I get a lot of worry out of my farm, too. I worry about frost, thaws, rain, drought, hail, storms and the rumors of storms. I worry about the rising price of hay and the sinking price of beef. And should there be an ailing animal on my place, my supper means little to me. Even one of lamb stew.

I'll admit, I complain pretty loud about such trials—so loud, perhaps, that my wife may think they overwhelm me. But for all its tribulations, the labor of farming has given me a satisfaction I have never found in any other occupation.

I like the thousand little things about a farm which can stop a man's heart in mid-beat and make him remember ever after. The trust of well-fed animals. The soft neighing of a mare to her exploring colt.

The sounds of the woods on the wild spring nights at mapling time and the smell of the fire-pink steam which lifts from the boiling sap. The power and the glory of a young bull as he blats and paws the earth to announce that he has now outgrown his age of innocence. The child-like swelling of pride which you can't quite hold back when one of your gleaming animals wins the judge's nod and a bright ribbon at the fair.

The smell of sun in a small boy's hair at berry picking time. The delighted cries of a little girl in a spring orchard as she peeks through clenched fingers at a bright bug or a tree toad or some other trophy of a child's eternal quest for something younger than itself.

I like the way the farm teaches my children about creation.

A few weeks ago there was quite a commotion at one of the neighboring homes. The center of the excitement was a cardboard box that the good lady of the house was trying to hide. But for all the precautions, a five-year-old boy managed a peek.

"Don't know why they're all excited," he said. "Just the cat having kittens."

That enlightened boy, I am glad to say, started his education on my farm.

All right. So it's a religion with me. But how does a man explain such a thing to his wife or to the real estate agent she sicks on him?

But why should I bother to try? Already there were people down the road who wanted to pass some kind of law that would prevent a rooster from crowing before seven in the morning. And twice in the last week our sheep had congregated on a neighbor's back porch. We might hang on another two or three years perhaps, but eventually our farm would have to succumb to the same law which had made it a farm. One kind of life must cease so that another might thrive.

It would be hard to say goodbye to the animals, I thought. One never knew what kind of people they would go to. But there was no use fighting the inevitable, especially when the family wasn't willing to fight with you. I decided to sell out.

Back at the house I still cherished the hurt the family had handed me and I didn't give them the satisfaction of knowing that they had won. I said nothing about it at all, but the next time I was in the city, I dropped in to see the real estate man and made the deal. Afterward I dropped around to see my friend in the feed business. Then at supper that night, I told the family.

"The farm is sold. We're slightly rich. I hope you're satisfied."

There was a sudden shocked hush, as if a funeral had unexpectedly come around the corner. "No!" my wife said finally. "You wouldn't!"

I was surprised at her. "But you wanted it this way! You were the one who sent the real estate man, weren't you?"

I thought she was going to cry. "But I didn't send him! I—I just called up to see how much the land might be worth. I didn't tell him to see you!"

The children had stopped eating too. "But what will we do with all the animals, dad?" Sydney asked.

"Sell them. What else?"

"Not my horse, you won't!"

"And not my chinchillas!"

The Big Fellow took a little more time to give me his opinion. "You might have asked me," he said. "I never did say that I didn't like farming. It was just that I didn't like the way we were doing it here and now."

And as I listened to them scolding me for being so impetuous, I saw that it was not as I had thought at all. Sure, my family had protested against the battle of the farm. They had protested it bitterly, just as I had. But like me, they loved it just the same. It had taken this to make them realize it.

I felt a little ashamed, and very, very happy. We had a half gallon of ice cream a little later and a box of chocolates for mother. And next day I called on the real estate man again.

"Some of these bigger farms you have on your list," I said. "Some of these places just aching to be sold— how about showing me a few?"

So the animals will only go to a new place, not to new owners. Not 40 acres this time, but 200, and every acre as beautiful as the combined hands of God and man can make it. Just the thought of it makes me feel breathless and a little guilty. Have we any right to expect so much?

And the money it will take—the money, the money! We may be the rest of our lives paying on the mortgage.

Which is why I am out in the barn now writing this as I wait through the cold dark hours with a lantern under my knees, beside a sow approaching the brink of maternity.

("The Time I Quit Farming" by Gordon Green, from *Farm Journal*, May 1958)

ROADS

Upon stopping at my mother's recently, I noticed that the road going by the house had been widened and repaved. The dull black surface is now smooth, without a blemish and a comfort to drive on. I'm sure that everyone living up and down the road is pleased, for the time being there are no craterlike potholes to slalom by or to jar one's teeth.

For a moment I really enjoyed the smooth ride, until I reflected back a few years when the road was truly a "country road." With the black, hard and unforgiving surface, the road has lost a bit of its original character.

Years ago, it was narrow and without ditches. The woods and brush grew right up to its edge. On a May Sunday afternoon, it was not unusual to see several cars parked along the neighbor's ancient lilac hedge while their owners picked fragrant bouquets. And on a fall Indian summer Sunday, those same folks would stop once more, further down the road, to gather the reddened vines of bittersweet to bring a touch of October into their homes.

A massive red oak stretched its reaching limbs over the narrow road. By day it was harmless and harbored scurrying squirrels, but at night its silhouette seemed formidable and oppressive as it lurked over the road.

I recall several summer evening hikes returning home from town with my younger brother, Scott. As we approached the eerie form of the dark tree, I often wondered aloud what it would be like to spot a dead man hanging by his neck from the limb that stretched over the road. At this point, Scott would plead in a quavering voice, "Tom, shuuuuut up!" But the more I tried scaring him, the more frightened I became, and soon we showed our heels to the heavens as we raced under the tree, down the hill, to the safety of our beckoning yard light.

In the winter, the snow-covered road would become packed ice hard from passing traffic. As there was no salt or gravel spread on the road, we sometimes had our own skating rink lane. Up and down the road we skated, watching closely for traffic and the occasional exposed rock or patch of sand.

Since those winter days, I've never known the effortless glide of a downhill stretch like the one provided by the slight hill just south of our driveway.

Change was inevitable as the Skoogs, Harders, and Schmidts sold portions of their woods and fields. Stakes denoting surveyed or measured lots started showing up. Basements were dug, and new homes seemed to pop from the earth. Traffic became heavier, and there was pressure to upgrade the narrow road. First, roadsides were cleared, ditches cut, and the road widened. The lilac hedge, the bittersweet, and the spooky oak all stood in the way and were erased. The road is safer now—

even if there are far too many yard lights to make scaring younger brothers worthwhile.

But it is the sugar sand that I remember best. A fine sand that thousands of years before had tumbled and sorted as it settled on the bottom of a misdirected Mississippi River. The original river course was temporarily dammed by a massive lobe of ice extending to the northeast, and the widened flow of meltwater was rerouted miles to the east of its present channel.

I like to think that we grew up on a river bed, long extinct perhaps, but nonetheless an actual river bottom.

It was a sand so thick and fine that it literally swallowed my bicycle tires. To forge through the sand, it seemed that we pedaled from a standing position more than from a sitting one. Coasting was a luxury, while strong calf muscles were the norm.

In the spring the sloppy road was made up of meandering ribbons of ruts that formed temporary rivers that we kids would dam to create pools until the next passing car would destroy our efforts.

And what a thrill it was to read the daily chapters authored in the sand by the crossing doe and fawn, the marauding fox, or the grit-seeking pheasant. Tracks left in the sandy road provided countless mysteries and puzzles. Only after seeing a plodding June bug swimming through the sand did I realize what had left the pair of squiggly lines across the road. What a treat to follow the shuffling tracks to the shy turtle burying its nest of eggs on the road's edge.

Dirt roads can be an improvement over books rich in natural history. If I can personally witness the clues, I will better remember that May and June are the months to watch for turtle tracks and nests. The pheasant leaves a chapter telling that it needs to bathe in dust or seek gravel bits in order for its gizzard to render the beans or corn to pulp.

Asphalt, however, leaves no tracks. The nighttime travels go unnoticed and the mystique is gone. I wonder how many kids on that road even know what a fox or raccoon track looks like.

As we accumulated new neighbors, daily traffic increased. For convenience and ease of maintenance, the road was coated in a layer of asphalt. The problem of blowing dust billowing up as cars sped by was ended. Gone were the muddy springtime ruts to contend with. The newly paved road increased the appeal of those acres adjoining it, and still more houses were built.

Oh sure, there are many benefits to a paved road. The question of paving a road or not paving it is a sore spot among county board members. The success of county commissioners is measured by how much money they can save while providing the maximum services to their constituents, which includes paving roads.

In the decade from 1967 to 1977, over thirty million acres of land were paved or built on in the United States. For every mile of interstate highway that stretches across the state, thirty-three acres of land were consumed. Prime farmland, wetlands, forests, and meadows were not immune to that reach of the freeway.

I enjoy a smooth ride as well as the next person, but perhaps we would lessen our traffic accident rate and better enjoy the countryside if we weren't in such a hurry to get where we are going. Sandy roads have a way of slowing one down.

I don't live on that road anymore but I do live on another unpaved road. It has enough sand to make "reading" worthwhile and biking a bit more work. I look forward to the day when my daughters will learn to read the daily journal of the road. They will learn, as I did, to ride a bike in the sand. I can be sure that they will each have a strong set of legs. There will be some spills during those first wobbling moments of the solo ride on two wheels, but the pain shouldn't be too bad. Whoever heard of someone skinning their knee in the sand?

("Learning Nature by a Country Road" by Tom Anderson, 1989)

RODEO

When the first settlers came to the prairies there were no nightclubs or movie theaters or gymnasiums to go to. Some of the boys were standing around with nothing to do one day when one guy spoke up and said: "I know. Let's find some really wild bulls and unbroken horses and make them really mad and then ride on them while we whoop and holler. And while we're at it we can jump from galloping horses onto galloping steers and grab them by the horns and wrestle them down and maybe hook some wild broncs up to big wagons and race them over rough ground at about 70 miles an hour. What do you think?" They locked him up, of course, but then they got to thinking, hey, TV isn't going to be invented for another 86 years and we've got to do something in the meantime. Maybe we should give it a try. And they did.

(Terry Chamberlain, *The ABC's of Farming*, 1999)

ROOTPICKING

A step in the process of clearing new land for farming which occurs after cutting or pushing down trees. Briefly, it is a contest in which a human being pits his or her brain, brawn, and axe against assorted pieces of tree roots sticking out of the ground. The roots, being smarter, often win the first round or two, but the human, being more stubborn, usually wins in the long run. Often done by machine these days, the procedure, when done the old-fashioned way, taught many farm boys and girls to persevere in the face of obstacles, to work hard for long-term gain, and to hate their fathers.

(Terry Chamberlain, *The ABC's of Farming*, 1999)

RUSTLER

One who steals cattle from a ranch. On the ranges of the early United States the solution was to hang the offender by the neck from a cottonwood tree, a practice which, while it prevented the rustler from repeating his error, did not do much for the rehabilitation process. The more enlightened modern procedure, at least for the rustler who is apprehended in Western Canada, is to sentence him (or her, this being a profession of gender-equal opportunity) to enroll in a program to cure his or her addiction to red meat. He or she is also sternly reminded that a second offense will result in being restricted to a 100% vegetarian diet.

(Terry Chamberlain, *The ABC's of Farming*, 1999)

SADDLE

Leather seat attached to horse, on which rider sits. A very practical device (though it does have a horn you can't toot), it can be simple and serviceable or very fancy and costly. As a major symbol of Western life, it is much treasured by cowboys, cowgirls, and the makers of Preparation H.

(Terry Chamberlain, *The ABC's of Farming*, 1999)

SCARECROW

She bade her friends good-bye, and again started along the road of yellow brick. When she had gone several miles she thought she would stop to rest, and so climbed to the top of the fence beside the road and sat down. There was a great cornfield beyond the fence, and not far away she saw a Scarecrow, placed high on a pole to keep the birds from the ripe corn.

Dorothy leaned her chin upon her hand and gazed thoughtfully at the Scarecrow. Its head was a small sack stuffed with straw, with eyes, nose, and mouth painted on it to represent a face. An old, pointed blue hat, that had belonged to some Munchkin, was perched on his head, and the rest of the figure was a blue suit of clothes, worn and faded, which had also been stuffed with straw. On the feet were some old boots with blue tops, such as every man wore in this country, and the figure was raised above the stalks of corn by means of the pole stuck up its back.

While Dorothy was looking earnestly into the queer, painted face of the Scarecrow, she was surprised to see one of the eyes slowly wink at her. She thought she must have been mistaken at first, for none of the scarecrows in Kansas ever wink; but presently the figure nodded its head to her in a friendly way. Then she climbed down from the fence and walked up to it, while Toto ran around the pole and barked.

"Good day," said the Scarecrow, in a rather husky voice.

"Did you speak?" asked the girl, in wonder.

"Certainly," answered the Scarecrow. "How do you do?"

"I'm pretty well, thank you," replied Dorothy politely. "How do you do?"

"I'm not feeling well," said the Scarecrow, with a smile, "for it is very tedious being perched up here night and day to scare away crows."

"Can't you get down?" asked Dorothy.

"No, for this pole is stuck up my back. If you will please take away the pole I shall be greatly obliged to you."

Dorothy reached up both arms and lifted the figure off the pole, for, being stuffed with straw, it was quite light.

"Thank you very much," said the Scarecrow, when he had been set down on the ground. "I feel like a new man."

Dorothy was puzzled at this, for it sounded queer to hear a stuffed man speak, and to see him bow and walk along beside her.

"Who are you?" asked the Scarecrow when he had stretched himself and yawned. "And where are you going?"

"My name is Dorothy," said the girl, "and I am going to the Emerald

City, to ask the Great Oz to send me back to Kansas."

"Where is the Emerald City?" he inquired. "And who is Oz?"

"Why, don't you know?" she returned, in surprise.

"No, indeed. I don't know anything. You see, I am stuffed, so I have no brains at all," he answered sadly.

"Oh," said Dorothy, "I'm awfully sorry for you."

"Do you think," he asked, "if I go to the Emerald City with you, that Oz would give me some brains?"

"I cannot tell," she returned, "but you may come with me, if you like. If Oz will not give you any brains you will be no worse off than you are now."

"That is true," said the Scarecrow. "You see," he continued confidentially, "I don't mind my legs and arms and body being stuffed, because I cannot get hurt. If anyone treads on my toes or sticks a pin into me, it doesn't matter, for I can't feel it. But I do not want people to call me a fool, and if my head stays stuffed with straw instead of with brains, as yours is, how am I ever to know anything?"

"I understand how you feel," said the little girl, who was truly sorry for him. "If you will come with me I'll ask Oz to do all he can for you."

"Thank you," he answered gratefully.

They walked back to the road. Dorothy helped him over the fence, and they started along the path of yellow brick for the Emerald City.

Toto did not like this addition to the party at first. He smelled around the stuffed man as if he suspected there might be a nest of rats in the straw, and he often growled in an unfriendly way at the Scarecrow.

"Don't mind Toto," said Dorothy to her new friend. "He never bites."

"Oh, I'm not afraid," replied the Scarecrow. "He can't hurt the straw. Do let me carry that basket for you. I shall not mind it, for I can't get tired. I'll tell you a secret," he continued, as he walked along. "There is only one thing in the world I am afraid of."

"What is that?" asked Dorothy; "the Munchkin farmer who made you?"

"No," answered the Scarecrow; "it's a lighted match."

("How Dorothy Saved the Scarecrow," from The Wonderful Wizard of Oz by L. Frank Baum, 1900)

SELECTIVE BREEDING

Choosing breeding stock for their inherited characteristics. If you raise draft horses for weight-pulling competitions you won't breed your mare to a Shetland pony stallion. Or, if you're totally unfamiliar with livestock and still don't get it, consider this: a woman who wants her child to grow up to be a star of romantic movies will not seek a sperm donation from Yasir Arafat. This principle, applied over the centuries, has resulted in heavier beef cattle, faster racehorses, bigger ears of corn, hotter peppers, and parsnips that taste even more like tarpaper than older varieties do.

(Terry Chamberlain, *The ABC's of Farming*, 1999)

SEPTIC TANK

You are advised not to read the following entry just before or just after eating.

Most urban dwellers flush their toilets and empty their kitchen sinks with no further thought of what happens to the contents. On the farm or ranch, believe me, you know what happens because you have paid thousands for the underground container (the septic tank) that the waste goes into, for the pump and pipes which empty the septic tank, and for the lagoon or pumpout which provides final disposal. Furthermore, you probably installed the system yourself and almost certainly have repaired it, unclogged or thawed pipes, and cleared fouled floats. These are not pleasant tasks as they involve working with and near the effluent. There are many farm jobs that can be performed among the glorious sights, sounds, and smells of the countryside, but septic tank chores are not among them.

The septic tank setup does, however, beat the outdoor privy used by earlier generations of farm families. Historians blame rural depopulation on mechanization of agriculture, but I think that little old two-holer shack and 40 below weather had a lot to do with it.

(Terry Chamberlain, *The ABC's of Farming*, 1999)

SHEEP

Orlando was a character worth knowing but not respecting. Lazy, good-for-nothing, fat and jolly, he added mirth to the neighborhood, for we all knew him and didn't expect perfection of character. We just took him as he was with no regrets and no expectation of change. His feats of strength, his quickness and agility, in spite of lack of exercise, were unexplainable. I have seen him squat on his haunches beside a bumblebee's nest and carefully poke it with his finger. A bee would emerge, Orlando would spat him between his two hands, deftly killing him without a sting.

Carefully he would stir them until all had emerged and been killed. If for a moment they came too thickly, Orlando made a strategic retreat for a few moments until quiet settled on the nest, and then resumed the process. Of course, the objective was to get that one little comb of exquisitely rich and sweet honey in each nest.

Did you ever get butted by an ugly ram? Many a farm boy has been rolled end over end by a swift blow from behind just before reaching the safety of the fence, and we were always just a little wary about crossing fields where sheep were grazing. Our neighbor, George, had an ugly ram, an old, cautious, wise patriarch who was respected by all the animals on the farm. The farm was across the road from our school and I can still see Ralph, the smart-aleck-pupil, visiting us from the school to the north, rolling over and over on the ground after venturing too near the old ram in an attempt to stir him up. The old ram stirred all right, but not until his judgment told him that Ralph had ventured well within the limits of the ram's rope. Then a rush, a thunderbolt through the air, a boy rolling on the ground with the expectation of sitting lightly on a chair for a week.

Well, the winter days were sometimes long and boresome. Old Ram was in fine spirits; the owner and his men treated him with great respect, rarely venturing into the pen. About the middle of a certain forenoon, Orlando strolled into the basement barn for a visit. In the course of the joking, someone spoke of the bad temper of Old Ram.

Said Orlando, "Want to let him out and see me tame him?"

Naturally, the men thought it would be fun to see Orlando's soft-looking, fat body rolling end over end, so the offer was immediately accepted. Orlando placed himself in the center of the wide driveway through the basement, and blatted like a sheep. Old Ram walked daintily out onto the floor, proud, competent, and more than ready. An imitation blat from Orlando provided the proper start, and Old Ram started on a trot, then faster and faster, until he left the floor in one final jump sighted for Orlando's middle. But at just that moment, quick as a cat, and light as a feather, Orlando leaped into the air and came down with his two hands on old Ram's head, jamming his nose into the stable floor.

Old Ram was shaken but not conquered. It was hard to understand, but backing off to judge the situation he again plunged to the attack. Once more that fat man wasn't there but Old Ram's nose was pushed into the floor until it bled. The men who had come to laugh stood in wonderment at the exact timing of each leap by Orlando and the accurate landing on Old Ram's head. One more attack and Ram had enough. With an unconquered but puzzled blat, he turned and trotted to the gate of his pen.

("The Old Ram and the Hired Man" from *Growing up in the Horse and Buggy Days* by C. E. Ladd and E. R. Eastman, 1943)

SILAGE

Green fodder (silage) is packed into a round tower (silo) to ferment, much as grapes ferment to make wine. When this fermented feed is consumed by cows they naturally get sloshed and stay that way most of the time. Really. If you don't believe me just smell a cow's breath sometime, or watch the swaying motion with which she walks. City people think a cow looks passive and contented because that's her nature. Actually, she is so bombed she has no idea

what's going on, and is in fact barely conscious. Dairy farmers will tell you that silage is high in nutrients, but the real reason, which they hide from the public, is to reduce the cows—which tend otherwise to be too obstinate and inclined to violence—to a near-comatose state, in order to make them easier to handle.

(Terry Chamberlain, *The ABC's of Farming*, 1999)

SKUNK

"We had an invasion of skunks one year. They nested under the back kitchen and we would tie a trap to a post and usually each morning we'd get a young skunk. My husband would haul them away—as long as you kept a skunk moving, he couldn't spray. So each morning, this was a ritual, he hauled away a young skunk.

However, they got into our ice well which was a hole built by the side of the house, probably ten, twelve, fifteen feet deep, and a pair of them had got in there, fighting. They'd fought and killed one another, and the smell nearly drove us out of the house. I complained bitterly about this, but my husband went off to the field in the morning and he left us with it.

So the girl that was working for me and I decided we would do something about it. We got all rigged up with old clothes because we would smell so badly; we put bandana hankies across our noses

so the smell wouldn't send us too far, and I got a rope on a pail and I went down a ladder into this well.

The idea was that I was to put the skunks into this pail and she'd wait till I got up, and then she would pull the pail up. However, when I put the skunks in the pail she got excited, and as I climbed up she pulled the pail up, so I came up with my nose practically in the pail of skunks all the way up, and that I can still smell."

("High on the Ladder" from *Remembering the Farm* by Allan Anderson, 1977)

SLOUGH

A "pond," as it is called in more civilized lands. Most farms contain at least one of these noble bodies of water, which range in size from that of a city lot to 100 acres or more; in fact many prairie "lakes" are really overgrown sloughs.

Sloughs are generally regarded as negative phenomena because (1) they take up land which a farmer would rather use for crops or pasture, (2) they have a nasty habit of spreading out into surrounding fields in the spring, which results in tractors and implements getting bogged down, (3) they are seen by mothers as a danger to small children, who are unfailingly attracted to them, particularly if warned to stay away from them, (4) they make excellent incubators and nurseries for baby mosquitoes, and (5) their aroma, especially in the drier part of the season, is less than delicate.

However, as any child who grew up on a prairie farm—especially in pre-TV days—will tell you, a slough is pretty much indispensable to a proper and complete rural childhood. Why? Because (1) you can swim in it—if you're brave enough to risk "the itch,"

that is, (2) you can raft on it, (3) you can sometimes find wild mint beside it to chew on, (4) you can hide in the long grass beside it to spy on the daily activities of ducks, mudhens, muskrats, and assorted other wildlife, (5) you can catch frogs and tadpoles in it to show your mother for her edification and entertainment, (6) you can pick cattails there, and (7) warm slough mud between your toes is a heavenly sensation. No family farm, obviously, is complete without at least one good old smelly slough.

(Terry Chamberlain, *The ABC's of Farming*, 1999)

STONE

Stones are little gifts from Mother Nature, sent, like hail and grasshoppers, to remind the farmer he should have taken up the occupation of ice cream vendor, as he planned to do as a child. Running an implement over unseen stones is very unpleasant; they break disks, snap off cultivator shovels, ruin the teeth on swather knives, and what they can do to the insides of a combine is just too horrible to describe. Thus, farm families devote much time, money, equipment, and back-breaking labor to digging up and carting away stones. And each spring the melting of the snow reveals that good old Mother Nature has burped up a new batch. It's a constant war. Farmers will always keep fighting it and may even

win a few battles but they will never, never win the war. Never.

(Terry Chamberlain, *The ABC's of Farming*, 1999)

SUBURBAN ACREAGE

A plot of land that varies in size but is generally bigger than a city lot and smaller than a farm. They are popular with city folk who like to play at being farmers, cowboys, or country gentlemen. When the urge for the rural life becomes irresistible the following process occurs: Step 1—City family escapes crowded, noisy city for peace, quiet, and freedom of country. Step 2—City family discovers excess of peace and quiet can be rather disturbing. Also discovers necessity of spending a fortune on construction and/or upkeep of their own sewer, water, garbage disposal, snow removal, etc. systems, also time and expense of daily commute to work plus travel for shopping, entertainment, etc. Step 3—City family escapes bloodsucking acreage and returns to convenient, comfort, and abundant facilities of city. But only, of course, after painting glorious mental pictures for some other poor dreamy-eyed city couple of peace, quiet, and beauty of countryside and unloading the place on them.

(Terry Chamberlain, *The ABC's of Farming*, 1999)

SUMMER VACATION

Happily, our summers were more than just work. The long evenings were perfect for playing whiffle ball (there were never enough of us around to play baseball), riding bikes, or fooling around. We'd climb up into one of the prolific cherry trees when the fruit ripened, eating our fill alongside the robins, after Mother had picked all she was planning to can for the winter. Green apples were another summer treat. We'd borrow the big green salt shaker from the downstairs dining room and climb up into any of a score of apple trees and eat as many, covered with a layer of salt, as we cared to without ever getting the threatened bellyaches.

Sometimes there were visitors, usually relatives from Massachusetts, our favorites being Dad's Aunt Stella, her husband, Sam, and their daughter, Marilyn. While Aunt Stella visited, Sam helped out haying or in the garden and before chores added a little festivity to the operation for the adults with his frosty green bottles of Ballantine Ale. Poker games went on every night when Sam and Stella were around, and Marilyn, and her cousin, Ruthie, older than the rest of us, would take us kids swimming at Bear Pond, where there was also a sorry little amusement park. On Sunday, everybody would pack up and cram into several cars and go to Sebago State Park or Old Orchard Beach as a group.

Traveling was never an option for us with all the work that needed doing, daily chores, and milking. But each year as the summer progressed our family would plan a week's worth of daytrips we'd hope to take before school started after Labor Day. Destinations included Old Orchard Beach and Reid State Park on the coast, Rangeley inland, and perhaps one or two of the early agricultural fairs. In reality we seldom managed to accomplish even this modest itinerary, and with haying dragging on right up until summer's end, we'd wind up settling for two or three of our choices.

Old Orchard Beach, with its miles of white sand beaches, amusement park, and concession pier, was our favorite, and I'd usually bring along Joe. Linda would invite Marilyn Davenport or another pal. At summer's end the place would be mobbed. In those days Old Orchard was an annual vacation destination for thousands of French-Canadians from Québec City and Montréal, and it seemed there was as much French as English spoken. Adults and children alike played in the big translucent-green breakers rolling in on the beach. And there were vacationers showing a lot more deeply tanned skin than we were accustomed to as they reclined on their lounges or sprawled on blankets and colorful beach towels.

Mother and Dad would lie in the sun and we'd head down to the water's edge where you were necessarily shoulder-to-shoulder with other romping bathers. Until I was ten or eleven, all it took was a sideward look or a playful splash from any of the noisier, more aggressive kids and I was out of the water and back up on the blanket with my parents.

The pier and amusements were the real destination. Supported by bundles of huge pilings, the pier jutted boldly out into the open Atlantic for what seemed like a hundred yards. Back when my parents were dating there was a big dance pavilion at the seaward end where they went to listen and dance to the big swing bands of the era.

But by this time the pavilion had been gone for years, swept away in a fierce ocean storm. Most of the rides and other amusements were clustered at the pier's base, and early in the afternoon that's where we would head. Above the colorful dense crowd loomed the regal Ferris wheel and the modest roller coaster. There was a bizarre funhouse named Noah's Ark, distinguished by a surreal representation of the vessel rocking on its cradle high above everything near it. From its deck and portholes peered an assortment of improbable animals, clowns, and other colorful wacky figures, larger than life.

We ate slices of thin greasy pizza and French fries sprinkled with vinegar, always tossing some to the bold seagulls that mewed and flashed just above the surging swells. We'd split up and take our time making our way out to the end past concessions, arcades, shooting galleries, and souvenir shops. Joe and I would go on a ride or two, and along with Linda and Marilyn, brave Noah's Ark with the hall of mirrors, huge, slowly rotating barrel, and scary surprises deep in its recesses. I'd take such a beating on the bumper cars that eventually the more adept young drivers tired of ramming into me and left me alone. Linda would buy a souvenir or two, and before we knew it the afternoon would be spent. We'd walk back to the parking lot, tired and thankful for the rest provided by the ride home, where we'd arrive to get a late start letting in the cows and doing the chores.

("Summer Vacations" from *Growing Up on Maple Hill Farm* by Jerry Stelmok, 2007)

SWATHER

For thousands of years grain crops were cut with a *sickle* (a large, curved knife), then with a *scythe* (a two-handed knife with a very long

blade), until in the 19th century Cyrus McCormick invented the *reaper* (a horse-drawn implement with revolving reels and a mechanical knife). Then came the *binder*, which cut the grain and bound it into bundles so it could be hauled to a threshing machine. In the 20th century combines came into use; they cut and threshed the grain in one operation. But in much of the prairie region, with its short growing season, it was necessary to cut the grain earlier to escape frosts and let it mature in the field. Thus the swather came into use. It is basically the same as the old-time reaper, with reels and a mechanical knife, but has three major differences: (1) it leaves the cut grain lying in *swaths* (windrows, which the combine can "pick up" with a special attachment when the grain is mature), (2) it is powered by its own gasoline or diesel engine or pulled by a tractor, and (3) it often has an air-conditioned, radio-equipped cab, and can cost more than a luxury car. You could buy a trainload of sickles for the same price.

(Terry Chamberlain, *The ABC's of Farming*, 1999)

SWIMMING

The pond was where we learned to swim; and a slow and arduous business it was, being entirely self-taught. With no guidance whatever, we had to reinvent the art from the beginning, for we were not often in water with children who could swim. Very few from our parents' generation had ever learned how, and my parents seldom showed up at the pond, much less at the water hole. They had nothing to teach us about swimming, except

"Be careful." As youngsters our swimming trunks were worn-out or outgrown bib overalls cut off above the knees. Recycling worn-out clothes was a standard policy, but not every application of the policy was as stylish as this.

We had surmised that there were two ways to learn to swim. The first and most direct way was to wade out to hip-deep water, lift our feet, and flail about with arms and legs as furiously as possible, hoping to keep our feet out of the muck and our head out of the water. This method is presumably very ancient, since it is absolutely impossible to imagine anything more primitive. Nevertheless, we proceeded to reinvent the method and to apply it assiduously. Results were meager. Summer after summer, swimming seemed to me a thing impossible to learn. Why, I sometimes wondered in those early days, would anyone really *want* to swim? Flying, for example, would be considerably easier.

Fortunately, there was another method, indirect and more sedate in its approach, requiring the use of a large log. Long before we had learned to swim, we had mastered the technique of traveling around the pond by "swimming" with hands (or chest or chin) on a large floating log, feet churning up a storm for propulsion. We had the idea that our feet had to be kept *above* the water, pounding the surface, lest they sink and pull us under. The transition from "swimming" to swimming was harder than it appeared: releasing hands and pumping furiously so as to keep our head up was the more difficult just because we had learned to be completely dependent upon the log. Moreover, it is not easy to swim trying to keep most of the body safely exposed to the air. Eventually, our stubbornness prevailed over our wretched techniques and we cautiously abandoned the idea that we had to swim *on* the water, like a log, noticing that we could swim *in* the water, like a muskrat; and we did all learn to swim. Upon careful reflection on our two methods and their associated theories, I find that I cannot recommend either.

Our point of entry to the pond was the sandiest edge, but it is doubtful anyone would have been so sanguine as to think of that area as a beach. It was, in fact, the place where the cows and horses drank daily, but it was attractive enough to suit our taste, which was, fortunately, well underdeveloped.

Frequently, to clear our spot for the day, we lifted a crisp, sunbaked cow-pie from the sand and tossed it aside. If we got a pie that was done to a turn, with no soggy undercrust, we could sometimes make it sail like a Frisbee. Unfortunately, we did not then know that a Frisbee craze was in the offing and that American civilization would soon demand that the Frisbee be patented and marketed in quantity. True, ours was a fragile sort of toy, to be tossed with care and caught with trepidation, but it was surely history's first and best Frisbee, free and disposable, recyclable, biodegradable, environmentally sound, a natural product. The legend that the Frisbee was invented at Yale with a pie plate isn't true; it was invented in the sands of unremembered barnyards, with a pie.

There was a household rule that we not go in the water alone—one of those rules that we unaccountably observed. Not that any of us, barely afloat "swimmers" that we were, would have been of much assistance to anyone in distress. But nothing of the kind was ever required, not even on the day when Nelvin was sure he was drowning.

He and I were about seven and eight, too young to have made any headway as swimmers, and we had been puttering about at water's edge. Our mother was in the house and well aware that we were both at the pond, when Nelvin suddenly burst in upon her with terror all over his face.

"How long after you fall in the water do you drown?" he demanded.

When one of two boys returns from a pond alone on a dead trot with fear in his eyes and that question on his lips, it does not take a mother long to reach the dreadful conclusion.

"Oh, it's Ronny!" she screamed, nearly upsetting Nelvin as she dashed for the door.

Out the door and down toward the pond she sped, shouting for reinforcements, certain as she was that Ronny was lying facedown in the bottom of the pond and that Nelvin had escaped to report it. Nelvin was even more alarmed and outraged by this reaction, and

There was a household rule that we not go in the water alone—one of those rules that we unaccountably observed.

he yelled for his mother's attention—which was hard to get because she was already past the lilac bushes, nearing the barn at full throttle, heading for the pond. She had nearly reached the straightaway between the elms when who should saunter into view but Ronny himself, perfectly safe and nearly dry, handsomely attired in sawed-off bib overalls, and the proud captor of five—count 'em, Mom, five—squiggly pollywogs, and happy to have an audience to explain how he had caught them. Nice of Mother to come way out here to see them. Could he have some cornmeal?

Meanwhile, back at the house Nelvin was in a state of panic, aggravated by parental indifference. He had heard it said once upon a time that, well, no, you don't always drown *immediately* if your head accidentally goes under and you get water into your mouth and nose; so his present problem was, then how long *afterward* might you drown? He

had slipped in accidentally in pursuit of a pollywog, had gotten his head wet and his mouth full, and, without telling me his worry, had sped off to the house to find out if he might drown. He'd had a terrible accident, for heaven's sake, and it just might be fatal; would someone please tell him if so, and when? His own mother had ignored him and callously raced out of the house instead. Surely the situation *was* alarming; didn't anyone care that he might drown at any moment, standing right there alone in the middle of the kitchen, howling for help? He followed her out of the house back toward the pond, afraid he might drown before he got there. That would serve them right.

He didn't drown. There had been a failure of communication somewhere. But it was Nelvin and not I who had to be rescued after all, and Mother did it by patiently explaining the facts of life and death by drowning, convincing him that he would survive. I gave Nelvin one of my pollywogs, now installed in a mason jar. He got a little one, which was not very lively. On the trip from the pond in my cupped hands it had gotten its head above water and taken in a gulp of air, and it looked as if it might expire at any moment.

("Pollywogs and Apples" from *Eighty Acres* by Ronald Jager, 1990)

TAX

Farmers, like the rest of us, pay federal taxes, provincial taxes, municipal taxes, income tax (in the years they actually have a net income), school taxes, health taxes, road taxes, and more than their share of sales taxes, fuel taxes, property taxes, capital gains taxes, inheritance tax, fees for licenses, permits, and many more. Many, many more. If they ever sat down, added up all the taxes they pay, and compared it with their net incomes they would probably welcome bankruptcy, social collapse, or death (the only escape from taxes. Well, not quite; their families would have to pay estate taxes, inheritance taxes, and sales taxes on funeral and cemetery expenses. You can't win).

(Terry Chamberlain, *The ABC's of Farming*, 1999)

TEXAS GATE

Common in ranch country. Used where a fence crosses a public road, it consists of a slatted steel or wooden surface that vehicles can cross but cattle won't. It is also a useful safety feature, abruptly setting bolt upright any driver who is in danger of falling asleep.

(Terry Chamberlain, *The ABC's of Farming*, 1999)

THRESHING

One year I began the passage from boy to man. We were short of help because another threshing rig was over on Pleasant Ridge, where we usually exchanged help. Father said he needed me. Mother made plans for a neighbor girl to come and help.

"What will I do?" I asked Father.

"I was thinking about the straw pipe. Think you could handle that?"

"Sure." I had a dim impression of cranks and levers.

"It's not easy. You have to pay attention every minute. Couple years back I saw a boy knock a man off the strawstack being careless how he swung the pipe. You got to stick to it no matter how hot it gets, how much dust and chaff comes back at you."

"I can do it."

The rig came in the late afternoon, a big chugging Rumely Oil Pull tractor with a square stack and a little box where black oil squirted mysteriously through glass tubes. It chugged through the barnyard to a field northeast of the barn, pulling the bright red threshing machine behind it.

The driver was my familiar big, greasy overalled man. He started getting ready for the next day, leveling up the threshing machine by digging holes for some of the wheels to drop into, then lining up the tractor and stretching the long belt from tractor pulley to threshing-machine pulley. Around the tractor were red milk cans filled with gasoline, unpainted milk cans full of water, and great boxes of tools and spare parts.

The long pipe that carried straw from the machine to the stack was cradled along the top of the thresher. I climbed up to the little platform where the straw-pipe operator was supposed to stand. There were three cranks and a rope. I didn't know which did what.

The big man swung the grain chute out and walked back along the top of the rig. "You going to run the pipe?"

I nodded.

"Ever do it before?"

I shook my head.

"You can do it. Let me show you. This crank here raises the pipe up and down. This crank swings her back and forth. This one makes her longer and shorter. And this rope— that opens up a little door at the end of the pipe. Pull that, the straw goes shooting straight out the pipe. Leave it closed, the straw goes down onto the stack. Got that straight?"

I nodded.

"All right. Let's try her. Raise the pipe off the rig a couple feet."

I turned the crank. The pipe lifted up.

"Fine. Now swing her around."

I turned another crank. The pipe began to swing in a great half circle, making a groaning noise.

"Hold it." He picked up his oil can and gave the collar of the pipe a big squirt of oil.

"Try her again."

The pipe turned more easily and I swung it until it stuck straight out from the end of the thresher.

"Now get the feel of cranking her longer and shorter."

I did that, chain links rattling along the top of the pipe.

"You'll do fine." He winked at me. "Now then, put her back on top the rig the way she was. You can crank her around in the morning. Folks'll think you been doing it all your life."

In my mind I cranked that pipe half the night.

First thing next morning, when the dew was off, we went out into the fields to tip the oat shocks over, butts toward the morning sun so the dampness from the ground would dry out. As I worked, I remembered the first time I had ever done that. It had been early in the morning, the sun still low and red. In an hour or so I had to go back to the house and help Mother. I started tipping the shocks, the butts directly at the sun. Lyle was with me. He watched for a few minutes, then came over, shaking his head. "Nope. Not right at the sun. Tip them where the sun's going to be a couple hours from now."

I looked at the sun. I looked to the right along the horizon where I knew the sun was going. But how far to the right?

"Like the face of a clock," Lyle said. He pulled out the inch-thick old watch that bulged from the top pocket of his high-bibbed overalls. The hands stood at seven o'clock. He turned the face so the little hand pointed to the sun. He pointed his finger from the center of the watch to the number nine,

"That's where the sun'll be in a couple hours."

I went back to tipping the shocks, looking at the sun each time, aiming the butts at that certain angle to the right. I'd never before had such a feel of the sun's absolute route across our days.

That had been three years before. I turned the shocks casually now, automatically aiming them ahead of the sun.

The wagons, with their wide hayracks, began to arrive. I helped throw bundles—from shocks that had been tipped the day before— onto the first wagon and rode in on the high swaying load.

The tractor was already running. The wagon pulled in close to the feeder apron. I slid off and ran to the pipe—raised it, cranked it around in a half circle, then extended it. I gave the rope a couple of pulls, opening the little door and letting it clang shut. Everything went without a hitch.

I looked down and found Father watching me. There was surprise on his face. He looked at me a moment, then at the thresherman, then back at me.

I nodded.

Father smiled his approval and I grew about two inches up there on that high platform.

Another wagon pulled in along the other side of the machine. The thresherman pulled the drive lever on the tractor. The threshing machine came alive under me, vibrating, rocking back and forth a little, the chaff—dancing on the metal top. Slowly it all built to a steady humming that was half sound, half feel.

The men on the wagons began feeding oats to the machine, their pitchforks swinging in an easy alternating rhythm. A steady line of bundles was carried by the moving apron into the hidden workings of the great machine. The tractor engine roared louder. New sounds began as bundles were ripped apart and oat heads shook loose from the stems. Straw rattled under me and went shooting out the pipe. The oat grains sifted through screens and fanners and poured into the measuring bucket on top of the machine. The bucket filled to a half-bushel weight and dumped automatically, registering on the counting dial. Then the oats poured down the grain pipe in a rich stream to the waiting sack.

As always, Father was there to meet those first oats. He reached into the sack and brought out a handful, still warm from the fields, bright gold in the early sun. He blew into his hand, checking for chaff and weed seeds. Satisfied, he nodded to the thresherman.

Father went next to the beginning pile of straw. He held his hat out in front of the pipe, then checked in it to see if any grain was blowing through. Again he nodded his satisfaction to the thresherman.

Father returned to the grain pipe and carefully lifted a full bag up and down. This was how he confirmed what his walks through the fields had told him earlier. Everyone watched his face. As he swung the first bag into the waiting grain wagon, we knew without a word ever passing that it was a good crop.

The bundle wagons came and went. The grain wagon raced off to the granary to unload and return.

Straw spread out on the ground in a long pile as I swung the pipe back and forth. Father and a neighbor moved into the straw, which was next winter's bedding for the barns. With their pitchforks they began to form the rectangular outlines of the stack, motioning to me when they wanted the pipe moved.

Once, straw stopped coming out of the pipe. The machine groaned and thumped. Someone yelled. I looked around. The thresherman was running toward me. He made a pulling motion. I grabbed the rope that opened the door at the end of the pipe, and a wad of damp straw went shooting out beyond the stack. The machine smoothed. After that, the sound warned me when to pull the rope.

The sun moved across the sky. The dust and chaff settled around me. Once, when the bundle wagons got behind, I had a minute to climb down to earth and get a drink of water from the ten-gallon milk can, like the other men.

Finally, it was time for dinner. The machine whined to a stop, my little platform strangely motionless after hours of vibration. Father slid down from the strawstack and gave me a nod and a smile. There was a burst of laughter from the grain wagon. Lyle lifted a baby rabbit out of one of the bags. "Look at that," he said to the thresherman. "Can't understand how your rig can get the oats clean if a rabbit can go straight through."

The thresherman grinned. "You're lucky. Few days ago a skunk, came through."

Lyle put the rabbit down and it hopped away across the field. He told me later that somebody had found it under a shock and brought it in.

I beat the chaff and dust off my clothes and washed up with the other men. For the first time in my life, I sat down at the first table. Mother put a steaming platter of food in front of me.

When the chairs scraped back, I went out into the yard with the others. There, under the shade of the big maple tree, I listened to the talk.

"Call this grain?" a hired man was saying. "Hell, you should see it out on the Great Plains. They got wheat fields that stretch from hell to breakfast. I've seen twenty horses hitched onto one combine. A man starts cutting and by God he's got to take a bed with him 'cause he'll only be halfway around a field by nightfall."

There was laughter. "You sure you're not stretching things a little?"

"Hell no. If anything, I'm holding back 'cause I didn't figure anybody would believe the truth. Fact is, those fields are so big, and it takes so long to get the seed in, that different parts of the field don't even get ripe at the same time."

Old Abe was there. He was listening and nodding. "My grandfather was out there once. He came West from Ohio back in the eighteen-forties. Tried to grub out a farm down in Haney Valley. Somebody came by and told him he was crazy. Said there was land out on the Great Plains level as a table, not a tree in sight. Well, sir, he went out there and just about went crazy before he turned around and came back here."

"What went wrong?"

Abe took a chew of tobacco and got it going. "Why, he said a man used to hill country could lose his soul out there. Said that country swallowed you up without even a belch. Said there was no surprises. Country shows itself to you all at once. No privacy either. A neighbor living twenty miles away can look out in the morning, see if you're up and got a fire going yet."

Abe raised his head. A long stream of tobacco juice went sizzling into the brown grass. "So he came back here, my grandfather did. Said hill country had a feel of home about it, didn't keep leading a man off toward a horizon that was never there."

From that year on I was part of the threshing crew. When the rig went to the next job, leaving our farm quiet again and sleeping in the hot summer sun, I went with it to run the strawpipe at each farm along the ridge.

("Rites of Passage" from *The Land Remembers* by Ben Logan, 1975)

TRACTOR DRIVING

"The first thing you need to learn about driving a tractor is how to shut it off," my dad said matter-of-factly, looking me straight in the eye and pointing a finger at my nose. This was how he began my inaugural tractor-driving lesson, which was a rite of passage for every farmkid. I knew that this was serious business.

It was summertime in central Iowa, and I had just finished fourth grade. The corn, soybeans, and alfalfa were in the ground; our flock of sheep was in the pasture; and since Dad had some extra time on his hands (and a ten-year-old girl to entertain), he thought this might be a good time to begin tractor-driving lessons. I had been on a tractor plenty—sitting on Dad's lap and "helping" him steer as he plowed a field or drove a wagon of beans the two miles to the elevator—but I hadn't been tall enough to reach the clutch and brake pedals and, therefore, hadn't been old enough for driving lessons. Like the amusement park signs that said, "You must be this high to ride," I had to pass the clutch-pedal test before I would be allowed to pilot the tractor.

So, before he imparted any further tractor wisdom, he motioned for me to climb up into the driver's seat of the IH Farmall 806D and show him that I could press the clutch all the way to the floor. I pulled myself up into the seat. It felt good up there. I looked to my right at our farmhouse and felt about as tall as the third-floor attic window. Over my left shoulder, I saw our border collie patrolling around the sheep in the east pasture, subtly herding them into a loose group. I enjoyed the scene for just a moment then took a deep breath, grabbed onto the steering wheel, and stomped on the clutch as hard as I could. It groaned as I pushed it down, down, down— all the way to the floor.

"All right," said Dad, "that means you're ready!" In one motion, he climbed up beside me and started up the engine, because, as he had promised, our first lesson would be shutting it off.

"How do you think you do it?" he said over the roar of the engine.

"Turn the key off!" I yelled. I tried, but the key didn't do it.

Dad moved the long throttle handle behind the steering wheel all the way to the left to cut off the fuel supply, and the engine stopped. He started it up again and let me kill the engine. Lesson one, check! I was anxious to get moving and tear out of the gravel driveway.

Well, as with most tractors, that Farmall wasn't exactly going to tear anywhere. I suppose that was the beauty of teaching me to drive a tractor rather than one of my grandpa's beat-up drag-racing cars. I wouldn't be moving fast enough to do any damage. The rest of the lesson creeped along, too, and went something like this.

Step one: Turn on the key so the battery connects to the starter.

Step two: Move the throttle a little to the right so the engine gets some fuel.

Step three: Push the clutch pedal all the way down until it engages the safety switch.

Step four: Keep your right hand on the steering wheel for bracing. Then with your free hand, push in the starter button.

With my skinny fourth-grade leg standing on the clutch, I had the best of intentions, but you know how the next few minutes went: Start, chug, stall. Start, chug, stall. Start, chug, stall. Until, finally, the tractor lurched forward, hiccupped, and kept going, breathing a black, smokey sigh of relief from its stack. We were on the move! Dad helped me steer the tractor onto the main road and then let me bump the throttle up bit by bit. The tractor roared louder and louder, vibrating every tooth in my head and every bone in my body. There was no sign of stalling now—I glanced down at the big back tires, and they seemed to be spinning at breakneck speed. On either side of the road, black fields were lined with straight, healthy rows of new plants, and red-winged blackbirds watched us from the fence posts.

We drove like that for a while, Dad offering up comments about the soybean crop or the cows eating grass near Beaver Creek, me loosening my white-knuckle grip on the steering wheel ever so slightly.

Then, trouble. (I might have gasped, but the tractor was too loud for anyone to hear it.) Coming toward us was a big green machine—our neighbor, Mr. Hunter, on his new John Deere. My heart raced as I wondered how two tractors could possibly pass each other on that thin strip of gravel. We chugged closer. And closer. I felt like I was playing the slowest game of chicken the world had ever seen. I could read the seed logo stitched onto Mr. Hunter's cap. I could see the dirt of a morning's work on his face. Dad guided the tractor farther and farther to the right, until I was sure we were going to topple over into the ditch. Our Farmall and Mr. Hunter's Deere finally met, with merely inches (I was sure of it) separating them. And then, the most wonderful thing happened: As our tractors squeaked by each other, Mr. Hunter looked at me, offered the hint of a smile, and lifted his index finger off of the steering wheel to say hello. I finger-waved back. The rite of passage was complete; I was a real farmkid now.

As the years went by, I graduated to faster-moving vehicles. By age twelve, I was allowed to drive Dad's 1960 Chevy pickup by myself as long as I stuck to gravel roads. If I had a friend with me, we were allowed to drive it only in the pasture. That was safe for innocent bystanders, but not for that poor old pickup. My best friend and I drove it as fast as we could over every bump in the field, knocking our heads on the ceiling and knocking the battery on top of the engine. It was a long walk to the house to tell my dad about that one; it made me think I should have stuck with tractors.

These days, I live in Minneapolis with my husband, Gary, and two young sons, but my parents are still on the farm. Not much has changed there, happily enough. The Farmall 806D and the '60 Chevy are still around, though they're now housed in a Morton building instead of the gray, weathered barn. The red-winged blackbirds still watch the comings and goings on the stretch of gravel that runs past the farmhouse, though the road is now called 210th Street instead of Rural Route 1. My husband, boys, and I like to visit as often as we can, and we celebrate every Christmas there. I particularly love being at the farmhouse toward the end of the summer, when the corn is high in the south field and the fireflies are thick in the evenings.

This summer, my oldest son Abe was two and a half when we were on the farm. Old enough to walk out to the old sheep barn with the log (and me not too far behind); old enough to eat three ears of corn on the cob in one sitting; and old enough, I found out, to learn how to drive tractor.

Although he wasn't even close to passing the clutch-pedal test, my dad (ever after known as Grandad) thought it was about time Abe had his first tractor lesson.

"That's all right with me," I said, and the two headed off to the machine shed.

"Now, Abe," I heard my dad say. "When we're done, I want you to tell me if the tractor was loud or if it was quiet."

"Okay, Grandad," Abe answered, as he practically galloped to the big, red tractor.

Abe scaled the Farmall and looked, I thought, particularly small in the driver's seat with my dad. The two had a grand time. Abe took his steering duties quite seriously, only taking a hand off the wheel to wave to Gary and me as they left the driveway and headed for open road, his smile stretching from ear to ear.

When they finally pulled back into the driveway and turned off the tractor, my dad posed the question, "So, Abe, was the tractor loud or was it quiet?"

"It was LOUD, Grandad!" Abe answered approvingly.

Later that night, Gary jokingly asked my dad why he had never been invited to drive the Farmall. Apparently, Gary had never driven a tractor before.

"What?" Dad exclaimed. "Never driven a tractor? Well, don't you worry, Gary. I'll be sure you get to drive the Farmall all you want at Christmastime. And I'll be sure there's a snow blade on it."

When we got back to Minneapolis after that visit, Abe was already thinking about the next time he would get to drive tractor with Grandad. I wondered if we should start practicing the index-finger wave, just to be prepared.

We put some pictures of Abe and the Farmall in a photo album and, later, I overheard him showing them to a friend.

"That's me, that's Grandad, and that's MY tractor," he explained. Could this former farmgirl's heart be any more filled with pride?

("Tractor Lessons" by Margret Aldrich, from *My First Tractor*, 2010)

TRACTOR RESTORATION

There's more to collecting and restoring old tractors than nuts and bolts. A lot more. In fact, nuts and bolts are the least of it. Ask our marriage counselor. Don't get me wrong: Lovely Linda is a wonderful wife and friend and she has endured more than any one woman should have to put up with. I'm the first to admit that life with me isn't easy. I admit that, even though I don't always believe it.

Things got tense when I began collecting Allis-Chalmers WC tractors. I had one WC for almost twenty years before it occurred to me that it might be nice to have two. And once I had two, I thought it would really be handy to have a couple of junked WCs around for parts, and along with the parts tractors I got a couple of "runners." So then there were six. And I got a good deal on one that had been sitting in a shed for nearly twenty-five years, and I think I have another couple lined up not far from here, if I can just work out the details.

It has taken the better part of two years, but just last week Lovely Linda finally sighed, "I give up. I've lost track. I have no idea how many tractors you have." It was a moment of triumph—but it was not without, as they say, its downside.

I first realized I was getting into trouble when I overheard Lovely Linda telling her mother, "It used to be that he'd go to bed, smiling and sighing. I'd look over and see that he was reading a *Playboy* magazine. Now when he's smiling and sighing, it's because he's thumbing through an Allis-Chalmers parts catalog!"

Over the past couple years, I have collected advice along with my WCs, and I think it is only neighborly that I pass along to you what I have learned. If you're married and are thinking about getting into the old iron business, forget trivial things like socket wrenches and bearing pullers and lay the groundwork for your new hobby by carefully studying the following rules, Roger's Rules for Collecting Old Iron!

Rule #1: Collect only one model and make of tractor—nothing but John Deere Bs or Allis-Chalmers Gs, for example. When all your tractors are the same color and shape, it's harder, if not impossible, for anyone (if you catch my drift) to figure out how many tractors you actually have.

Rule #2: Similarly, never line up your tractors, ever. Nothing distresses a difficult spouse more than seeing twelve old tractors lined up, looking for all the world like a burning pile of hundred-dollar bills. Scatter the tractors around—a couple behind the shed, one or two in the shed, another beside the garage—so that it's not possible for anyone (if you know who I mean) to see more than two or three from any one perspective. Your hobby will be less "irritating" that way.

Rule #3: For pretty much the same reason, don't number your tractors. Give them names. You'd be surprised how much less trouble you will have if you talk about "Steel Wheels" or "Sweet Allis" rather than "Allis-Chalmers WC #14."

Rule #4: Early in your collecting, buy a tractor you don't want. Sell it again as quickly as you can; don't worry about making money on the transaction. The main

thing is to get a tractor and get rid of it. Then, for years, you can say, "Yes, Angel Face, I do have six John Deere Bs, and they are in the shed while our car is out in the weather, but that doesn't mean that I will always have six John Deere Bs. *Remember the one I got rid of a few years ago? I'm thinking of selling another one any day now so we can put the car in the garage.*"

If you have a friend who collects tractors, make arrangements for him to drop off a tractor now and again. That way you can say (if anyone asks) that you bought it. Then have it hauled off again, and say you sold it. With this system, you will re-establish your reputation for moderation every couple of years or so.

Warning: About the time I accumulated my sixth or seventh Allis WC I thought I'd be smart, so I bought a lovely little Allis C. Linda and our nine-year-old daughter Antonia were in the farmyard as I unloaded this lovely little item that needed only some wheel work and a new wiring harness.

"I see you bought yourself another tractor that doesn't run," said Linda.

"Guess what, dear?" I beamed. "I didn't buy myself another Allis-Chalmers. I bought *you* an Allis-Chalmers! She's yours, and ain't she cute?"

I could tell by the look on her face that she was about as excited as she was the Christmas I gave her a new drain cleaner attachment for her vacuum sweeper, but I wasn't at all prepared for what she said next: "How much can I get for it?"

"Er, uh, I didn't get it for you to sell, Honey Cakes. I was thinking, if you don't want to drive it all the time, I can take it into town now and then just to keep the oil stirred up for you. It won't be any trouble at all."

"Well, thanks, Rog, you're really too sweet. I don't deserve a darling like you. How much can I get for it?"

I almost broke into tears at the thought of someone loading that great tractor onto a trailer and driving off with it. I was thinking that I should have gone with my first impulse and said that it had followed me home and asked if I could maybe keep it, but thank goodness, about that time my mind kicked into road gear. "Actually, I thought that if you wouldn't mind sharing, it could also be Antonia's tractor. Right. That's it! Eventually it'll be Antonia's tractor."

Antonia leaped into the C's seat with a squeal and started twisting the steering wheel and making tractor noises. Linda snorted something about me fixing my own supper that night—that is, if I was intending to stay over—and headed back toward the house while I helped Antonia bond with her lovely new tractor. That was a close call, and my advice to you is not to buy your wife a tractor. In fact, you're better off sticking with the idea of the drain cleaner attachment for the vacuum sweeper.

Rule #5: Pay for tractors with a cashier's check, postal money order, or cash. These leave far less evidence than checks drawn on the family account. Once you have gotten possession of a tractor and paid for it, *eat the stubs, carbon copies, or receipts immediately.* Such things have a way of becoming an embarrassment later. Take it from me.

Some collectors like to point out to skeptical marriage partners that what with interest rates so low these days, buying old tractors is actually an investment, a way of being sure the spouse will be "taken care of and comfortable should something . . . something terrible happen." Doesn't work with Lovely Linda. She thinks Allis-Chalmers WCs *are* the "something terrible."

Rule #6: Now and then, buy a wreck "for parts," even if you don't need the parts, even if it has no salvageable parts. In fact, you might consider hauling an extra wreck or two whenever you haul home a good machine, if possible, on the same trailer or truck. This is called "liability averaging."

If your spouse says something about it being strange that you have money for yet another tractor but not enough for a new refrigerator, point indignantly to the tractors on the trailer: the beautiful one on

steel and in running condition for which you paid $1,600, and the two rusted hulks you got for $50 each. Then huff (or whine, depending on what has worked in the past), "Snookums, I got those for a little more than $500 each and the one in the back is easily worth $2,000 just as it stands. That's a tidy profit of $400—*which is more than four times what I paid for the other two.*" See? Doesn't that make you sound like an investment wizard?

Some collectors find it effective to add something like, "It's pretty hard to find a good refrigerator for $500!" But it has been my experience that a smart-aleck attitude can fairly directly lead to the purchase of a $500 refrigerator.

Rule #7: When things get critical in the household, consider dragging home a tractor without a transmission or rear wheels. If there is complaint, you say something like, "Tractor? What tractor? That's not a tractor! That's only a front end. Not even close to a tractor." Then, a couple weeks later, bring home a rear end, minus the radiator, engine, and front wheels. "What tractor?" you say. "That's no tractor! That's only a rear end. Not even close to a tractor:' Don't try this, however, more than once every couple years.

Rule #8: Have an implement dealer, salvage yard proprietor, or friend call you now and then when you're not at home and tell your spouse, "Rog told me to keep an eye on the Allis WC going at the auction up at Centerville Saturday, but it sold for $1,200 and I know there's no way a financially cautious and responsible guy like Rog would pay that much for a tractor so I didn't even make a bid on it for him."

Not only will this make you look real good, but the next time you do buy a tractor, say something like, "Lovie-Bear, this beauty only cost me $300, which means we're $900 ahead of where we would have been if I'd gotten the one that came up for sale at Centerville. Why, if I keep saving money like this, we'll be able to go on a Caribbean cruise next winter." If you say it fast enough, it might work.

Rule #9: If your mate insults your tractor work by referring to it as "rustoration" or "tinkering," laugh a lighthearted laugh that makes it clear that tractors are not to you what shoes are to Imelda Marcos. Remind her that you could sell all your tools and tractors any time you want and that you really resent her slipping those twelve-step program brochures under your pillow every night.

Rule #10: Your situation may deteriorate to the point where your mate asks, "What do you love more, me or your blasted tractors?" Whatever you do, don't ask for time to think it over.

I have tried to couch the above information in nonsexist language. Yes, I am dealing with my wife Linda—and what a darling she is! But there is every indication that my daughter Antonia is going to be a tractor nut like her Old Man and will be using these same devices to smooth things over with her husband.

The above suggestions are not dishonest or deceptive, exactly. They are ways to make life easier for your spouse. In fact, now that I think about it, these little acts of diplomacy are actually a kindness, a way to smooth the road for someone you love. Following Roger's Rules is a way of being a better person. People who follow Roger's Rules are *good* people. In fact, I feel so good about myself, I think I'll go out and buy myself another tractor! It'll be a good investment. I'll have it hauled in at night. That way I won't bother Lovely Linda.

("Roger's Rules for Collecting Old Iron" from *Old Tractors Never Die* by Roger Welsch, 2001)

TRANSPORTATION

Grain and livestock were once transported on railways, which were generally located far from busy streets and highways. Now these commodities are increasingly carried by lumbering tractor-trailer trucks which compete for street and road space with cars, pickup trucks, vans, campers, buses, bicycles, motorcycles, and wildlife. This is called progress.

(Terry Chamberlain, *The ABC's of Farming*, 1999)

UNDERWEAR

Underwear. A close relationship exists between the regulation of bodily temperature and the kind of underwear worn. *Woolen* underwear would be ideal for winter were it not for 5 facts: (1) It is very difficult to keep clean. Wool fibers, owing to their structure, absorb the sweat and oily secretions of the skin and hold them, and bacteria thrive in woolen underwear. (2) Wool does not absorb or give up moisture rapidly.

(3) Strong soaps and boiling water cannot be used in washing wool. If woolen underwear is laundered carelessly, the fibers mat, the air spaces are closed, and the garment loses its feeling of warmth. (4) Some persons cannot tolerate wool next to the skin on account of its irritating properties. (5) Woolen underwear is expensive.

Wool mixed with cotton or silk makes good underwear, especially for aged people, children and invalids.

Cotton underwear is more generally used than any other kind. When woven with an open mesh, cotton acquires a feeling of warmth, the large air spaces making it resemble wool. More dirt clings to cotton than to linen, but cotton launders easily and hence is a very sanitary material. Cotton underwear has from 15 to 30 percent more heat than linen. In a close, tight weave, cotton is a good conductor of heat, which is the reason a garment of this kind feels so cool in summer. It is cheap, very durable and easily laundered.

Linen underwear is more expensive than cotton. It is used in very warm countries. The chief objections to it are that it (1) may cool the body too quickly, (2) musses easily, and (3) does not last as long as cotton as it frays on the edges.

Silk underwear loses its moisture more rapidly than wool and therefore is more sanitary. For those who cannot wear wool next to the skin and to whom cost is no consideration, silk is an excellent material for undergarments. It is more easily cleaned than wool; and being light, though warm, it takes up little space.

The subjects of personal hygiene (bathing, etc.), and hygienic underwear should be considered together in order to get the best results and maintain good health.

("Clothing the Farm Family" from *Farm Knowledge* by E. L. D. Seymour, 1919)

VALUE-ADDED

One of those trendy new agricultural terms. Because the price of grain never seems to keep up with inflation, the experts have decided we must do things to the grain to make it fetch a higher price. With any other products that can be easily done with one of those little gadgets that whacks a new price sticker down over the old one, but with grain and other farm products the procedure is more complicated. Thus there are individual farmers and other *entrepreneurs* busy making wheat into noodles, straw into building panels, crabapples into cider and so on. The proponents of Value-Added seem to believe it will reignite the rural economy, attract new investment to small communities, provide employment, save the family farm, bring about world peace, and cure male-pattern baldness. Sarcasm aside, they are probably right to a considerable extent. Certainly something must be done when you consider that the elevator door price of 1997 wheat in August of that year was about the same as it was in 1917. (Not a joke, unfortunately, but true.)

(Terry Chamberlain, *The ABC's of Farming*, 1999)

VEGETABLES

"The difference between the rich and the poor is vegetables," said some astute observer of the scene—Truman Capote, I think—the implication being that people with cultivated tastes know and appreciate good vegetables and are willing and able to afford them.

My mother wasn't rich, but she had a great respect for vegetables and prepared them superbly. We ate like the Duke and Duchess of Windsor. I think of her each June as I hustle my fresh young peas into the freezer.

I remember being sent to deliver a kettle of creamed new peas as a gesture of condolence to a home where they'd had a death. At the time it impressed me as a strange offering, but in retrospect I know those peas were more welcome than a dozen angel food cakes.

I calculate my young peas at a dollar a pint (excluding labor) and well worth the cost. We raise them for market, so I feel I can afford the luxury. When I say young, I mean downright premature. By the time they fill the pods, they're beginning to lose their delicate sweetness. When the morning's load comes from the field, I search it for the baskets with thinner pods, the ones picked by the beginners. Paul grumbles about the "darned kids" who pick them so young, but I rejoice.

It isn't just the flavor of this supreme vegetable or the anticipation of winter feasts that gives me pleasure, but the whole June ambience. It's a season of high hopes. The crops are coming along in great style, still outdistancing the weeds. The first potato blossoms are opening. The spring rains have established grass in places where grass will wither in late summer. The wheat is heading and hinting of yellow, and the fragrance of linden and honeysuckle scent the air.

Spirits are high and kids are eager. It's not difficult to coax Leslie and Kelly from their porch across the road to come sit under the maples and shell peas. Their fresh young faces and secretive giggles are part and parcel of the pleasure. Paul and Orrin come from their field work and flop down to help. The dogs lie companionably at our sides. I wonder what the poor people are doing today.

("High on the Vine" from *Harvest of Bittersweet* by Patricia Penton Leimbach, 1987)

VETERINARIAN

A doctor who has decided to treat animals instead of human beings because animals never ask for a second opinion or sue for malpractice. He or she sometimes works all day and all night; sometimes climbs into stalls with gigantic sick (and therefore irritable) bulls; sometimes stands in the cold for hours with his or her hands inside a cow. This is a weird person.

(Terry Chamberlain, *The ABC's of Farming*, 1999)

WASHING

When a woman wants to buy a piece of calico, the first question she considers is, "Will it bear washing?" If men, when they set out to hunt a wife, would make this a leading question, if they were as fearful of getting possession of a fading woman, as we are of fading chintz, it would be one move towards leading our sex into habits that conduce to long continued freshness and vigor. But the problem is a deeper one for man to solve. How can he tell which of the rosy cheeked girls he so admires will shrivel up and wither away on his hands, or which retain her buoyant step and cheerful voice, on even into those late years, when the hair is silvering, and the roses have faded from her cheek. Well, I can't tell the boys much about things, because they don't read this womanish column, but I can say to you, dear girls, that if you wish to make women of yourselves, who will be ornaments to society and of sterling value both at home and abroad, you must not be lazy. There is nothing in the world that I have so little admiration for as a lazy woman—except it be a lazy man. They are dead weights for somebody to carry, and the bearers must often want to drop the burdens ere the journey is ended.

A woman who wants refinements and luxuries and enjoyments, but wants somebody else to do all the work and drudgery that attend these things, is not my style of a woman; nor is she one that will hold her color to the end. There is nothing in this world worth having but labor is the price we must pay for it. But says one, "I was born rich. If I go to ironing, and sweeping, and making my own dresses, I shall turn somebody else out of employment; it would be mercenary and mean on my part to thus rob those who labor to live." Well, there is something in this, but if you have no need to work at home, there is a broad field of benevolent labor where just such women are needed. Some of the hardest working women I ever knew are those whose circumstances financially would place them above toil; but they knew, as every well balanced head must understand, that selfish idleness will sooner or later end in a weak body and enfeebled mind—the only way is to "Play the sweet keys wouldst thou keep them in tune."

The lamented Garfield once said: "The most valuable gift which can be bestowed upon woman is something to do." Why, bless your hearts, good women, there is plenty for all, if you will only look around and be willing to do the work that lies nearest your hand.

Women grow wishy-washy and lose their elasticity and vivacity because they live too much within themselves; think too much of food, and dress, and the four walls of home, and not enough of the human family at large. You can count them in perhaps, if there is a ball, or party, or theatrical in the wind, but if there are sick to be visited, poor to be fed and clothed, or some sin stalking abroad that only combined effort can grapple with, you must look elsewhere for help. I tell you, girls, it is not those who spent their young years in making tidies and embroidering aprons, whose color will stand the test of a few years' housekeeping and motherhood. Your young days are the prelude to riper years. If they are spent in trifling amusements and gratifications, what does your womanhood promise? Now, don't say that I am cross, and don't want you to have a good time, and enjoy yourselves heartily, for that is just what I most desire, but I want you to so mix your pleasures with solid work and worth and study, that they may be long continued, and that the Power above can bless you, and you can stand among your fellow beings as intelligent, useful, and lovable

women, and your last days be as happy as the first.

In consideration of the great number of women possessing natural gifts and capacities, we do not cut very substantial figures in the world. Oh, yes, we do, though! Think of Elizabeth Fry, Florence Nightingale, Harriet Newell, Clara Barton, Lucretia Mott and Frances E. Willard, superb women of today; why, there is nothing at all to be ashamed of about women. Yes there is a long list who "had a mind to work," and who made, and are still making, records we love to recall— but what are you doing? Their work will not add to your size. Are the women of your neighborhood wide-awake? Are they engaged in good pursuits? Do they spend their leisure in helping along the world's Christian work? Are they improving their intellects? And is the little world in which they circulate happier and brighter for their presence? Only a few can the attain eminence, but all can fill in their niche. "She hath done what she could"—this is the simple duty that is expected of us.

A kindly concern for the welfare of the whole human family, with heart and hand ready to succor the distressed, lights up the human countenance, develops thought, and makes woman of lasting value. "Ideas," says Voltaire, "are like beards—men never have any until they grow up, and women none at all." If we have none, it is our own faults; we have not cultivated the germ; we have been lazy and unmindful of our talent, and the approving "well done" is not for us to hear. We have an increasing lot of some sorts of culture—we have Latin, and physics, and esthetics—plenty and to spare, but have we more women, now-a-day's, who can turn a hand to anything that the home demands, and not die in consequence? Have we more who can get up a meal if a husband or brother happens home with an unexpected friend without looking as if they were the most injured of mortals? Have we more who are sound in body and cheerful in mind than of yore? For these are the kind needed to perpetuate the race; these are the kind who know that before they are fitted for wider spheres of usefulness they must fill the bill of requirements in the one in which nature has placed them. In short, such are the women who will "bear washing," and will not become at the first dash a mere piece of dilapidated household furniture.

("Women Who Will Bear Washing" by Mary Sidney, from *Farm Journal*, 1886

WEANING

In cattle raising, the process of getting a calf to give up its mother's teat to take milk—and subsequently other food—from a container. The person—often the young son or

daughter of the farmer—forced to teach the calf this new skill is, of course, the weaner. And often feels like one, because wrestling a calf away from its mother and trying to convince it your milk-dipped fingers are a good substitute for mama's nipple is a messy and not-very-dignified task.

(Terry Chamberlain, *The ABC's of Farming,* 1999)

WEATHER FORECASTING

An art vital to the farming industry. There are two general ways to go about it:

1. The Traditional Method—Observing the habits of animals and birds, the phases of the moon, sunspots, sundogs, hoarfrost, and other natural phenomena. These are time-honored and charming modes of prediction, but I've tried them, and to be honest they don't seem to work all that well.

2. The Modern Method—Depends on barometers, thermometers, humidistats, space satellites, computers, other sophisticated equipment, and university-trained personnel. It doesn't work very well either but provides more employment than Method Number 1.

Apparently, however, the science of meteorology (the classy word for "studying the weather") is improving; those who work at it say so themselves. They say they are right 80% of the time, while 25 years ago they were right only 50% of the time. That's chiefly because they used to say either "rain tomorrow" or "fair tomorrow" (50% chance of being right); now they say "possibility of rain tomorrow 30%." Thus, if it doesn't rain they can say "Told you it probably wouldn't," and if it does they can say "Told you there was a 30% chance it would, so we weren't wrong." With that method they should be right 100% of the time; to get only 80% they have actually to work at being incompetent.

(Terry Chamberlain, *The ABC's of Farming,* 1999)

WEED

A hard thing to define. Canada thistle and stinkweed are always weeds. Barley and wheat are only weeds sometimes, such as when they grow in a canola crop. So you could say weeds are things that you don't want to have around in certain places at certain times. But that would mean several of my relatives are weeds, so I'll have to keep searching for a better definition. (Still, the idea of a chemical spray to zap out my cousin Bert sure is tempting.)

(Terry Chamberlain, *The ABC's of Farming*, 1999)

WHEELBARROWS

If they made wheelbarrows the way they used to, I'd have bought one at the nearest store, but the fact is that I went a hundred miles (all the way to Pennsylvania) to get an antique 1875 wheelbarrow. That sounds pretty ridiculous, but some men like mustaches and I happen to like wheelbarrows. Mustaches get into your coffee while wheelbarrows are utilitarian, so if you are a reader

with a mustache, just don't be quick to criticize me.

There's something personal about a wheelbarrow. You can't, for example, use a wheelbarrow with another person. Just have a friend take one handle while you take the other, and the result will surprise you: it just won't work. Working with the wrong wheelbarrow is like wearing an ill-fitted suit.

When you live in the country, you should have certain things—like a station wagon and a good stout cane and a tweed coat with suede patches on the elbows. But above all, you must always have a sturdy wheelbarrow. Whether for carrying sod or firewood or gardening equipment, there is no other way but with a good old-fashioned wheelbarrow. At the moment I have three modern barrows as well as my newly acquired antique, and I also have a bump on my head. The bump is the result of trying to carry a load downhill in a most modern, deluxe, pneumatic-tired wheelbarrow. My undersized ten-inch wheel encountered a ten-inch depression and I did a ten-foot arc in midair over said vehicle.

I am certain that everyone using modern wheelbarrows is constantly annoyed at those small toy wheels which sink into the slightest hole. But my hardware man says we live in an age where we "have to take what we can get" and "we can't fight City Hall." I think both of these statements are un-American and completely disgraceful. And that's why I went to Pennsylvania for a properly wheeled barrow that I can use without courting disaster and in which I can carry my apples without joggling them into applesauce.

The tiny wheel problem has gone unnoticed for a long while, so allow me to present it as I see it. In the early days, wheels had to be big because the roads were rough. Wagons and other vehicles could go through forests or over bad roads with very little trouble because of their enormous wheels. Even the early automobiles had big wheels. But except for the low pressure and wider circumference of the modern tired wheel, the new tiny automobile wheel (often smaller than regular motorcycle size) is much less efficient than the old Model T sized wheel! In the first place, your new wheel turns more times to get from here to there; therefore it logically wears out more rubber—the same quality of present-day rubber on a large wheel would last twice as

long. Second, the ride would be better: a small wheel has to ride into and out of a small hole that a large wheel could go right over. Finally, a larger circle offers more ground traction so that a small wheel gives less braking surface and is more liable to skid.

The automobile experts will not argue with all this, and they do admit that the small wheel is mostly the product of styling. The only real advantage of a small wheel is to get the car lower to the ground, but we seem to be already too low for proper vision. (If you get on your *knees* in the road alongside the driver of the average full-size car, your eyes will be on the same level or lower than his!)

If you have ever wondered why the biggest trucks can pass you so artfully with a full load at eighty miles an hour, remember the truck driver's benefit of wheels that are turning much slower. He also has more traction area needed for braking and control. The big truck's superiority on the highway is due mostly to its huge wheels. It's also why you'll find the world's fastest racing cars using oversize wheels. So I'm sold on big wheels and, darn it all, a fellow *can* fight City Hall. Or buy antique wheelbarrows.

("Wheelbarrows" from *The Cracker Barrel* by Eric Sloane, 1967)

WIND

Always under close scrutiny by famers, who use it in the vital art of forecasting the weather. If the wind is from the north they predict that it will be too cold, possibly doing frost damage to the crops. If it is from the south it will be too hot, drying out the fields and singeing the heads of the plants. If it is from the east it will rain, drowning out the young plants, or it will possibly even snow. If it is from the west the weather is about to change, probably for the worse. Farmers are real positive thinkers. As near as I can figure, the only good wind would be one coming straight down.

(Terry Chamberlain, *The ABC's of Farming*, 1999)

XMAS

Something in the celebration of Christmas invites chaos and disaster, as though there has to be an opposite to the reverence. Someone once suggested that it's like even God gets tired of all the piety and He lets the devil win some of the time.

Christmas trees were always falling down. Unsupervised children munched on ornaments. Santa's pillow-paunch was always slipping. Dogs wandered into school Christmas programs. The children forgot their lines and substituted something highly inappropriate.

Church Christmas programs were not immune to the chaos. Such events can simply take on a life of their own. A friend, who is a United Methodist minister, found this out. He agreed to play the role of a beggar for the church program. At the proper moment he was to shuffle up the aisle, awed by the splendor of candles and decorations, stare down for a reverent moment into the manger at the baby Jesus, and say something appropriate to the occasion.

Rehearsals went as planned, but a few days before Christmas the minister came down with a serious case of the flu. On the night of the program he had a raging fever and hardly knew what was going on. The family left him in bed in the parsonage, next to the church.

Events proceeded without him, the performers prepared to skip the scene where the minister was supposed to enter. But right on cue, dressed in his beggar clothes, he appeared, shuffling along the aisle, staring vacant-eyed around the church, truly seeming a stranger.

There was total silence as he shuffled up to the front. Weaving unsteadily, he peered for a long time into the manger. Then he slowly turned and stared at the congregation, eyes blinking. His mouth moved and no sound came out. Finally he said, "He's—he's a scrawny little devil, isn't he."

He lowered his head and seemed to be looking at his clothes in confusion. He looked again at the people and said, in a monotone, "I don't think I should have said that."

Then he turned and, using the ends of the pew backs to steady himself, shuffled back down the aisle and out the door. He returned to the parsonage, crawled into bed and went to sleep.

The silence persisted in the church. People looked at one another. Was it funny or was it some serious theological breach? Then, one person began to clap his hands. Others followed until everyone was clapping and soon that sound was joined by raucous laughter.

The minister, of course, denies the whole event, claiming he remembers nothing about it. No matter. For that community a new and often to be repeated story of Christmas had been born.

The time Santa came to visit my father was like that.

It happened in a year long after Mother had died. Father had remarried, had sold the farm, and was living in the little town of Blue River. The Christmas season that year was filled with promise. I had come back from my wanderings as a seaman on merchant ships. My brother Lee was there with his wife, Millie, and their two young children.

Millie was a lovely and definite Englishwoman with clear ideas about Christmas and some doubts about the ability of Americans to "do Christmas properly."

Father, that evening, had just ended a noisy session with the two children in his lap and was deep into a Zane Gray western novel which he said he had to finish "to see what happens."

There was a loud knock. The door crashed open and Santa Claus stumbled in. He pushed past the open-mouthed children, walked up to Father and clapped him on the back. "Hello there, Sam!" he said in a loud voice. "How the hell are you?"

Santa pulled a chair up close to Father. "You know, Sam, I was just thinking about that time we all went fishing for a week on the Wisconsin River. Remember, nobody wanted to be cook. So we drew lots for the first meal and said the first one to complain about the food had to cook from then on. Well, Boots got the short straw. He put about half a pound of salt into the stew. You took a bite and spit it out and said 'My god, that's salty!' Then you remembered and you said 'But that's just the way I like it.' Remember that?"

Father was nodding and laughing. Santa was laughing and clapping Father on the back again. There was a strong smell of whiskey in the room. The children were staring at Santa. Millie was momentarily immobilized. It was her first American Christmas and I resisted whispering to her that this was the way we always did Christmas in Wisconsin.

Santa, we learned later, had been at a community gathering to hand out gifts to the children. Then, without changing clothes, he had gone to the tavern where people had found some impish pleasure in buying drinks for Santa Claus.

After quite a while in the tavern, Santa had come to see Father.

The storytelling went on. Both Father and Santa seemed oblivious to Millie's dark glances and the presence of the children. The two men were busily visiting the past. They covered Halloween pranks such as putting buggies up on barn roofs, calling on girls in sleighs, then back to fishing.

"Say, Sam," Santa said, "That same fishing trip, there was this game warden came by. We played some kind of trick on him. Who was that?"

"That was D. M. Cranston;' Father said. "He was Stella's father."

Stella Cranston, of course, became my mother.

"My god, Sam," Santa said. "She was such a beauty, Stella was.

Santa looked at Millie blankly. He stared down at his red suit, pushed at his white beard, seeming confused, as though he had forgotten he was supposed to be Santa. Then he bowed to Millie, a little wobbly, touched each child on the head and left, calling back from the door, "Merry Christmas!" The door closed. From the outside his voice came back one more time. "You take care of yourself, Sam."

Millie gathered the two children close to her, prepared to repair disillusionment. But it was all right. Ginny, the oldest grandchild, said in an awed voice, "I didn't know Granddaddy knew Santa Claus."

Father picked up his book, unaware of any tensions in the room or of any contradictions. He was smiling. The book was up in front of his face but he was looking somewhere beyond, seeming very pleased to have been reminded of those earlier days.

("The Time Santa Came to See Father" from *Christmas Remembered* by Ben Logan, 1997)

I still remember that time we had a big bonfire going someplace on the Pine River. It was all frozen over. We was trying to learn to skate. She was sitting by the fire, her hands tucked inside a black fur muff. She was laughing at us. She wouldn't help us learn how to skate because she said then she wouldn't have the fun of seeing us fall down."

"We were married that year," Father said. "On Christmas Day."

Santa was still. For a moment the presence of Mother was in the room and all the memories of her on other Christmases.

Millie decided it was time. She went to Santa, smiled at him, helped him up and suggested that perhaps he needed to be off to deliver presents to children who were waiting all over the world.

YIELD

In farming, the amount of crop produced in a given area, expressed in bushels per acre (which any sensible person can understand) or tonnes per hectare (which nobody can understand—nobody my age, anyway).

(Terry Chamberlain, *The ABC's of Farming*, 1999)

ZERO TILL

A non-traditional method of planting crops and controlling weeds without actually digging up the soil. This is a revolutionary new development, though you could hardly call it groundbreaking.

(Terry Chamberlain, *The ABC's of Farming*, 1999)

ZINNIAS

Many lovely flowers may be easily grown in the garden with the vegetables. One of the best of these is the zinnia. This beautiful showy flower received its name from a doctor named Zinn but it is also called *Youth-and-Old-Age*. Can you guess why? Because you will find the baby buds and flowers on the same stem that the old blossoms are on.

Growing zinnias will provide you with many pleasant surprises. Not until the flowers open will you be able to guess how many different colors you will find. The colors vary considerably and there will be many shades of pink, red, yellow, orange, lavender, and purple. Some of the blossoms will be variegated although these are not considered so lovely as the solid colors. Some will be single and others double. If you are successful in caring for them, you may have blossoms as large as four inches across.

Zinnia seed may be purchased from the florist or any store that sells vegetable seeds. One small package is all you will require. This will cost five or ten cents.

The plants are easy to grow and will do well in any soil where vegetables or other flowers succeed. They need a deep good soil either loamy or sandy.

Plant the seed in the bed or row on the first of May. Scatter the seeds carefully and thinly; that is, do not allow them to be too close together. Cover them with a thin layer of soft earth and pat it down firmly. Now you will have fun watching for them to come up.

The zinnia is a rather large heavy plant and for this reason it must not be crowded either in the row or in the bed. As soon as the young plants are from one and one-half to two inches tall, they must be thinned out so that they are not standing closer together than twelve or eighteen inches. With a sharp stick or a small trowel carefully dig up the little plants that are too close to each other and quickly plant them in new places where they can be farther apart. If you let them dry out while moving them, they will die. Press the earth firmly about each plant after you have set it in its new place.

Now watch them grow! See how fast they develop and watch for the first buds to come. By the first of July you should be able to pick the first blossoms and from then on, until the frost comes, your flower bed should be very beautiful with the gorgeous blooms.

There is just one thing that may spoil your garden. That is weeds. You could not grow big and strong if you had to divide your food with six or eight other hungry children, could you? Neither can your zinnias be strong and full of blossoms if you allow a lot of weeds and grass to steal the food and the moisture from the soil. Every time you go to the garden pull out the weeds. They come out easiest in the early morning or after a light rain.

If you follow these directions, you will be rewarded. It will be so much fun that you will want to gather some of the old dead blossoms and place them in an envelope to save their seeds for the next year's garden.

(By Robert M. Adams, from "A Garden Primer for First-Year Garden Club Workers," Cornell Junior Extension Bulletin 24, 1927)

Z